SEARCHING FOR
BOWLBY

BY

C. V. Wooster

Disclaimer

This publication is intended to provide an accurate and well-researched portrayal of historical events and figures. While every effort has been made to ensure the facts are presented as faithfully as possible, historical interpretations can evolve over time, and new information may emerge that could further illuminate the subject matter. The events and characters depicted herein are based on the best available records, but certain elements of the narrative are interpretive, as is common in historical storytelling. For artistic purposes, some conversations and characters are composites, and while many characters are based on real individuals, certain dialogue and events have been fabricated for story continuity.

Any resemblance to actual persons, living or dead, other than public figures and those clearly identified in the text, is purely coincidental, unless otherwise noted as part of public record.

The author and publisher do not assume any responsibility for any inaccuracies or discrepancies that may arise. The stories shared in this book reflect the perspectives and understandings at the time of writing. Any opinions or conclusions expressed are those of the author and are not intended to serve as definitive judgments.

Newsletter Sign Up – Stay connected and hear about exciting projects, offers and stories at https://subscribepage.io/cvwooster

Dedication

For more than six decades, I lived with words unwritten, chapters left unfinished, and stories that never found their way into the world. I wrote, but I did not publish. I carried books inside me as if they were a secret inheritance; always waiting, always postponed.

Perhaps it was fear. Perhaps it was the weight of my own beginning.

My first thought was to dedicate this book to my parents. In some ways, it would have been fitting. They gave me life, but also left me with the fractures and shadows of a traumatic upbringing. Their love was complicated, and their absence even more so. From them came the attention disorders and the lifelong struggle for steadiness that I worked decades to overcome. They shaped me, for better and for worse. Yet even as I acknowledge them here, I know this book belongs to another.

It belongs to Rozlyn, my late wife, who became my healing and my home. Her quiet strength, her calm but principled way of moving through the world, and her unfailing care for others taught me what it meant to be truly seen, truly loved. She renewed my life, helped me place the past where it belonged, and showed me how to move forward with hope.

Her passing left me broken, a chasm carved into the very center of my being. And yet, over time, her memory began to fill the void she left. Losing a spouse is both the worst and the best of life's experiences. Worst, because the absence is unbearable. Best, because it reveals the depths of love, courage, compassion, and kindness, both in ourselves and in others. We discover that grief can become a forge, reshaping us into something truer, more substantial.

Without her, this book would not exist. Without her, I may never have had the courage to let my words step into the light. If my sixty-plus years of searching and stumbling brought me to this moment of publication, then it was Rozlyn's presence, and even her absence, that made the journey complete.

And so, this book is for her: my sweetest of angels, the quiet revolutionary in my own life, the one who showed me how love can heal even the deepest wounds.

Foreword

My search for John Bowlby began, in truth, as a search for myself. From the start, it was a journey: part inward, part outward, a search for meaning through the life of a man whose work has shaped countless lives yet remains elusive to many. Some may ask why someone like me—a teacher, not a psychiatrist or psychologist—should presume to write the biography of such an esteemed thinker and historical figure. It is a fair question. I have no clinical practice, no academic tenure in psychology, no pedigree stamped with the letters Dr. before my name. Instead, I have wandered like a pilgrim through my own life, wrestling with the very questions Bowlby himself tried to answer: what sustains human connection, what shatters it, and what it means to repair what is broken.

For decades, I stood in classrooms, pen in hand, drawing maps not only of empires but of human choices. I tried to help young people see the patterns that ripple through time: the victories, the betrayals, the fractures that shape both nations and individuals. And though my training was not in psychiatry, perhaps that is why I feel compelled to tell this story. I do not come as a clinician cataloguing theories, but as one who has walked the fault lines of attachment myself, carrying the cracks forward like scars in stone. To some, that may appear a weakness. I would argue it is my strongest credential. For Bowlby knew as well as anyone that love, loss, and belonging are not sterile subjects for laboratories; they are the heartbeat of every human life, mine included.

As part of my credentialing, I studied the giants of child development: Maslow stacking his pyramids of need, Pavlov ringing his bell, Piaget mapping stages of thought, Erikson sketching his cycles of life. And yet, curiously, Bowlby was rarely mentioned. His absence grew louder with each year, an empty chair in the lecture hall. Meanwhile, in my classroom, I could see his invisible fingerprints everywhere. I taught the avoidant, children who built walls high and thick, fortresses against disappointment. I taught the anxious, whose darting eyes searched endlessly for approval like ship lanterns sweeping a dark harbor. I taught (too many) disorganized bodies and voices tangled with chaos, their laughter fragile as glass. And yes, sometimes, I taught the secure; but not nearly enough. In those classrooms I felt the quiet urgency of the search: Bowlby's name missing from the textbooks, yet his presence alive in the children before me.

I approached Bowlby's life as I approached history, my chosen craft: tracing not only what he said, but the time that pressed upon him, the world that shaped him, and the legacy that followed in his wake. History, after all, is not just the study of events; it is the study of why those events mattered. To write Bowlby's life is to chart both the man and the age he tried to heal, to hold his story against the larger canvas of the twentieth century.

After a childhood of my own marked by fractured bonds, I came to Bowlby hoping to find clarity in the ruins left by flawed parents and a turbulent upbringing. I wanted to understand where the language of connection was born, why it could mend or wound, and how it might explain the fault lines in my own life. Somewhere along that search, Bowlby became more than ink on a page. He became something fatherly, a guide across the wreckage, a lantern over difficult terrain.

And yet, when I mentioned his name in conversation, I was often met with blank stares. It is a sad fact that despite his towering contributions, Bowlby remains a shadow figure to the public, his silhouette cast behind the brighter lights of Freud and Jung. Their names appear in novels and films, in punchlines and pub debates. Bowlby, meanwhile, lingers behind the curtain, unspoken, even as his work quietly remade entire fields. And so the search deepened not only for his theories, but for the man himself: the life behind the framework, the human story behind the science.

This has always puzzled me. For Bowlby's accomplishments were not minor echoes but seismic shifts. He gave us not just a lens for myth or memory, but a framework that changed psychology, psychiatry, social work, education, even medicine. His theory of attachment explained what binds us from our first breath, and how the absence of those bonds leaves marks that last a lifetime. He knew this in his bones. As the old saying goes, we give what we did not get. Bowlby himself sought to mend his childhood deficits by gifting the world a new language for love and loss.

Yes, there are other excellent biographies and analyses of his life and work like *John Bowlby: His Early Life: A Biographical Journey Into the Roots of Attachment Therapy* by Suzan Van Dijken and *Encounters with John Bowlby: Tales of Attachment* by Arturo Ezquerro. These are formidable books and I heap high praise on them. But the search feels unfinished. Each book captures facets of him, yet none, to my mind, completes the portrait. They left me searching still.

For a long time, I vacillated between two titles: *The Quiet Revolutionary* and *Searching for Bowlby*. The first carried a certain elegance; it spoke to his profound but understated role in reshaping psychology and child development, his quiet defiance against prevailing dogmas, and the way he altered the field without theatrics or fanfare. Yet, in the end, I chose *Searching for Bowlby*. Because that is, in truth, what this book is. It is both my search and, I suspect, the reader's search: for the man who gave us the language of attachment but who still remains a mystery to many outside the academy. His work is everywhere, yet his name is strangely absent from the conversations that matter most. *Searching for Bowlby* felt truer: a title that acknowledges the quest, the discovery, and the unveiling of a figure still hidden in plain sight.

But I believe none have captured the cinematic sweep of his story, spanning the thunder of two World Wars, the long shadows they cast, and the quieter but no less decisive struggles of the years beyond. That story alone deserves to be told: not merely the soldier, the doctor, the witness to upheaval, but the man who carried those histories into his work. And beyond that, the rest of his life—his friendships and doubts, his moments of triumph and failure, the contradictions that made him whole. For Bowlby was more than a set of theories; he was revolutionary yet reserved, influential yet misunderstood, brilliant yet deeply human. His life, in all its breadth and paradox, deserves to be seen, not in fragments, but as a full reel played from beginning to end.

And today, though his name is dimmed to many, his work shines everywhere. Therapists, counselors, and even dating coaches draw daily on his insights. A generation raised on YouTube discovers his ideas through creators who frame failed romances or anxious texts in the language of attachment theory. An entire cottage industry has sprung from the soil he tilled. He might have distrusted its fads, recoiled from its self-promotion, but I think he would also have recognized its power: that even watered down, his ideas still bring people back to themselves.

The book *Attached* by Amir Levine and Rachel Heller carried his framework into yet another wave of public awareness, climbing bestseller lists and giving readers the vocabulary of "secure," "anxious," and "avoidant." It was, for many, their first glimpse of concepts Bowlby articulated decades earlier. And that is good. People are learning, healing, finding new ways to understand themselves and those they love.

And yet, for me, it remains a bittersweet success. The architecture of attachment is everywhere, but the architect himself remains largely unknown. His ideas fill classrooms, counseling offices, and living rooms around the globe, but his name stays in the shadows, hidden behind the curtain.

This book is my attempt to change that. To pull back the fabric, to let Bowlby step into the light—not just as a theorist but as a man, flawed and luminous, who walked through his own wounds to give us a language for ours.

And so my search for Bowlby continues: not as a scholar hunched over footnotes, but as a seeker tracing faint footprints through the dust of history. I searched for him in the silences of textbooks where his name should have echoed, in the unlit corners of lectures where his absence spoke louder than words, and in the fractured gazes of children I once taught, where his theory lived though his name was never spoken. I searched for him in my own story, where attachment was not theory but ache, not abstraction but a wound carried in the body.

It has been both an outward journey into the archive of his life and an inward journey into the corridors of my own. And somewhere between those two paths, in that meeting place of history and humanity, I believe Bowlby waits. This book, then, is not the end of the search but its continuation: an invitation for you, too, to search for him, and in doing so, to search for yourself.

C. V. Wooster – October 2025

Table of Contents

Prologue

It was the tail-end of the 1950s, and the room was quiet save for the soft hum of a clock ticking on the far wall. The sound was barely audible beneath the distant murmur of London traffic filtering through the half-open window. A faint, damp chill hung in the air, typical of London winters, clinging to the edges of the small, dimly lit office. The scent of old leather and wood polish filled the space, mingling with the antiseptic remnants of earlier sessions.

Dr. John Bowlby sat in a large, red-brown leather chair, its old skin creaking as he leaned forward, observing the boy who sat across from him on the floor. The child's small fingers listlessly pushed a toy car back and forth, the motion mechanical, devoid of any particular joy. Every now and then, the car's wheels would snag on the uneven grain of the wooden floor, and the boy would pause, seemingly waiting for something to happen, before continuing with the same muted energy.

He was thin, and his cheeks had an unhealthy pallor. As he observed him, Dr. Bowlby was leaning forward slightly, elbows resting on his knees, his fingers loosely intertwined. The old psychiatrist cut a distinguished figure in his dark, pinstriped suit, his bushy grey eyebrows low over friendly and interested dark eyes. He had a high, crinkled forehead that disappeared after some way into his receding white hairline, and one finger tapped absently at the armrest as he watched the child play.

He had been sitting there for what felt like an eternity, watching, waiting, hoping for some sign of life. But Timothy remained detached, isolated in his own world, where even his interaction with the toy seemed like an interaction with a stranger.

"Do you like cars?" Bowlby's voice was soft, measured, as though afraid that even the gentlest words might push Timothy further away. He had learned long ago that a child in this state could not be reached through force, only through patience, understanding, and the careful offering of connection.

The boy didn't respond. His gaze was fixed on the car in his hand, but the doctor could tell his mind was somewhere far away. The silence remained, not uncomfortable but rather resigned, as if Timothy had long since come to see words as unnecessary, perhaps even burdensome.

The doctor resisted the urge to sigh, glancing around the room instead; it was a modest space furnished with an assortment of toys meant to encourage play and imagination. But here, among the blocks, the stuffed animals, the miniature trains, Timothy had simply picked a toy up at random and seemed to be content to while away the time.

2

He tried again. "You know, I was very interested in cars when I was young. I would have liked the one you have there."

For a brief moment, Timothy's hand paused, but the child almost immediately resumed his slow, monotonous play. Bowlby settled back into his chair, his expression calm, though internally he was wondering at the boy, trying to piece together what had gone so wrong, so early.

He knew the facts, of course. There had been reports. Timothy's parents were rarely home, both consumed by demanding careers that left little time for anything else. Nannies came and went like the changing of seasons, none staying long enough to form any meaningful connection. The child was fed, clothed, and sent to school by his Nanny, but in all the ways that mattered, he was abandoned. It was a familiar story, and his mind flicked back to Minnie, the beloved nanny who had been more of a mother to him than his own mother ever was. The contrast between Minnie's warmth and the cold distance of his parents still struck him, even all these years later.

Timothy put the car away and reached for a stuffed bear, its fur worn and patchy. He held it by one leg, dragging the bear along the floor as though it were just another object, something to fill the space rather than something to hold close. There was no tenderness in his touch, no sense of attachment. To Bowlby, it was as though the boy had never learned what it meant to hold something, or someone, close.

"How does the bear feel?" Bowlby asked, his voice gentle yet probing.

This time, there was a flicker... a tiny, fleeting shift in Timothy's gaze. His eyes flicked toward Bowlby for just a second before returning to the bear. His lips parted slightly, as if he might speak, but the moment slipped away before any words could form. Slowly, quietly, the boy pulled the bear closer to his chest, hugging it in a gesture that seemed more reflexive than affectionate.

Bowlby's chest tightened. He had spent years, decades even, studying the intricacies of attachment, the delicate bonds that formed or failed to form between parent and child. He had seen the effect of the war on children, of poverty, and the struggle of hard times. And yet, today, something deeper stirred within him. Timothy's silence, his isolation, felt all too familiar. It was as though he were looking into a mirror, seeing his own childhood reflected back at him.

After all, he had been Timothy once.

He remembered the smell of wet wool and freshly pressed clothes had once filled the air as he sat alone in the large drawing room of his family's home, surrounded by toys he never touched. John could still remember the way the air in his childhood home felt stale and heavy, despite the wealth and privilege surrounding him. His parents had been distant, absorbed in their own lives, much like Timothy's were now. The emptiness of those years, the gnawing absence of warmth, had left him hollow. The memories were always there, just beneath the surface, waiting to rise when he saw a child like Timothy.

He shifted in his chair, the leather creaking softly beneath him. He wanted to reach out, to pull the boy from the void he was trapped in, to give him something to hold onto, but he knew that this was not how it worked. Healing, if it came, would take time. Patience. Understanding. Bowlby had learned this through years of working with children like Timothy, children who had been deprived of the most fundamental human need: connection.

But patience was a cruel master, especially when the need for action felt so urgent.

The doctor knew there was no need to probe further today; the boy had revealed enough, though not in the way most might expect. His silence, his withdrawn demeanor, had told Bowlby everything he needed to know.

"That's all for today, Timothy," Bowlby said, his voice soft as he stood. "I'll see you again next week, yes?"

The boy didn't respond. He never did.

Bowlby rang for his assistant, calling in the boy's nanny. A cheerful young woman entered the room, offering a polite nod to the doctor as she gently took Timothy's hand and led him from the office. The boy didn't look back. Now, Bowlby leaned back in his chair with a slow exhale. The weight of Timothy's isolation hung in the air, familiar and suffocating. Bowlby had carried that same weight throughout most of his childhood.

He sat there for a long moment, staring at the empty space where Timothy had been. Memories of his own childhood drifted back, sitting alone in the grand but cold drawing room, surrounded by toys that meant nothing without someone to share them with. It was a strange, hollow feeling, knowing that the past and present could mirror each other so closely.

He could remember it all so clearly...

Chapter 1.

Seen and Not Heard

In 1907, London stretched out over the Thames like a creature half-awake, its veins and arteries winding through streets veiled in mist and the damp breath of the river. The city was a split between splendor and grime, and the Empire's ambition pressed against the claustrophobia of its narrowest lanes. It was the Edwardian era, a time of gilded facades and deeper anxieties, as England perched on the edge of change, facing a future shaped by technology and a past knotted with imperial entanglements.

Edward VII, Victoria's eldest, wore the crown, and he was a man unsettled by the world unraveling around him. The 'Uncle of Europe', as they called him, did not enjoy the absolute power his crown had promised. His power now faced pushback from all sides, liberals challenging authority, labor movements igniting discontent, the shadows of the Boer War still lingering in public opinion. Prime Minister Sir Henry Campbell-Bannerman and his Liberal government had set out with optimism, promising reforms, yet found themselves grappling with the South African colonies and the pressing demands of the industrial age.

The industrial machinery that had thrust England into modernity continued to hum, reshaping the skyline and the people alike. London, a teeming metropolis of over seven million, was an emblem of both innovation and inequality. The cityscape rose in spires and turrets, the Houses of Parliament, the dome of St. Paul's, the steel-and-stone span of the new Tower Bridge, all standing as symbols of the Empire against the soft drizzle. But London was defined just as much by its collisions and divides: Mayfair's stately residences and gas-lit promenades contrasted with the East End's dark alleys and crumbling tenements. The privileged zipped through the streets in gleaming motorcars, their fashion statements in steel, while nearby, laborers rattled along in horse-drawn carts through clouds of soot and smoke. And all through this, the Thames meandered with indifference, its dark waters reflecting a city torn between its monuments and its slums.

It was a time when science and art stretched the limits of human ambition, pressing against what had been and what might be. Just four years prior, on a sandy field in North Carolina, the Wright brothers had lifted the first powered aircraft into the sky, a machine that stuttered and wobbled but held the promise of something unprecedented: that humans could conquer the air. News of their feat rippled across oceans and borders, sparking conversations in every pub, drawing rooms, and lecture hall...and this was only the start. Soon, inventions that were once novelties, the telephone, the telegraph, became lifelines, threading people together across cities and continents, accelerating the very heartbeat of human communication.

Electricity was slowly illuminating city streets and humble kitchens alike, a glow that banished the soft flicker of gas lamps and pointed to a mechanized future. But beyond these mechanical marvels, society was swept up by an undercurrent of introspection and escapism. The music halls of London bustled with audiences who craved laughter and satire, where songs like "Ta-ra-ra Boom-de-ay" and the antics of performers like Marie Lloyd offered a few hours' release from life's drudgeries.

Yet underneath the Edwardian glamour, fissures were beginning to form in society's glossy surface. Laborers, armed with voices sharpened by unions, demanded fair wages and humane conditions, clashing against the rigid class walls that had defined them since the Victorian age. Women, too, began rattling their gilded cages; the suffrage movement gained momentum, steered by resolute figures like Emmeline Pankhurst.

Yet the state had its own troubles; across Europe, alliances were drawing invisible battle lines, casting shadows over the continent's peace. As one half of the Anglo-Russian Entente, Britain sought to curb Germany's swelling influence, even as faint murmurs of war echoed through political chambers and coffeehouses alike.

Look around now, and you would see a city layered with elegance and grit, where silk frocks and feathered hats brushed past soot-stained wool coats. In the opulent corridors of London, oblivious gentlemen in tailored suits ambled past factory workers destined to die in the wars to come…outside, the scent of baked bread mingled with coal smoke, as children darted around cobbled streets, their laughter mixing with the clamor of carriage wheels and street vendors.

And this was John Bowlby's London, a city caught between tradition and transformation, where the stability of the old ways was increasingly challenged by the forces of progress and change. Little did young John realize the role he would come to play in shaping the changes that lay ahead in the dawning century.

***

The Bowlby house of John's childhood rose from its quiet London Street like a monolith, a brooding grey thing that had long since settled into itself, exhaling cold air from its ancient bones. Even in summer, when the sun strained against the clouds and the rest of the world seemed to thaw, the house remained indifferent, immune to warmth. The stone walls drank in the light and spat it back as shadows. John imagined the house could breathe if it wanted to; its heavy silence pressed against his ears like a whispered threat, warning him not to expect too much from its cavernous halls.

Perched at the very top of this fortress was the nursery, the highest room, tucked away like an afterthought. It was here that John and his elder brother Tony spent most of their days, an exile of sorts, far removed from the bustle below, where the adults lived their mysterious, untouchable lives. The nursery felt more like a tower than a room, a place that belonged to neither the ground nor the sky. There, Tony and he, so close in age that sometimes John forgot where one of them ended and the other began, would fight and make up, one moment wrestling and the next, laughing together.

The room was dim despite the windows; they were tall but faced a dull courtyard, and the light that managed to creep in was more shadow than sun. The wallpaper, once adorned with delicate patterns of flowers and birds, had long since faded, curling at the edges like a forgotten memory. The room's furnishings were sparse, their once-fine materials showing signs of neglect, as though even the nursery had resigned itself to a state of quiet decay.

In this desolate kingdom, Nanny Friend, whom they called Nanna with no sense of affection, hovered over them like one of the dark corners come to life.

Nanna had sharp eyes and sharper words. Her footsteps usually arrived with a sigh, and she would wrap her hands, thin as claws, around John's arm if he misbehaved; her grip was cool and indifferent, as if she were handling a piece of misplaced furniture rather than a child. John missed their old nanny terribly, though he could never say it aloud. Minnie had been soft, warm, and smelled faintly of lavender; Nanna smelled of starch and had a weary, whip-like way of talking.

"Now, you sit straight, John," Nanna would say, her voice thin but pointed as she adjusted his collar with a tug that left it too tight.

John would stiffen but say nothing. He had learned that silence was better than protest; Nanna would find something wrong either way. She treated them all the same, though John felt her eyes linger on Tony with a rare flicker of approval.

Tony, the golden boy.

The six Bowlby children were divided into an informal structure of three pairs; the youngest, Jim and Evelyn, were referred collectively as 'the babies,' while John's elder sisters, Winnie and Marion, were always called 'the girls'. Finally, Tony and John, only thirteen months apart, were 'the boys,' and they were in constant battle. Tony was the eldest son, and John couldn't forget it, not for a second. The weight of being the second son pressed down on him in ways he couldn't understand but felt every day. If Tony won a game, John sulked; if John ran faster, Tony would make sure no one noticed. There was love between them, and then there was a rivalry.

A race through the gardens had left them muddy and sweaty, and after they'd had a stern disciplining from Nanna and were deposited back into the nursery, John sulked as Tony gladly returned to his toys.

"It's not fair," John muttered. "I was going to win, Nanna finding us distracted me..."

Tony didn't look up from his toy soldier, which he was inspecting with a sense of childish victory. "Don't be a baby. I came first, didn't I? That's that."

That was Tony: always first. First to speak, first to take, first to be noticed by their mother in that single hour she gave them after tea.

Life in the Bowlby household was rigid, ruled by the expectations of the Edwardian era. The children were to be seen, but never heard. It was a rule enforced not just by Nanna, but by John's mother, Lady May Bowlby, whose beauty and elegance were matched only by her emotional distance. Tall and graceful, she floated through their lives like a figure from a portrait, admirable but unreachable. Her affection was rare, her smiles fleeting, and when she did bestow a pat on John's head or a brief word, it felt mechanical, like a duty rather than an act of warmth.

"Affection spoils children," she would often say, not to John directly but to Nanna, as if explaining away the faint discomfort she felt around her own offspring. The Edwardian way of schooling continued to affect the way children were raised in England, and it was believed that the best way to raise the best of children was not to spoil them with intimate care.

Yet as distant as Mother was, Father was even less tangible. John knew that Father, one Sir Anthony Alfred Bowlby, was surgeon to the King's Household, and a very important man. In fact, he could recite many facts about him, yet he couldn't quite picture his face most of the time, only the outline of a man who would sometimes arrive suddenly at the house after months, only to disappear yet again. Father was a presence in their lives, but not an active one; he moved through their days like a shadow, brief and fleeting, leaving only the scent of tobacco and leather behind him. Only many years later would John realize that perhaps Sir Anthony's own childhood loss, the loss of his father to war, had cast a shadow over him.

The children's infrequent forays into the city afforded little comfort. Chaperoned by Nanna or their humorless tutor, the children would sometimes be afforded walks through the city, made to read out the faded signs of various shopfronts, yet what they were reading, really, was the city around them.

Over the decades, London had morphed into a giant between two worlds, caught in the last breaths of the Edwardian era, on the cusp of a strange new modernity. It was a place of stillness and motion, of old buildings with crooked chimneys and new steel bridges rising from the water like iron bones. The streets, wide and cobbled, were lined with rattling horse-drawn carriages, while impressive new motorcars were the way of the future.

On their walks, John would look shyly as older children in stiff collars and woolen knickerbockers walked by, kicking pebbles into the gutters. As they passed by the markets, they would see carts laden with vegetables, bread, and the occasional goose. The scent of fresh-baked bread would mingle with the sharp tang of fish, with scales glinting under the weak afternoon sun. Sometimes he would see the poorer women bartering for apples and squabbling over pennies, children clinging to their sides. In such moments, his own mother's distance would rankle sorely in John's heart, and he would look away.

For John, life felt like a series of walls, both real and invisible, erected to keep him in place. The tall, gray buildings of London, with their chimneys puffing out smoke, only added to the sense of being trapped. On foggy days, the mist would roll in from the Thames, swallowing the city until only the faint glow of gas lamps remained, their flickering lights like distant beacons. It was as if London itself was trying to hide, to retreat from the world's gaze.

On such days, there would be no walks, but from the window, the children would hear the clack of boots on wet cobblestones, the sharp call of a newsboy shouting the latest headlines, even the world itself was dulled by the thick blanket of mist. At other times, it would rain, and the

14

miserable weather would lock the children in for days on end. This was particularly dreaded by the children, who would inevitably go stir-crazy and invite the irritable wrath of Nanny Friend. As always, Mother would be either in her own world or gone for stretches to visit Father, whom the children rarely saw.

And so, life in the house was a life lived among ghosts and memories and people who weren't there, not really there, at any rate.

Yet in July, things would change.

***

In July, the family would visit the New Forest, and the days leading up to the trip were always a strange kind of torment, for summer in London was little better than its rain. The city pressed in on you from all sides, the grey buildings, the narrow streets, the air heavy with the smells of horse manure and coal smoke. But in the New Forest, everything was different. The sky was wider, the air clearer, and even Mother seemed less distant, sitting by the brook with her sketchbook while John and Tony splashed in the water. The girls never accompanied them; they were sent off to be with their grandparents during these visits.

John loved the brook. The way it twisted and curled, never staying still. He would crouch at its edge, poking at the sticklebacks darting between the rocks, feeling more alive than he ever did in the nursery. The dragonflies hovered over the water like living jewels, and the sunlight through the leaves cast rippling patterns on the surface that seemed to move with a life of their own.

Tony, of course, always tried to outdo him. If John found a worm wriggling near the water, Tony would find two. If John managed to climb a low branch of an oak tree, Tony would be three branches higher before he could even look up.

But there was something about the forest that made the rivalry less bitter. Here, it didn't matter so much that Tony was first; here, John could breathe. They had a mail cart, a wooden contraption on wheels, a gift from Father last Christmas, and they would race it down the hills. Tony always won, but even then, the wind on John's face was victory enough.

In London, there were walls and rules; in the forest, there was freedom. They were allowed to roam on their own, exploring every corner of the vast woods. They would ride donkeys, their short legs kicking at the animals' sides, pretending they were knights off on some grand adventure. And at night, when the air cooled and the shadows lengthened, they would sit by the fire and listen to the sounds of the forest, owls hooting, the rustle of leaves in the wind.

Mother accompanied them, but even so she rarely spoke, her attention fixed on her sketches. Father, of course, never came. He had always stayed in London, buried in his work, but of late, he was away from the country. The moment in 1914 war had broken out and Great Britain had joined, the elder Bowlby had joined active service and had disappeared without so much as a word to the family.

When the children asked Nanna about the war, all they got were confusing readings from the newspapers, which promised a *swift and glorious victory,* and that the boys *would be back by Christmas.*

"Will father be back by Christmas?" Tony asked excitedly.

"Likely not," Nanna said bluntly, rolling the newspaper away. "Men may start wars, but I doubt they know how to end them."

The children did not understand half of the things she said when she was in one of her moods, and attempts to pry would be met with a glare. The one time John had made the mistake of asking about the war from Mother, she had paused, her eyes growing misty, before she left the room without a word. He had felt terrible about it after.

The only other outdoor recreation John looked forward to was at the behest of his maternal grandfather, or as he called him, Grampie. These activities could range anything from fishing, to shooting, to birdwatching. In any and all cases, the mornings with Grampie always began the same way: early.

When such mornings came, John would wake with his eyelids heavy but excited, his small boots clumsy against the wooden steps of the old house. Grampie would already be waiting, standing on the edge of the porch, his long frame straight as a fencepost. He was a tall man, lanky but hardy in the way his generation of men were. He wore the same outfit every time for these excursions, a dark hunting jacket, faded but carefully patched in places, and a tweed hat pulled low over his brow. A thick white mustache bristled above his upper lip, giving him the stern air of an old officer, but his eyes betrayed a gentleness to him: sharp and twinkling, they were always amused.

John adored him. His grampie had a way of filling space, not with words, he wasn't a chatty man, but with a steady, grounding presence. In the absence of John's father, Grampie was a quiet rock in John's small and often lonely life. He wasn't indulgent, not the kind of grandfather who let you stay up late or sneak extra sweets, but he was consistent; he had a way of showing love through action, through time spent and lessons taught.

"Got your binoculars?" Grampie asked that morning, his voice low and gravelly, more of a rumble than a sound.

"Yes, sir," John replied, lifting them like a badge of honor. The lenses were scratched and smudged, but they worked well enough for a boy learning to see the world.

"Good lad," Grampie said with a curt nod. Then, with a swift turn, he began walking, his long legs setting a brisk pace that John scrambled to match. The two of them headed out toward the woods, where the birds sang their morning songs. The cool air smelled of damp earth and pine, and John felt alive in a way he never did back home.

Grampie always moved like he belonged in the forest, his boots barely crunching the underbrush, his shoulders rolling with the confidence of a man who had spent more hours outdoors than in. John, by contrast, was noisy; he tripped over roots and sent startled sparrows flitting out of bushes. Grampie would pause, glancing back with a raised eyebrow but no scolding, just a silent reminder to tread more softly.

18

"Listen," Grampie said after a while, holding up a gloved hand. John froze, tilting his head to hear whatever magic his grandfather had caught. At first, there was nothing, just the faint rustle of leaves in the breeze. Then, faint and lilting, the song of a blackcap.

"That," Grampie said, pointing toward a thicket of brambles ahead, "is worth your trouble. Keep your eyes sharp."

John raised his binoculars, clumsily focusing them on the source of the sound. The bird came into view, a small, plump thing with a slate-gray cap that seemed too neat, too precise, to belong to something wild. John's heart raced with the thrill of discovery.

"Beautiful, isn't it?" Grampie murmured, and John agreed.

They spent hours like that, wandering through the woods, spotting finches, robins, and thrushes. Grampie taught John to notice the subtle details, the flash of yellow on a goldfinch's wings, the way a robin's song seemed brighter in the spring. Then, by noon, they would be back on the porch, the sun high and warm. Grampie would light his pipe, the smoke curling lazily upward as he sat in his rocking chair. John would then sit beside him, silent but satisfied in a way he could never quite explain.

***

The return to home felt particularly dismal after such adventures, and John would ache with a repressed

19

belligerence at being forced back into the cage of the house. Nanna would tut and roll her eyes when the brothers returned full of energy, turning to mother with exasperated complaints.

"The forest has run them wild, ma'am!" she'd say. "Why, they left here as angels, and have returned as little savages..."

For her part, Mother would listen with a distant look, scold the children lightly, and go about her day.

While their father continued to serve across the channel in France, his letters came occasionally in neat little envelopes, scrawled across in haste, their edges smudged from their long journey. Each time the postman knocked, the same ritual played out. Mother would sit in her chair by the fire, tear open the envelope with dainty fingers, her face giving nothing away. As Nanny Friend kept a vigilant eye on the children, Mother would sit by the fire like a distant goddess, her eyes scanning the letter. Then, with a sort of weary impatience, she'd fold it back up and tuck it into a drawer, silent.

The children waited every time, gathered like sparrows around her. As little Evelyn stared with wide eyes, John and Tony would wait for her to speak, for her to read the words aloud. But she never did. Not only were children not meant to be heard, but it seemed words were not meant to be read, at least to those too young to understand the calamitous world outside their strict home confines.

One rainy afternoon, as the grey clouds pressed low against the city, John couldn't hold back any longer. The latest letter had just disappeared into its drawer, swallowed whole by the wood.

"Mother," John ventured, his voice quieter than he intended. "What does he say?"

She paused, fingers still lingering on the closed drawer. "Nothing for you to worry about," she said, her voice clipped.

"But..." John started again, taking a step forward, feeling Tony's eyes on him. "Does he...does he ask about us?"

Mother's hands tightened, just barely, but John noticed. She stood, brushing invisible dust from her skirt. "Finish your lessons," she said briskly, walking from the room.

"What a loving and noble son," Nanna commented with her usual, cutting sarcasm. "How easily you wound your mother!"

To this, John grew flushed and sulked the rest of the day. Nanna's words had the additional effect of not just scorning her victim, but pillorying him; for the rest of the day, Tony and his sisters fixed a disapproving look at John that nearly drove him to tears.

Whether it had been a consequence of one of these letters or a piece of advice from the other ladies with their husbands abroad, it was decided that the children needed a formal schooling outside of their homes, perhaps in an attempt to toughen them up. Whatever the case, the strict governess in charge of the children's education was told that she would no longer be teaching the boys, to which John and Tony both rejoiced.

The school selected for them was one day school in Somerset Street, known mostly as Edge's.

A week in this place proved that while it was a reprieve from their lonely, grey lives, it wasn't any kinder. Edge's was a place with an underlying sense of menace, and John could feel it even though he was only seven. The building sat stoically on Somerset Street, an institution of pale brick and polished stone with a front as prim as a line of marching soldiers. Its iron gates, painted a deep, haughty green, swung open each morning to reveal a tidy gravel path that crunched beneath John's polished loafers. Set back from the road, the building itself seemed to watch the street with a sense of severity, its arched windows gleaming like rows of half-shut eyes keeping silent watch.

Inside, the hallways were as polished as old silver, faintly glowing with the patina so associated with London's grime. Meanwhile, in the classrooms, the desks were arranged with rigid precision, their dark wood worn smooth by countless eager and reluctant hands. High shelves filled with leather-bound volumes lined the walls, thick with knowledge and the faint, musty smell of old paper. Light would filter through tall windows onto the faces of students who sat in prim rows, giving the place a harsh glow as the students would cough in the chalky air. This was a place of quiet, orderly ambition enforced with punishment. Here, you were small, and everything was designed to beat you into shape.

The headmaster, proprietor, and namesake of the school was one Mr. Edgeton, a man who didn't so much walk

22

as he loomed. He was the picture of a gentleman, only he was a picture and nothing else; where he had the bearing of an aristocrat, he also had the temper and brutishness of a butcher. When he passed by, the other boys would shrink into themselves, tensing like rabbits caught in a trap. Mr. Edgeton was a man who believed fear was more useful than kindness, and the cane he always carried was a reminder of the adage he believed in so earnestly—*spare the rod, you spoil the child.*

Institutions like Edge's, with their rigid hierarchies and spartan conditions, were not merely centers of learning but also factories of character, or so their proponents believed. Often steeped in tradition and located in grand, Gothic buildings, these schools were seen as the ideal environment for molding young minds, believed to instill discipline, stoicism, and a sense of duty, qualities deemed essential for leadership in the British Empire. A man like Edgeton would be the center of such places, a figure of awe and sometimes fear. His authority was absolute, and corporal punishment was a tool wielded with the aim of instilling obedience and a strong moral compass.

Generations of British boys and girls would pass through these institutions, their formative years shaped by the regimented routines and austere surroundings. The experience would leave an indelible mark on their personalities and worldview, while also forging a sense of camaraderie among peers. The system produced a cadre of leaders who went on to shape the course of history. Politicians, military commanders, and business tycoons emerged from these hallowed halls, carrying with them the values and attitudes instilled by their alma maters. Yet, it also bred a certain aloofness and a tendency to suppress

23

emotions, a legacy that would influence British culture for decades to come by furthering the isolation of the child and thus raising a generation that would in turn be alienated from their own children.

For John, this alienation only compounded his sense of everyday isolation. Tony, as ever, was as much a problem as he was a comfort. The teachers at Edge's, in a thoughtless mistake, had decided to place them in the same class. It might have been sensible, but to Tony, it was unbearable; after all, he wanted to be the older brother in every sense, to stand taller and walk faster; to be right when John was wrong.

That first morning, seated on the hard, uncomfortable bench, John's eyes roamed the room. The walls were bare save for a few charts tacked haphazardly, lessons on mathematics and grammar that seemed to have no interest in being learned. The light slanted through the high windows, dust drifting lazily in its path. Everything about the place felt stifling, the air itself heavy with rules and expectations. There was no room for error here; no room for being small or uncertain.

The other boys sat in rows, stiff-backed and silent. They knew better. They'd learned quickly that Edge didn't tolerate fidgeting or whispering, and they especially didn't tolerate curiosity. You were meant to sit and learn. No questions asked. The lessons, delivered in a monotone, were less about discovery and more about survival. If you could sit through the hours without drawing attention to yourself, you'd made it through the day unscathed.

After this prolonged purgatory, the walk home through Hyde Park was a relief. The park, on a soft summer's afternoon, was a world apart from London. The trees would cast dappled shadows across the sun-drenched grass, their branches stretched wide like outstretched arms, coaxing the afternoon into the timeless hush that only nature commands.

The lake shimmered beneath the sunlight, a lazy mirror capturing the cerulean sky. This was named the Serpentine, a forty-acre body of water commissioned in the 18th century by Queen Caroline. Now dappled with ducks and the occasional rowboat, nearly two hundred years later, it seemed almost to smile under the soft weight of the summer sun.

Hyde Park was an oasis, a place where beauty stretched in wide, careless sweeps across the land. To the upper echelons of society, the sprawling 350 acres, bordered by bustling streets and the genteel neighborhoods of London, served as a salon under open skies. Ladies in wide-brimmed hats and men in tailored morning coats paraded along Rotten Row, their steps deliberate and their expressions carefully composed. The Row itself, a long, tree-lined bridleway, carried the reputation of exclusivity. To be seen there, atop a fine horse or in a finely tailored suit, was to assert one's place in the social pecking order.

Of course, for the masses, Hyde Park was something else entirely. It was freedom from the drudgery of industrial life, and on weekends, families crowded its greens, laying out threadbare blankets under its ancient oaks. Around them, the air would carry the faint scent of blossoming lilacs and warm earth, mingling with the comforting traces of woodsmoke from nearby houses. Lovers lingered under the shade of elms, while friends exchanged stories over picnics, voices mingling like a gentle stream. Soldiers on leave strolled quietly, their minds for once not on battles, but on the dance of leaves and the serene sway of the grass, tall and untroubled. Often, Hyde Park's Speakers' Corner would also attract the radicals of society: the orators, artists, socialists, anarchists, and suffragettes, who would speak their minds even if they rarely got through to either the rich parading their wealth or the common folk trying to enjoy their day.

Like many, John and Tony liked Hyde Park for the reprieve it offered. It was only here, under the vast, open sky, that the boys could stretch their legs, feel the cool air on their faces, and for a little while, forget the tightening grip of the classroom. But even in this lesser Eden, the brothers would inevitably clash heads.

One day, as the sun hung low over Hyde Park, the brothers walked side by side, their black shoes crunching on the gravel path. The other boys from Edge's trailed behind, their chatter and laughter faded and distant. The air smelled of damp earth and autumn leaves, but for John, it held little pleasure. Tony had been picking at him all day, little jabs, little digs, nothing anyone else would notice, but John felt every word like a pebble in his shoe.

"They're stupid, especially Edgeton," Tony muttered, just loud enough for his brother to hear. "A year older and they put me in the same class as you! *In-com-petent.*"

He said the word in the same tone as Nanny Friend, mildly proud at how old it made him feel. He had not yet noticed that John was clenching his fists, the words stinging him more than they should.

Tony glanced at him sideways. "It really is thoughtless, don't you think? You should be a year back, at least." He smirked. "Or back home with the girls."

John stopped. He couldn't help it. His feet just refused to take another step. "Let off," he said, his voice trembling slightly but strong enough.

Tony stopped too, blinking in surprise.

"What are you on about?"

"Stop digging at me like that. Or else."

Tony frowned. He hadn't expected John to answer back, not like this; he was tempted to shove his brother back, but he could see the other boys further down the path. If John answered back, as he always did, the last thing Tony wanted to risk was being seen rolling through the ground wrestling with his brother. He'd be laughed at, no doubt.

"What's the matter with you?" Tony said, a faint sneer crossing his face. "Can't you take a joke?"

John shook his head. "It's not a joke," he said, his voice firm now, the tremor gone. "You always act like you're better, but you're not."

Tony's eyes narrowed, but John didn't flinch. For a while, they stood there, staring each other down; then, Tony took a step back, his grin flickering before he turned away, pretending like nothing had happened.

"You're too jumpy," he said dismissively. "Let's go home, or we'll be late for tea. I don't want another thrashing from Nanna."

27

John nodded mutely, and the boys continued on the way. Edge's had taught John something important, even if it wasn't what Mr. Edgeton had intended. It taught him that the world wasn't fair, that power was something people wielded to keep you small, but it also taught him that standing up, even when it was difficult, was the only way to face it. Conformity risked losing yourself, to be beaten and molded into something else, and his identity was the one thing John had always insisted on and would never compromise.

Chapter 2.

Lindisfarne

As the years passed, the war was no longer a distant thing, far across the Channel; it was a living, breathing thing that had crept unchallenged into every home in London.

John Bowlby, now eleven, could feel it in the silence that lingered after supper, the way his mother stared at the mantelpiece as Nanny Friend read the newspaper to her with her usual bored tone. The letters from Father were fewer now; they came sporadically, thin paper folded tightly into old envelopes. John no longer asked what they said; whatever words they contained seemed to only deepen the quiet in the house, like stones dropped into still water. Sometimes, John imagined him somewhere in France, deep in the mud and chaos of the front, but his mind couldn't grasp it.

And then there was Nanna. Unlike the rest of the world, she hadn't changed, at least not in ways that John could see. She was as sharp-tongued and rigid as ever, her cold sarcasm a constant in a world that seemed to be unraveling. Sometimes, John caught himself wondering if Nanna felt the fear that gripped everyone else, but he couldn't imagine it. Nanna seemed beyond fear, beyond any human frailty.

What had changed, unmistakably, was London. The city felt hollowed out, as if the war had drained its lifeblood. The streets, once crowded with well-dressed men and women, were now occupied by tired, weary women in dark skirts, clutching their ration cards and hurrying through their errands. The men who had once filled the streets had either gone to war or were conspicuously absent. Even the posters of Kitchener, which had once stood proudly on every corner, their bright colors urging men to join the fight, were now faded and peeling, their message a sad echo of a forgotten call. The war felt closer, the air heavy with the scent of coal smoke and fear. There was talk of the front, always, and of those who hadn't come back, neighbors whose faces John vaguely remembered from before the war, now reduced to little more than names.

But it was the sky that unsettled him most. The air raids so far had been few and far between, but the rumors promised that worse was to come; after all, the past year had seen the dropping in the dead of night, shattering glass, and tearing through the familiar streets. Now, the nights were unlit in London, as people feared to give a well-lit target to the German bombers. A sense of quiet paranoia had settled in, and the city was bracing itself like an animal before a storm.

When the bombs would come, the children would be forced down into their cramped and musty cellar, with the babies crying and girls squealing anytime they felt something brush against their leg in the darkness, in fear of rats they never saw. The boys did their best to put on a brave face, trying to emulate Mother, who would eventually lead them out from the cellar the next morning, pale but resolute.

Tony was always the first to say what they were both thinking. "They're going to double down, mark it down," he muttered one evening on the way back home. "The boys are saying the Hun's going to launch a full attack on London. I think they're right."

John didn't respond. He'd heard the same stories from their classmates at Edge's; boys who had relatives in the East End, boys who talked about fires in the night and people crushed beneath rubble.

"It's just stories," John said, trying to reassure himself more than his brother. "They can't keep bombings going…"

Tony didn't answer.

***

It was late spring when the decision came. John and Tony were being sent to prep school, far from London, far from the looming raids. The announcement came at dinner, in the usual quiet and formal atmosphere of their dining room. The large oak table, worn from years of family meals, stretched between them like a chasm. Tony sat beside John, their elbows brushing as they ate in silence, the clinking of silverware the only sound. The babies fidgeted in their seats, while the sisters focused intently on their plates. At one end of the table sat mother; at the opposite end, Father's chair was empty as ever.

31

When it came, the announcement wasn't really an announcement at all. Mother simply mentioned it as she passed the vegetables, as if she were remarking on the weather.

"You'll both be going to a prep school soon. It's been arranged." Her voice was clipped, efficient, the way it always was when she wanted to avoid questions.

John didn't know how to feel. Part of him had expected it; the war had reached the point where London no longer felt safe, even in their quiet, grey house. But another part of him, the part that still clung to the familiar, to the small routines that made sense in a senseless world, felt something close to panic. It felt too much, too fast, but he said nothing. Tony would speak, as he always did, and John would follow.

Sure enough, Tony looked up from his plate, his brow furrowed. "Where?"

"Lindisfarne preparatory," Mother replied. "Worcester."

"What about Father?" Tony asked quietly. "Does he know we're getting carted off?"

Mother's hands paused. "This is your father's suggestion. I will hear no more on the topic."

And that was that. Now, as John glanced across the table at his sisters, they pushed their food around their plates, their discomfort visible in the way they avoided looking up. It struck John that while he and Tony were being sent away, the girls would remain at home. The unfairness of it gnawed at him. The boys, often favored for their gender, now felt punished for the same reason. But there was nothing to say, no way to change what had already been decided.

That night, as John lay in bed, the weight of their parents' decision settled over him like a leaden blanket. The thought of leaving London, of being sent away to a strange, cold school, filled him with dread. He didn't want to go. He didn't want to leave behind the small, familiar world that had once felt secure, even though it had grown colder and more uncertain with each passing day.

He considered how his parents had never really been much in favor of the trend of boarding schools, being fiercely doting as they were on him and Tony, yet apparently, they had arrived at the conclusion that the rough and tough living of the boarding houses was a more reasonable risk than staying in London where the threat was less of other schoolboys and more of a bomb dropping down on them.

Even so, a part of John still wondered if it wasn't better to take the risk of staying here rather than going out into the unknown. But agency was not something afforded to the young; all John could do, like the rest of his siblings, was to abide by the decisions made by his parents and hope for the best.

But the days passed far too quickly for John's taste, and it was soon time to leave. The family took a large carriage to the station, but even so Winnie and Marion had to be left behind to make room for the boys, the babies, Mother, and Nanna. This was John's first time to the station and it was as full of wonder as it was somewhat frightening; the great building thick with steam, the clatter of wheels and hissing engines filling the air. As they waited for their train, John stood stiffly beside Tony, both boys clutching their small leather cases, eyes cast downward. They each wore their most proper suits, and John's baker-boy cap was low over his mousy hair.

Mother stood a few feet away, her back ramrod straight, gloved hands folded over her handbag. She said little, as usual, eyes focused somewhere beyond them, never quite meeting theirs. Next to her, Nanny Friend held little Jim's hand, who was sniffling loudly. His face was red, wet with tears he couldn't hide.

The train arrived soon like a screaming serpent, and John resisted the urge to jam his fingers into his ears like little Jim or Evelyn; the last thing he needed was another teasing from Tony. As boarding began, Mother turned them to look at her.

"Be good boys, both of you," she said, her voice even. "No fights, no ill manners, and certainly no missing classes... I shall be informed at once. And write when you arrive."

John nodded, throat dry. Beside him, Tony stood taller, chin slightly raised, already looking past the whole affair. He always did that. Brushed it all off, as if leaving for boarding school was just another dull day.

Then, the train whistle blew. Nanny Friend tightened her grip on Jim as he let out a fresh sob, sighing. "Time to go, boys," she called out impatiently, glancing at the clock as if it were all just another errand. "Hurry now, the stationmaster's not as patient as me..."

Quietly, John shook little Jim's quivering hand and followed Tony toward the train. As they boarded, he dared one last glance at Mother. She gave a small nod, lips tight but not unkind. And then they were moving, the wheels grinding against the tracks, and the platform, with its tears, its silences, slipped away into the fog.

Looking down at his polished shoes, John whispered, "None of this feels real."

"Well, it is," Tony said with a frown, looking out of the train's window. "It's real. Don't be a baby."

Too conflicted to argue, John sulked instead. Soon, the slight was forgotten, and the boys found themselves playing cards with a rather rakish young man, who had undertaken it upon himself to teach the game to the brothers. As the light waned and London grew steadily distant, John did his best to study his hand, smile, and try not to think about the future.

***

The train's steady rhythm had lulled John into a half-daze by the time they reached Worcestershire. When the brothers stepped off the carriage, they were quickly rounded up with other Lindisfarne students by a twitchy old coachman. All in all, there were six of them, and they were quickly led out to the cramped old coach that would take them to the school.

Leaving the station, the air hit John first, clean, crisp, and grassy. There was dirt here, but no grime; no clatter of horse-drawn abs or the suffocating press of people. The sky stretched out above him in pale blues and soft greys, clouds hanging low and soft as wool. John took it all in, his boots sinking slightly into the soft earth of the road.

Beside him, Tony kicked at the dirt, already half-bored. "Not much here, is there?" he muttered, though John could hear the curiosity underneath his brother's mask of indifference.

"' Urry now, young masters," the old coachman said, lighting a pipe as he looked down at them. "Up an' in you go."

As the children were reluctantly shoved into the coach like sardines in a can, they began their long and bumpy ride down to Lindisfarne. John was fortunate enough to have a seat at the narrow window, and he stared wistfully at the fields rolling out in every direction. Every once in a while, they'd pass by stretches of hedgerows lining the paths like old soldiers, neat and unbending. Yet beyond them, the world was wild; small hills swelled and dipped, and in the distance, he could see the stooped silhouettes of trees.

Yet this wild splendor grew more tamed as they reached Lindisfarne. The school stood on the crest of an ancient rise, crowned by a red-brick clock tower rising against the sky like a monument over the sprawling land. From a distance, the school seemed perfectly in tune with the earth; nestled among hills, it was part of the landscape but also something apart. The building was grand, but not ostentatiously so; its lines were sharp, its angles precise.

It didn't invite. It commanded.

The old clock tower looked down at them as the coach rounded a bend, passed by the low stone walls, and came to a stop.

"Out ye go, out ye go," the old man said, opening the coach doors and puffing impatiently on his woody pipe. "Stand straight, young masters, an' head down to the hall…"

As a bell rang with a clear, crisp sound, the children dismounted the coach with groans and jostles. John, now standing on the gravel path that wound toward the main building, looked around. Ever-sensitive, he could feel it all pressing down on him, the sense of history, the structure of the place. The wind stirred faintly, rustling the leaves in the nearby trees and carrying the scent of wet earth and old wood.

"Come, John," said Tony, who was already striding ahead, hands in his pockets, eager to take the lead. John followed with a sigh, not too far behind.

***

In time, John would grow quickly familiar with Lindisfarne's grounds. The North Lodge, where the boys were to stay, was tucked discreetly at the entrance to the estate. The estate buildings scattered around were neat and purposeful, but carried the weight of age in their stone walls and ivy-covered roofs. The lodgings were military in precision, but given to rowdiness considering the many schoolboys staying there; however, such behavior was met with a quick and eager cane by the masters, and so John and Tony stayed well out of such trouble.

But the heart of everything was Abberley Hall, the old country house that had been their first port of call upon reaching the school. As the groundskeeper explained, the building was built on old foundations, and some of the old stone could still be seen around the base, dark and mossy.

The main structure of Abberley Hall rose in terracotta tones, its rectangular windows lined in white and staring out across the grounds with a measured indifference. The house's form was classical in every sense, symmetrical and balanced, with vine-tangled columns and pilasters on the façade. The chimneypieces were commanding, carved from dark, veined marble that caught the dim firelight like ink on paper. Above them, the cornices framed the high ceilings with crisp, geometric perfection, their intricate carvings catching the shadows and drawing the eye upward. There were no frivolous flourishes in the house's design; nothing seemed to exist purely for the sake of beauty.

From the outside, the Hall seemed timeless, caught somewhere between the present and the past. Yet within its calculated symmetry and disciplined structure, there was an undercurrent of life: the worn stones, the creeping vines, the faint scuff marks on the grand staircase where generations of feet had risen and fallen.

The Headmaster's residence was, by contrast, a jarring interruption to the house's careful elegance. It was hard to say whether it had been attached to Abberley's garden front with a sense of innovation or as a reckless exercise in modernity; the structure was an abrupt block of raw concrete that neither flowed with the land nor honored the vision of the main building. It did, however, match the headmaster himself; Mr. Kilby was a tall, austere man who moved through the school with an air of quiet authority. His voice, sharp and clipped, cut through the classrooms like a blade. Discipline was paramount at Lindisfarne, and the boys quickly learned the consequences of disobedience.

***

The boys found themselves confined, again, in a place of absolute order. The dormitory where John and Tony would sleep was a long, narrow room, lined with rows of identical iron beds. Scratchy woolen blankets were neatly folded at the foot of each bed, and the walls were bare, save for a single crucifix that hung at the far end of the room.

Here, the boys would wake in the morning and immediately find themselves stuck in a rigid schedule of lessons, chores, and outdoor activities. With the pale light filtering through the old dormitory windows, John would dress up in the uniform: stiff collars, starched cuffs, all white and grey and navy. His days began in silence, punctuated only by the occasional stifled yawn, and ended with sore limbs and a deadened mind.

Tony adapted with relative ease; the school seemed to suit him, and he thrived in the rigid structure, slipping into it as naturally as if he'd been born to it. John would watch his brother stroll into the dining hall each morning, nodding easily to boys and masters alike. Tony had a charm about him, and though John was liked enough by the other boys, he did not have much of what might be called friends.

To make matters worse, the nature of the school depressed him; he felt every rule, every timetable, as a weight pressing down on him. His day was sliced into

39

precise portions: breakfast at 7:30, assembly at 8:15, and classes beginning sharply at 9. He moved from classroom to classroom, from Latin to arithmetic, then history and geography, and the exodus never seemed to end. The classrooms were small, with only about a dozen boys to a room, so there was no hiding in the crowd, no drifting into the background. The masters saw everything, every slip in attention, every poorly concealed yawn. More than once, John saw Headmaster Kilby descending on some poor boy who had had the temerity to yawn during class.

"I suppose you find all of this terribly boring," he would say, indignant as he would tap at his table with his wooden scale. "Hands."

"Please, sir, I didn't mean…"

"I said *hands*, young man."

What would follow were the sharp cracks of a ruler striking the boy's pale palms until they were red and blistered. The others would cringe at every strike, and would know that this was the cost of not conforming.

This pressure for conformity was not just present in studies; Lindisfarne's dedication to physical prowess was just about as intense as its academic rigor. The school boasted an Astroturf pitch and an indoor swimming pool; hockey, golf, and croquet filled the autumn afternoons, while riding, fishing, and archery occupied the weekends. Even as the chill of winter crept in, there was no excuse for idleness. John dreaded those outdoor sessions, the crisp air biting at his face as he fumbled with the hockey stick, struggling to keep up with Tony and the others who seemed to glide across the field as if they'd been born with the sticks in their hands.

Tony, naturally, was a star at this. He took to hockey with a competitive ferocity, his eyes gleaming with the thrill of the game, his movements quick and precise. He was always the first to score, always the one the other boys gravitated towards, admiring, even imitating. Tony knew how to take the ball, how to read his opponents, how to move in a way that seemed effortless. For him, these games were just another way to shine, another way to prove himself. John found himself fuming at this, and often the other boys would be found chuckling as they watched John trying to outdo his brother.

Mondays and Thursdays were Letter Days, but word from home arrived infrequently. As they scarfed down bread and butter for breakfast alongside their slices of cold ham, the letters would arrive and John would receive them with the same hope of a swift return to London. But there was no such luck; almost always, his mother's words were brief and formal, offering little in the way of comfort or reassurance. Then, on Fridays, they had archery practice. Rows of boys lined up with bows in hand, aiming at targets that seemed impossibly far away, like English bowmen on the eve of Agincourt.

Taking a deep breath, John would stretch back an arrow until the bowstring went taut…and then he would release it with a sharp crack, sending it, more often than not, somewhere near the rim of the target.

"Missed, Johnny?" Some of the other boys would laugh sometimes, only shutting up when Tony sent an arrow firmly to the middle of the board. Then, he would jut his chin out proudly as they fawned over him, and this would only irritate John more than anything.

What really rankled him, though, was the lack of *time*. The evenings, which John longed to spend quietly reading or writing, were swallowed up by the preparations of certain text sections assigned by the Masters. These sections would need to be adequately prepared before class the next day, and the few hours of their freedom would inevitably end up sacrificed at the altar of these expectations. As the sun set, the dormitories would be silent, and it was during these quiet hours that John felt most alone; while Tony joked around with his friends, John was left with his work and his thoughts.

Saturday mornings brought more games, cricket in the spring, soccer in the fall, and Tony was always there, at the center of it all, running and shouting commands as though he were born to lead. John played his part dutifully, but his heart wasn't in it. He longed to escape, to wander the grounds alone, to explore the hills that rolled beyond the school's carefully trimmed hedges.

And the Sundays were the most unyielding of all. Each boy was expected to memorize the Collect for the day—more than once. John saw one of the boys getting a beating for being lax or for standing out, and so John dutifully studied, memorized, and played along. Then, the afternoons brought the weekly letter-writing ritual, as each boy would sit down to pen a letter home. Sometimes, they wrote about the small battles of the week, the triumphs and failures in the classroom, the bruises from rugby, or the mundane details of daily life that, once committed to paper, became yet another duty.

And like this, life continued to pass…

Chapter 3.

Time and Fate

It was around this time that the war finally drew to a close. It was November 1918; the world had held its breath for four years, its lungs filled with the smoke of gunfire and the thick stench of trench mud. Armistice, the word they all hoped for, had been spoken at last; and on the eleventh day of that month, the guns fell silent.

The news reached Lindisfarne prep in the middle of a cold morning as John sat in the corner of a quiet classroom, hunched over a page of Latin verbs.

"It's over! The Hun surrendered!" came a distant yet excited call down the hallway, drifting into the classroom.

John froze. At first, he barely lifted his head as voices rose around him in class, uncertain and hushed, as if saying it too loudly might undo it somehow.

"…You hear that?"

"…Up to his old antics…"

"...Is it really over?"

As speculation grew, John glanced up, catching the eye of a boy across the room who'd heard it too, the same questioning glint in his eye, the faintest hint of hope hanging in the air.

Then, without warning, their English professor looked inside, catching the eye of their severe Latin teacher.

"Master Gregory, did you hear?" he called, grinning widely. "Our boys have done it... the Germans have capitulated!"

A sudden cheer broke out, and John found himself joining in as well, sharing in the joy of the other boys with their fathers away at the front lines. Some of the boys near the door broke into hip-hip-hoorahs.

In London, there were parades, of course. The streets filled with people waving flags and shouting themselves hoarse, as if to convince themselves that they could feel joy again. Old men and young women, children too small to understand the breadth of what had happened, all gathered in squares and boulevards. For a moment, they allowed themselves to forget the apologetic telegrams that had shattered so many hearts, the empty chairs at dinner tables, the faces that had left and would never return...

But even as the streets and glades of England were ecstatic, there was little celebration left in the front lines. After the first throes of desperate joy and drinking, soldiers now lay sprawled in their foxholes, the trenches stretched across Europe like endless scars, raw and exposed. Prisoners of war sat sullenly under guard, while the English battalions looked at one another with the disbelieving eyes of

44

survivors; after all, they had come to know death intimately, like an old relative who had overstayed his welcome. Now that the relative had left, but he had not left them whole.

The fields of the content were battered beyond recognition, trees snapped like matchsticks, fields torn open as if by some godly rage. The once-green Somme had become oceans of mud, where he air smelled of rusted metal and burnt earth. Villages lay in ruins; farmhouses were skeletons, their beams jutting into the air like broken ribs.

The question now was of what came next. As soldiers shuffled back home with tired eyes, politicians and generals gathered around tables in grand halls, dividing up the world on maps, carving up empires with the precision of surgeons. They spoke of treaties and reparations, of justice and blame, and other ideas far too large and abstract to truly quantify. The ordinary people remained more concerned with more everyday worries; would the women, who had upheld industry on their backs, be corralled back into their kitchens? How would the returning soldiers be received and kept? Would the government find jobs for them?

For John Bowlby, the question of what came next was more complicated. The war was over, and he had assumed that this meant that his father would be returning, but a letter from home informed him that though his father had arrived, he would be leaving again in a week to tend to his duties, which meant that he wouldn't be home during John's next visit.

Though John understood that his father was an important man and was glad that he had gone through the war unhurt, his father's continued distance still rankled. As other children would go home and meet their fathers again, they looked forward to their breaks eagerly; John and Tony, however, had no such thing to look forward to. Tony brought up to the others about how important and busy their father was, but John saw even that for what it was, a way to cope with the idea that all that awaited them when they got back home was Father's empty chair.

***

The pupils of Lindisfarne were allowed visits home only during the holidays. As John returned home from Lindisfarne that winter in December, the world outside the train felt quiet and still. The holidays stretched before him, an empty slate; Lindisfarne was behind him for the time being, but its presence loomed, its influence reaching back with invisible fingers, tugging him, even now, toward its stony walls, its strict rules, its endless structure.

His father was still away, and John and Tony were received by Nanny Friend and Mother, who lightly embraced her sons before they took a motorcar back home. Watching boys his age play or walk about behind their fathers through the icy windows of the car, John was again reminded of his father's absence.

"Has Father written about when he'll be back?" Tony asked, seemingly casually. Clearly, he had the same thing on his mind.

"He will write when he is able," Mother responded, looking straight ahead. The boys knew that was about the only response they were going to get.

46

It was during this winter holiday, with his father absent and his mother lost in quiet worry, that John's godfather stepped in. He was a friend of the family, an infrequent but warm presence that brought some stability to the house. He was a sturdy man with a robust laugh and a way of talking with his hands that John quite liked. Quietly, John looked up to him almost as though to a father, and welcomed the invitation to spend a day together.

"Have him back in time for tea," Nanna said with her hands on her hips as John eagerly followed his godfather out of the door. "And do make sure not to leave him in any foul company; all sorts of beastly people around these days…"

"Yes, yes, my good woman," his godfather said easily as he put on his hat. "Your boy shall return in pristine condition."

Nanna sniffed at that, but they were already off. The duo was headed to a soccer game, and his godfather was to play. For John, the prospect was thrilling: the clamor of the crowd, the crisp winter air biting at his cheeks, and the thrill of watching the game up close. It was the kind of outing that felt special, something beyond the confines of Lindisfarne's rules and structures, something meant just for him.

"You play soccer, John?"

"…Yes sir," John replied, not mentioning the fact that he quite disliked the game by now, thanks to being consistently shown up by Tony at Lindisfarne.

The day around them was bright but cold, the sky a pale gray that stretched unbroken above the field. They arrived at the grounds, a patch of green surrounded by cheering spectators wrapped in scarves and thick coats, their breath clouding in front of them in the sharp air. John watched from the sidelines, his hands shoved deep into his pockets, his eyes following his godfather as he jogged onto the field, as strong and vital as ever.

And then, something happened. One moment, his godfather was there, running with the ball, and the next, he tumbled, rag-dolling across the field until he crumpled to a heap…

John heard the gasps ripple through the crowd, felt the sudden chill settle over him like a cold hand. Time seemed to slow down as people rushed onto the field, as his godfather lay motionless on the grass, his face pale, his body still. John didn't understand; it was like watching a scene in a play, something unreal, something that couldn't possibly be happening in front of him.

But it was real.

The stretcher came, the murmurs rose and fell around him, and John stood there, rooted to the spot, unable to move or speak. He didn't cry. There was a strange numbness that settled over him, a kind of fog that blurred the edges of everything, making it all feel distant, unreal. Calls were made to the Bowlby residence, and Nanna came to pick him up, without her caustic attitude for once. Seated in the motorcar beside her, John looked down the whole ride.

By the time he returned home, the silence was thicker than ever. Evelyn came to him crying with a hug; apparently, she had misheard the facts and had thought that it was he who had fallen lifeless and not their godfather.

"I thought, I thought…" she blubbered.

"Shhh, it's alright, I'm here," he replied, his voice somewhat unsteady.

As he cooed and comforted his sister, his mother's face was drawn, her eyes rimmed red as she looked into the fireplace.

"What a thing life is," she muttered almost to herself. "Hale as you like one day, and the next…and heavens, his poor wife…"

From then on, Mother spoke of the tragedy only indirectly, in fragments that barely made sense. She never sat John down to tell him how to grieve, how to cope. In fact, no one spoke of the tragedy openly. It was as if the grief had been folded up, tucked away in a box, and placed on a high shelf, out of reach, out of sight. But John could feel its presence, even if he couldn't touch it, couldn't open it…and so he tried to make sense of this new revelation, the specter of Death, in his own way. He asked questions: why did this happen? Was it preventable?

But there were no answers. A man was gone, and nothing he could do would change that. And so, John carried the weight of this event with him to Lindisfarne, tucked away somewhere deep inside, like a bruise that never quite healed.

Back at school, the days resumed their steady, relentless pace. Lindisfarne was indifferent to personal tragedies; it had its own rhythm, its own demands, and John was expected to fall in line, to carry on as if nothing had happened. The bells rang, the classes began, the sports matches continued, and John moved through it all with a new weight in his chest, a heaviness that he couldn't explain to anyone, that he wasn't even sure he fully understood himself.

If he, too, was shaken, Tony didn't let it show. He threw himself back into his own world, immediately busy thriving in the rigid structure, excelling at everything he touched.

Meanwhile, John watched him from a distance, feeling a strange kind of detachment. And as he wrote another useless letter back home that would receive a similarly perfunctory reply, John felt a sense of dreary aimlessness beginning to creep over him.

**

The next time John and Tony returned home was in the summer of 1919. This time, father would be waiting for them, and both boys were nervous about meeting him again, though they tried to ignore this by arguing throughout the way about small and inconsequential things, the way only siblings could.

After a long ride by rail and another ride by motorcar, they were again deposited at the Bowlby residence. As they entered the house and greeted their mother, they found their father, Sir Anthony Alfred Bowlby, waiting at the table with his tea and a newspaper.

Father was dressed in his civilian outfit, in his favourite tweed hunting coat. His face was carved into austere lines, sharp cheekbones, a firm jaw, and a thick white mustache that entirely hooded his lips. His eyes were steady, distant, the pale gray of old steel, framed by a hint of crow's feet that seemed less from smiling and more from years of squinting at wounds, medicines, and fine print. This was a man who didn't allow himself the luxury of softness, not with his children and certainly not with himself.

"Welcome back home, Father," the boys said.

They then stood waiting a bit awkwardly, shifting in their boots as Father regarded them in silence for a long moment; finally, he gave a short, approving nod. They had grown, and it pleased him, though he wouldn't say it.

"You are both quite taller," he finally said. "I believe you have much of your mother in your faces."

"Both of them look quite like you, my dear," Mother said, pouring herself some tea as well.

"I suppose so," Father replied with a frown, "I do not quite see it, but I suppose so..."

Then, he nodded again and returned to his newspaper. And that was that; greetings were over, and the boys were off to wash and take off their dusty travel clothes.

The next few days passed in a parade of quiet meals and polite exchanges. Sir Anthony's satisfaction was distant, buried behind layers of reserve. He spoke to them rarely, though he seemed pleased that Tony excelled at sports and that John was diligent in his studies, but even this approval felt like a ledger that was balanced, checked, and quickly closed.

Then, one evening, John was called into his father's study alone. The room was dim, lit only by the orange glow of a single lamp and the thin blue ribbons of pipe smoke that wove through the air. Sir Anthony sat at his desk, poring over a stack of documents. He didn't look up when John entered, only gestured to the chair opposite him.

51

"How is your education progressing?" he asked finally, his voice formal.

John felt himself straighten in his seat. "It's going well, Father. I've been keeping up with the work."

Sir Anthony nodded, his gaze drifting for a moment to the window, where the sun was slipping below the horizon. "Your brother has been thinking about the army, you know," he said, almost to himself, and then his eyes flicked back to John, sharp and appraising. "Smart boy. What about you?"

John hesitated. He still felt that peculiar sense of aimlessness, that sense of having no anchor or attachment to any future at all. The only thing he could think of was medicine, that was what he'd been thinking, after all. What had begun with his trying to emulate his father's interest had transformed into his own interest. The way humans worked fascinated him, and he felt drawn to the idea of understanding people.

"I'd...like to be a doctor," John said.

Sir Anthony's face didn't change, but John sensed a slight disappointment; it was there in the slight tightening of his jaw, in the way his fingers drummed once, sharply, against the desk.

"Medicine?" Sir Anthony's voice was calm as he took a long puff from his pipe, exhaling a cloud of smoke that drifted lazily toward the ceiling. "Why? It has been my profession, and I can assure you it is hardly the best fit for you."

John wanted to ask why... why would it not suit him? But he knew better than to question his father. Those words,

52

so often heard in his childhood, returned to him. *Children are seen, not heard.*

"Have you considered the navy?" Father suddenly asked, looking up with his clear eyes. "Why, when you were a boy, I used to call you my little Jack Tar." He allowed himself a rare smile, as if the memory amused him. "Do you remember?"

John shook his head, though it felt a little familiar, like something from a half-forgotten dream. Then he remembered how Nanna always used to say that he'd be an admiral someday, and Tony would be a bishop. Suddenly, he realized, it didn't matter what he had said to his father at all. The question that had been asked of him was a formality, and this suggestion was anything but. His fate had been sealed since he had been an infant, he was always supposed to join the Navy.

John gulped, and for a moment, he felt a flicker of rebellion, a desire to tell his father he didn't want the navy, that he wanted something different for himself. But his father's approval was as elusive as it was powerful, and the thought of disappointing him felt like a betrayal.

"I hadn't thought of it," John managed.

Sir Anthony nodded, as if that settled the matter. "The Navy is a fine career, John. A career for a man with discipline, and it is a fine life from what I understand." He took another puff on his pipe, his gaze steady and unyielding. "I think you'll do well there."

"Yes, Father," John replied timidly.

Father leaned back in his chair, a faint smile tugging at the corners of his mouth. "Good man," he said, nodding. "That's what I like to hear."

As John rose to leave, he took a few steps and glanced back at his father one last time. Sir Anthony was already absorbed in his papers, his attention fixed on the orderly rows of figures and letters, as if nothing else in the world existed. John felt a pang of something he couldn't quite name, a longing, perhaps, for *something*, some sort of connection to this stranger he knew as Father. In the space of a lifetime, he had barely known his father; now, in the space of an afternoon, this same stranger had decided his whole life from that moment onward.

And now as he opened the door, John Bowlby found himself staring in the face of a fate prewritten for him.

Chapter 4.

The Officer Who Never Was

And so, by May 1921, John Bowlby found himself attending the Royal Naval College in Dartmouth.

Dartmouth in the day was a small but industrious port town nestled along the steep banks of the River Dart in Devon, England. The river, winding inland from the English Channel, was flanked by rows of tightly packed terraced houses with slate roofs, their chimneys sending thin columns of smoke into the crisp spring air. Fishing boats and small cargo vessels crowded the harbor, bobbing gently as they awaited repairs or unloading. The quays buzzed with life, dockworkers hauling goods, fishermen tending their nets, and shopkeepers selling wares to sailors passing through. The town reflected the naval character of the college it housed, with uniformed officers regularly seen along the cobbled streets and the harbor. Despite its modest size, Dartmouth held historical significance, its roots tracing back to medieval times as a launching point for Crusades and later as a strategic naval port.

Above the town, overlooking the river and the wooded valleys beyond, stood the Naval College. Built on the plateau of Mount Boone, the imposing structure dominated the landscape, its symmetrical façade of granite and Portland stone glinting in the sunlight. The college had been established in 1863 at nearby Osborne House with the purpose of preparing naval cadets for service in the Royal Navy, before the college was eventually moved to Dartmouth in 1905.

The college's design reflected both functionality and grandeur. Its main building, constructed in the Edwardian Baroque style, featured a central clock tower that rose above the symmetrical wings. The architecture was austere but purposeful, and again John found himself inside a structure that existed to reinforce a sense of discipline and order.

Within the college building itself, the halls echoed with the sharp staccato of wood-sole boots on polished floors. Lecture rooms featured rows of wooden desks and blackboards covered with diagrams of ship rigging, navigation charts, and mathematical equations. The College blended the traditions of a public school with the practical rigor of a technical institution, and so the daily routines at the college mirrored the discipline of naval life, with cadets rising early for physical drills, inspections, and carefully scheduled lessons. Even the youngest cadets were introduced to engineering, spending hours in workshops learning to operate and maintain the machinery essential to modern naval warfare.

The teaching staff brought a strong public-school ethos, many of them having served at elite preparatory institutions, while cadets were addressed in the same manner as public-school pupils, creating a blend of severity and camaraderie. The curriculum balanced traditional subjects such as Latin and mathematics with naval-specific training, from navigation and gunnery to seamanship.

The college also had expansive training grounds that extended to the water's edge, where the river served as a natural classroom. Here, cadets practiced maneuvers on sleek, wooden training boats moored in precise lines along the docks. The boats, known as whalers and cutters, were painted in navy colors and equipped with brass fittings that shone in the sunlight. Drills often involved rowing exercises, navigation challenges, and semaphore practice, all conducted under the watchful eyes of instructors.

The town of Dartmouth viewed the college with a mix of reverence and practicality. Local businesses thrived on supplying the institution, while families took pride in the sight of the cadets marching in formation. However, for all its grandeur, the college was also a somber place. Many of its alumni had perished during the Great War, their names etched on plaques within the college chapel.

From the wide windows of the college, John would look at the view of the Dart Estuary, a reminder of the world he might soon be a part of. Surrounding the college were terraces of neatly trimmed lawns, interspersed with gravel pathways and bordered by young saplings. Here, John would walk sometimes, looking around him and feeling a sense of *otherness* when he looked out into the expanse that promised to be his life. In the evenings, the college settled into a quiet routine. Gas lamps would illuminate the paths, casting long shadows across the grounds, and the River Dart, now a dark ribbon under the rising moon, carried the faint echoes of John's supposed future, a life of duty on the open sea.

But when he wasn't dwelling on the future, John actually enjoyed Dartmouth. Perhaps it was because, for once, he was out of Tony's shadow, or perhaps because he was excelling academically. The schedule was both grueling and gratifying; the days were defined by routine and rigor, yet something about the place: its rhythms, its demands, brought out the best in him. For all its naval strictness and stiff formality, Dartmouth had given him something he hadn't always felt at Lindisfarne: confidence. He had risen quietly to the top of his term in most subjects, a feat that carried its own kind of satisfaction, though he was careful never to gloat. Dartmouth wasn't the kind of place that rewarded gloating; it rewarded discipline, precision, and sheer skill.

Academic life was a constant exercise in hierarchy. Each subject had three grades: the top, the middle, and the bottom. John, ever meticulous, had managed to secure the top grade in nearly everything, thanks to long hours spent with his nose in a textbook. Only French had eluded him, a thorn in an otherwise immaculate record. This wasn't for lack of trying; he'd spent weeks wrestling with verb conjugations and idiomatic phrases, but the language refused to bend to his will. He often wondered if it was stubbornness on his part or the language's. Either way, the result was the same: a solid place in the bottom grade.

But Dartmouth wasn't just about academics; it was about leadership, about the ability to command respect without demanding it. John's promotion to cadet captain was an honor, though it came with its share of burdens. As cadet captain, he had to lead his term in various capacities, whether marching them down to engineering and seamanship lessons or ensuring that no one stepped out of line during morning inspections. Of course, leadership at Dartmouth wasn't about authority; it was about responsibility. It meant marching a group of cadets across the grounds, and to carry the weight of their collective success or failure. One misstep, and the blame fell squarely on his shoulders.

Never the loud, charismatic type, John didn't inspire through grand gestures or stirring speeches. Instead, his strength lay in quiet competence, in the way he set an example simply by doing what needed to be done. He moved through the halls of Dartmouth with a kind of understated grace, his uniform always pressed, his boots polished to a mirror shine. He didn't shout to be heard; his voice carried because it was calm and measured, because it spoke of certainty even when he felt anything but.

For all his successes, John remained grounded. He was proud of his academic achievements, yes, but he was also acutely aware of his limitations. He often reflected on his essays, pieces he'd poured himself into late at night when the rest of the cadets were asleep. Writing had always been a quiet joy for him, a way to wrestle with ideas and pin them to the page. He wasn't outstanding, he'd admit that freely, but he was good, better than average, even. His essays were thoughtful, carefully constructed, each sentence a brick in a wall he was determined to build straight and true. Writing was a family trait, he supposed; his paternal grandfather had been an enthusiastic writer, and John liked to think that some of that passion had trickled down to him.

Still, he didn't linger too long on praise or recognition. Dartmouth was not a place that encouraged self-congratulation. The cadets were there to learn, to be forged into something harder and sharper, and there was no room for softness. The days were tightly regimented: morning drills, hours of classes, practical lessons in engineering and seamanship, each segment of the day flowing into the next with the precision of a naval timetable. It was a world of sharp edges and unyielding expectations, where even the smallest mistake felt like a crack in the hull of a ship.

The physical landscape of Dartmouth mirrored its ethos. The sprawling grounds were dominated by crisp, white buildings, their facades as immaculate as the cadets' uniforms. The air always carried a tang of salt from the nearby sea, a constant reminder of what lay beyond the safe confines of the campus. Of course, for John, Dartmouth was a crucible. It stripped away what was unnecessary and left him with a clearer sense of who he was, or, at least, who he was becoming. It taught him the value of precision, of quiet determination, of rising to meet a challenge even when every muscle in your body begged you to stop. It was there, among the cadets and the salt air and the relentless expectations, that he began to understand the shape of himself.

In the evenings, when the day's duties had finally receded, he often sat in the dim light of his shared quarters, pen in hand, thinking about how to frame the day's events. The room smelled faintly of seawater and sweat, the scent of uniforms hung to dry mingling with the salt that crept in from the nearby coast. Here, he would write letters home, before sealing them in thick envelopes, neatly addressed in his careful script, the ink dark and deliberate.

Each letter carried the tone of a young man trying to sound composed, as if to remind his mother that she needn't worry. They were filled with dry humor and practical updates, small snapshots of Dartmouth life that veiled the underlying grind.

"Marching the term to engineering lessons is, I assure you, less glamorous than it sounds," he wrote one July, the line as much for his own amusement as hers. He didn't mention the weight of responsibility that came with leading forty cadets, the constant need to keep the formation tight and the pace exact, even when the summer heat pressed down like a hand on his back. A sense of pride, though, still slipped through the cracks of his self-deprecating humor. He wanted her to know, not just in words but in the spirit of the letters, that he was doing well. Not thriving in the carefree sense, but holding his own in a place where failure wasn't just personal; it was visible, public, and deeply humbling. After all, Dartmouth wasn't designed for the fainthearted, a fact he didn't need to spell out.

But John's time at Dartmouth wasn't just defined by his academic achievements; his talent in sports stood out early, and now, out from under Tony's shadow, he was a fixture on the rugby field, playing in the 1st XV. The sport demanded precision and force, but it also required a kind of camaraderie that John embraced fully. He had a knack for games that demanded agility and quick thinking: hockey, tennis, and cricket all counted him among their regular players. Even sailing came naturally to him.

But where some cadets may have narrowed their focus, limiting themselves to the rigors of sport or study, John seemed to move effortlessly into realms less traveled. A friend named Donald McGavin had introduced him to birdwatching, an unlikely pursuit given the high-energy environment of Dartmouth. Yet it quickly became one of his quiet joys, reminding him of birdwatching with his grandfather many years ago.

The birds themselves were the first surprise. Nuthatches, John noted in a letter to his mother, "little birds with blue backs and chestnut breasts which creep along trees," captured his attention with their peculiar, almost deliberate movements. Unlike the predictable march of his termmates or the drilled patterns of formation, the nuthatches moved as though answering to no one but themselves, skittering sideways along branches, pausing to inspect the bark for hidden insects. Their independence and vibrant plumage completely charmed him.

The process of birdwatching, too, held an almost meditative appeal. Standing among the trees, John had to quiet his body and his thoughts. The first lesson his grandfather had taught him many years ago was patience. Birds, after all, did not appear on command; they came when they chose, flitting into view only after the watcher had faded into the background. John learned to listen to the subtle rustling of leaves, to track the faint calls of unseen creatures, and to discern between the trill of a wren and the sharper chatter of a sparrow. Armed with a well-worn notebook for jotting observations, a pair of binoculars, and a kind of reverence for the natural world, John grew to love the activity.

In the quiet under the canopy, with the wind brushing softly against his face, he watched as the birds, oblivious to the hierarchies of men, moved freely, and John, in watching them, felt a subtle kind of freedom himself.

***

The Passing Out examination was the culmination of years of rigor, a distillation of discipline, sweat, and the sheer weight of expectation. It loomed over the cadets like a shadow, pressing on their backs as they marched through Dartmouth's cobbled courtyards or sat hunched over their books, the chill of the Devon air seeping through the stone walls. For John Bowlby, the examination was a crucible that promised to shape his future, and in his private moments, this worried him. For as he prepared, a nagging question gnawed at the edges of his thoughts:

Was this the life he truly wanted?

But there was no time to dwell on this. After all, the days leading up to the exam would be a blur of study and practice, punctuated by letters exchanged between John and his parents. His father's correspondence, as ever, was written with the deliberate hand of a man accustomed to order. His mother's letters were more neutral and reflective, offering a sense of distant encouragement.

In the quiet hours after lights-out, John would lie on his narrow cot, staring at the ceiling as the murmurs of his fellow cadets ebbed and flowed around him. Some nights, he replayed the conversations he had had with his father in his mind, scrutinizing each thread of his life as though it were a line in a code he had yet to decipher. Other nights, he thought of the sea... its vastness, its unpredictability, and the sense of having been thrown out onto it.

This mood of uncertainty was not limited to John, either. As he and Donald sat in the corner of the common room one day, they found themselves discussing the future in the light of a single desk lamp that carved their faces into sharp contrasts. Around them, the space smelled of linseed oil and the faint metallic tang of seawater, as though the ocean was already reaching for them through the thick stone walls of Dartmouth.

"This isn't quite what I imagined when I first came here," Donald was saying. "The drills, the exams, the bloody knots…I can manage all that. But it's the training ship that worries me…once we set foot on a ship, it's a whole other world. It's final. You've thought about it, haven't you?"

John nodded, his fingers toying with a brass button that had come loose from his coat. He turned it over in his hand, tracing the embossed anchor as if it held the answers he was looking for. "I have," he said. "More than I should, probably."

"And?" Donald pressed, leaning forward now. "Do you feel certain?"

John didn't answer immediately. Instead, he leaned forward, deliberately resting his hands on his knees as he thought it out in his usual, methodical manner. "It's not certainty," he said finally. "Perhaps you're not supposed to know until you're out there."

Donald raised an eyebrow. "It seems to me that that would keep you from committing one way or another."

"I'm committing to the process," John replied, a hint of defensiveness creeping into his voice. "To seeing it through. Isn't that enough for now?"

"Maybe," Donald conceded, though his tone suggested otherwise. "But do you ever think about what else you could do? There's more to the world than this navy-blue bubble we're living in."

"Of course," John said, his voice quiet. "You know, I had other considerations before joining. But that doesn't mean I'd rather be anywhere else, at least not right now."

For a moment, neither of them spoke.

"You know," John said after a while, "there's something to be said for just doing it. For taking the next step and figuring it out as you go."

Donald snorted. "You sound like one of the instructors."

"Maybe they've got a point," John said, shrugging. "What's the alternative? Sitting here, debating what might be? We'll never know until we're out there. Until we've had a real taste of it."

Donald leaned back again, his gaze fixed on the ceiling. "You make it sound simple."

"It's not," John admitted. "But that doesn't mean it's wrong."

Another pause stretched between them, heavy but not uncomfortable. They had spent long enough birdwatching together to be able to sit in silence without the need to fill it. Finally, Donald stood, his chair scraping against the floor as he pushed it back. "You know, John, for someone who doesn't claim to have all the answers, you sure sound like you do."

John smiled, the corner of his mouth twitching upward. "I wouldn't go that far."

"Fair enough," Donald said, clapping a hand on John's shoulder as he passed. "But for what it's worth, I hope you're right."

After all this deliberation, the examination itself came and went with little fanfare. John passed in all subjects, his performance solid if not spectacular. There was relief in knowing he had met the standard, but it was tempered by the knowledge that passing was only the first step. The next phase, the training ship, loomed ahead, and with it the reality of naval life. It was one thing to read about the routines of seafaring; it was another to live them.

Before the cadets were dispatched to their assignments, John sat down to write to his parents. His pen hovered over the page as he tried to find the words to express the clarity he had arrived at in his conversations with Donald. *I have, I think, definitely decided to carry on in the Service,* he wrote, his tone careful but resolute. *I am interested in the work & am confident in myself that I shall get so absorbed that I shall not want to quit.*

It was not a declaration of undying loyalty to the Navy; rather, it was a pragmatic choice. John knew himself well enough to recognize that his curiosity and determination would sustain him, at least for the time being. He refused to let himself drift into the Navy without thinking or bothering about anything, as he put it in his letter to his father. Now, the weeks that followed were filled with preparations for the training ship. John immersed himself in the routines of naval life, from knot-tying to navigation to a hundred little things that would be tested. His letters home grew to be filled with observations about his experiences and reflections on the challenges he faced. Now, as John Bowlby first stood on the deck of the training ship, the wind tugging at his uniform and the horizon stretching endlessly before him, it seemed very likely to him that there would be a future as an officer waiting for him, just as his father had imagined.

66

And yet…

Unknown even to the young man breathing in the salt air, a far different, and arguably more interesting fate awaited him.

***

The training ship was cleared with just as much ease as his examinations, and by the May of 1924, John's world consisted of salt, steel, and the quiet rumble of the Atlantic beneath his feet.

He had started his training as a midshipman alongside Donald and two others, boys who still smirked and squabbled like schoolboys but walked now with a stiffness that uniforms seemed to demand. The HMS Royal Oak, her name carved into the annals of the Atlantic Fleet like a permanent dent, was their classroom, their dormitory, their theater of disappointments and small triumphs. She was not a beautiful ship; beauty belonged to things with curves and movement. The Royal Oak was angular and firm, a fortress floating on slate-gray waters.

The ship cruised from one coastal town to the next across England and Scotland, an endless loop of granite cliffs, stubborn lighthouses, and villages that shrank when viewed from the deck. Such towns were their frequent ports of call or rest, such as Aberdeen, where the wind punched through wool coats like a needle, or Scarborough, where gulls swirled endlessly over the gray and white beachheads, screeching witnesses to the cadets' education.

In terms of education, though, the cadets learned quickly. Watches were kept with a practical precision; gunnery drills were carried out with blanks that exploded with dramatic noise but no consequence. John found a rhythm in the labor, his body moving before his mind could weigh the task. Loading and unloading; standing watch, counting waves like steps on a staircase. He took comfort in the monotony of the tasks and the unchanging nature of the sea; the horizon stayed exactly where it always had been, just out of reach.

But what stood out to him most was the strange role they played in this awkward post-war world. They weren't warriors; they weren't explorers. They were, in many ways, ferrymen.

In the afternoons, the HMS Royal Oak opened her steel belly to the public, and cadets like John were given the task of rowing townspeople to and from the great ship. They came in clusters, men in thick coats who carried the weight of the war on their faces, women clutching handkerchiefs as if ready to wave farewell, and children with eyes too bright for the solemnity of the scene. They boarded the ship like pilgrims, wandering the decks and corridors with a reverence usually reserved for churches. Sometimes John would watch them, ordinary people looking for something larger than themselves. He didn't blame them. The war had left holes that needed filling, and if a tour of the Atlantic Fleet's pride could offer even a momentary feeling of grandeur, John supposed it was worth it. Donald, however, saw things differently.

"We're the world's most expensive amusement park ride," he grumbled as they rowed back toward the pier one evening. The wind picked up and sent spray into the boat, dampening their trousers and erasing any sense of dignity they had left. "This isn't what I signed up for. The Navy's a lot of things, but a ferry service shouldn't be one of them."

John didn't reply. He had been thinking the same thing, but didn't have the words for it yet.

Evenings on shore offered something close to relief. The towns they visited put on dances and concerts, as if to thank the Navy for its patience. In Scarborough, the hall was cramped and smelled of damp plaster and gin, with yellow bulbs swinging from the ceiling like low-hanging fruit. Most of the cadets loitered on the edges of the room, their boots scuffed and their caps crooked as they chuckled and made merry.

On nearly the opposite end of the room, Donald shook his head and leaned in close to John. "Look at them. Dancing! What is this, a play?"

"Maybe it is," John wryly replied.

He believed it too. The whole ship, the whole tour, as enjoyable as it often was, he was beginning to realize that there was something terribly repetitious about it, as though they were a travelling troupe of actors reenacting the same performance port to port.

In his letters to his mother, he would try to wring some sort of meaning from the easy monotony of life on sea. He wrote: *One's work is so entirely different from anything one has ever seen or heard of before that it does not seem like work, in the sense in which one has been used to think of it, at all.*

And he wasn't wrong. For weeks, the tasks repeated themselves with such predictable precision that John had begun to mark time not by the rise and fall of the sun, but by the bells and whistles that instructed him when to move.

The Royal Oak was heavy and still, sitting on water like an animal that no longer hunted; for all its might and mass, the ship spent its days idling at harbors, waiting for curious tourists or government officials to justify its existence. John and Donald were thus doomed to wander the vessel's halls like two men searching for a door that didn't exist. For boys who had joined the Navy on the promise of sharp discipline and quiet dignity, life aboard the Royal Oak was not just disappointing, it was slack. That was John's word for it: slack, loose, something sagging where it shouldn't.

There is very little to do on a ship in peacetime, he wrote to his mother in exasperation one evening. *Slack and demoralizing.*

Donald had his own thoughts on the matter, which he would share when he and John would sit near the gunwales during their breaks, staring at horizons that refused to move.

"We're wasting away here," Donald said one evening, tipping his cap back to let the wind find his forehead. "If I wanted a life of idling, I'd have stayed home and learned to mend fences."

John could only agree in silence. There seemed to be no point in being a naval officer during peacetime, no contribution to mankind, no stories to write home about, no higher purpose to serve. Men with steady hands and sharp minds had been reduced to chores that children could do. The officers supervised drills with blanks; the enlisted men painted the ship again and again until it seemed to shine like a question no one was asking.

70

But it was more than the dullness of it that gnawed at John. It was what the Navy had promised him, or rather, what he had imagined the Navy would be. He had imagined that the sea might carve him into something greater, for he wanted to improve himself and thereby do his part to improve society.

John's naval instructor, a rugged but kindly man of few words, had overheard these exchanges; nothing came of it at first, until one day as he was walking past, he put a great paw on John's shoulder.

"You're a young man," he said, frowning slightly. "But a smart one. I see that. Everyone sees it."

"Thank you, sir," John replied, unsure of how to respond.

The instructor leaned in. "What I'm saying is, you're right...leave the Navy. Go to university. Use that head of yours."

While John was still floundering for an answer, the man had already moved on, leaving him with even more doubts. In his discussions with Donald, these doubts only grew.

"There's nowhere for us to *go* in this job," Donald argued, seated one evening on their shared bunk, his voice low. He had been flipping through his officer's manual, bored beyond belief. "If we stay, we'll never rise above lieutenant-commander. That's the ceiling."

The ceiling, as Donald called it, was a rank with just enough prestige to keep a man proud and just enough stagnation to keep him bitter. To rise above it was nearly impossible now; the war had ended, and with peace came

71

cuts. By 1919, the Royal Navy had employed over 268,000 people. By 1924, that number had shriveled to 99,000. The numbers were stark and unforgiving, just like the Navy itself. John guessed that this very shrinking was why the Royal Oak now ferried civilians aboard like guests at a tea party, an awkward gesture to prove its relevance in a world that no longer required ships like her.

On the morning John made his decision, he found Donald leaning against the gunwale, his cap tipped back just enough to catch the low-hanging sun. The day's monotony clung to the air, a thick, invisible fog that weighed on their shoulders. It wasn't yet time for their evening tea break, but Donald had already slipped away, his impatience with protocol a quiet rebellion that no one seemed to notice or care about.

"I'm leaving," John said, cutting straight to the point. There was no preamble; he had little time for small talk, especially when it came to matters like this.

Donald turned his head slowly. His eyebrows arched just slightly, the only indication of surprise.

"Leaving what?" he asked, though he knew.

"The Navy."

Donald didn't respond immediately. Instead, he traced his finger along the edge of the railing, where rust was beginning to form, the kind that no amount of painting could hide.

"And you'll tell your father... what, exactly?" Donald finally said.

"That I'm wasting my time here. That I've been wasting it for months."

Donald shook his head. "Your father won't care about time. He'll care about the prestige of your position, the fact that he can say he has a son in the Navy. And he will also care about money…you know, there's a fine."

John grimaced; he hated how right Donald often was. To leave Dartmouth before completing his service obligations meant a fine of forty pounds for every term. John had done the math; it wasn't a small amount, even for their family.

"I'll convince him," John said, though his voice lacked the steel he wished it had.

"Good luck with that," Donald said, turning back toward the horizon. "If it works…well, we'll see."

That evening, John sat at his desk, pen in hand, staring at a blank sheet of paper. The ship moved beneath his feet, a constant reminder of its presence, its permanence. He wasn't sure where to begin. His father, a man of few words and fewer indulgences, would need more than sentiment to be swayed.

He started with the practicalities.

Dear Father, he wrote. *I hope this letter finds you well. I write to discuss an important matter concerning my future in the Navy.*

He pressed on, explaining his dissatisfaction, his belief that staying aboard the HMS Royal Oak would lead only to stagnation. He wrote about wanting more, an education, a career that would challenge him. Medicine, he

73

decided, was the angle to take again, this time with a more rational confidence. His father had discarded medicine for him as he had believed that John would do better in the navy, and so, John believed that an adequate explanation of the state of the navy as he had experienced it would be enough to shift his father's opinion on the subject. But he hesitated now as he reached the part about the fee. Forty pounds per term, eleven terms completed, four hundred and forty pounds. The number loomed large on the page, stark and unavoidable.

Taking a deep breath, he now signed the letter simply, 'Your son, John,' and folded the paper carefully.

The response came two weeks later, delivered by a junior officer who handed it over without ceremony. John retreated to his bunk, the envelope trembling slightly in his hands. His father's handwriting was as he remembered it: neat, deliberate, each letter spaced just so.

John, the letter began, blunt and unadorned. *Your request came as a surprise. While I do not agree with your decision, I have decided to support it.*

John exhaled, the tension in his chest loosening. He read on.

The sum of £440 is not insignificant; you should know this. I hope you will treat this opportunity with the seriousness it deserves. I more than most know that medicine is a noble field, but it is also a demanding one. If you fail to meet its challenges, I will consider this money wasted.

The letter ended without sentiment, just a terse note about arrangements and expectations. John read it twice more, the words sinking in deeper each time. He felt relief, yes, but also a weight, a new kind of pressure that came not from the Navy but from the man who had just bought him out of it.

Donald was ecstatic when John shared the news and applied to Cambridge alongside him.

"Don't get me wrong," he said one evening as they packed their belongings. "I still believe the Navy's a noble calling. But if I have to spend one more day saluting tourists, I shall surely go mad."

John smiled but said nothing.

As they stepped off the gangplank for the last time, John turned around. The Royal Oak loomed there, massive and unmoving, as if watching them leave. For all its size, the ship seemed smaller now, diminished somehow. The ship would go on without them; that was its nature. But for the first time in months, John felt like he, too, was finally moving forward.

Chapter 5.

Cambridge

After stepping off the gangplank of the HMS Royal Oak, John found himself untethered, a young man no longer bound by military routine but not yet anchored to a clear future.

It was 1924, and a return to London proved less to be a visit homewards and more of a new trial. He found himself enrolled, now, at University College London out of necessity. Cambridge was his ultimate goal, but it had barriers, literal and figurative, stacked like ancient walls. Latin was one of them; learned in a rushed and haphazard manner at Lindisfarne, his Latin was passable enough to impress his naval instructors but nowhere near the precision Cambridge demanded. Here, Latin was tradition, intellectual heritage, and a way to weed out the unworthy.

At University College, John tackled it with a ferocity that surprised even himself, sitting for hours beneath the dim gaslights of rented rooms, parsing verbs and declensions until his head throbbed. Meanwhile, the College itself stood like a grand assertion of neoclassical ambition amidst Bloomsbury's flat lanes. The portico dominated the scene, with a colonnaded crown rising above the courtyard like a temple of Zeus, giving the structure its unmistakable silhouette against the crisp English sky.

John had little time to appreciate the architecture; however, Cambridge loomed like a shadow over every decision he made. He worried about the test, the one known as the "Little-Go." The name sounded almost frivolous, but the examination was anything but. Latin, Greek, modern languages, mathematics, physics, chemistry, English, divinity, and history, each a fortress that had to be stormed. The breadth of it was staggering, yet John knew failure wasn't an option, not with his father's stern letter folded neatly in his suitcase.

He wasn't alone, though. Letters from Donald arrived sporadically, filled with the same dry wit that had kept them sane during endless naval drills. Donald had promised to join him at Cambridge if John managed to break through, which he was quite determined to.

In January 1925, John sat for the Little-Go. The room where the exam was held was intimidating, high-ceilinged with wooden beams that seemed to press down on him. His pencil felt foreign in his hand, and for a moment, as he stared at the Latin translation question, his mind went blank. Then, almost instinctively, the preparation took over. He found himself scribbling furiously, pausing only to glance at the proctor's stern face or the clock ticking too quickly on the wall.

When the results came, he unfolded the letter with shaking hands.

Passed, it said without fanfare, but John was ecstatic nonetheless upon seeing the word he had worked toward for nearly a year.

***

By the autumn of 1925, John was walking through the gates of Trinity College, Cambridge, an eighteen-year-old medical student with a sharpened sense of purpose.

The world of Cambridge was unlike anything he had ever known. Students in dark academic gowns hurried across cobblestone paths between lectures, their conversations a mix of philosophical debates and lighter banter, echoing off the ancient stone walls. The shadow of the Great War still lingered, and debates about science, literature, and politics reflected a world grappling with change.

But even with change, the colleges' roots ran deep; after all, this was a place full of history. First greeting John Bowlby at Trinity College was the Great Gate, its stately presence speaking to centuries of ambition, mischief, and reinvention. Above the carved stone entrance, Henry VIII presided from his niche, clutching a chair leg. Beneath his statue, coats of arms memorialize Edward III and his sons, one shield notably blank, a silent elegy to William of Hatfield, who never grew to bear arms of his own.

Stepping into the college's Great Court was to enter the ambitions of Thomas Nevile cast in stone. With its imperial symmetry, the expanse was vast enough to make any newcomer feel both insignificant and awestruck. Built between 1599 and 1608, the Court was layered with history.

78

But if the Great Court embodied Trinity's permanence, Nevile's Court speaks of its evolution. Crafted in 1614 and expanded later by James Essex, the Court bridged the temporal gap between Thomas Nevile's vision and modern necessity. Its cloisters offered sanctuary, providing a sheltered path from the Great Hall to one of Cambridge's most storied treasures: the Wren Library. Designed by Christopher Wren and completed in 1695, the light spills across its delicate limewood carvings. Here, the air faintly smelled of aged parchment, and there were treasures housed within: Shakespeare's First Folios, Newton's letters, and manuscripts older than the college itself. Meanwhile, the Cloisters opened onto the river and the Backs, offering a view so tranquil it seems to belong to another world entirely.

South of Nevile's Court lay New Court, also known as King's Court, a Tudor-Gothic space that seems to revel in its myths; at its center stood a sprawling horse chestnut tree, often misattributed as the site of Newton's gravitational epiphany. Then was the Chapel, a mid-16th-century marvel of warm, aged stone that embodies both reverence and remembrance. Inside, memorials to fallen Fellows shared space with a statue of Isaac Newton, his face caught in the temporal flux of stone.

Beyond the courts and cloisters lay the grounds, a patchwork of cultivated beauty and academic rigor. The Fellows' Garden, tucked away on the west side of Queen's Road, offered a retreat from the college's grandeur. Here, amidst manicured lawns and quiet paths, tutors would occasionally host summer garden parties among the rustle of leaves.

Finally, came Trinity Bridge, a triple-arched marvel of Portland stone spanning the River Cam. Built in 1765 by

James Essex, the bridge was both functional and symbolic, connecting the college to the wider world while standing as a reminder of its architectural ingenuity. Beneath its arches, the river flowed steadily alongside the reflections of spires, trees, and students punting lazily on sunny afternoons…

And as John Bowlby drank this all in, he knew he had started a new phase in his life, one that would likely determine the rest of it.

Donald arrived a month after John, suitcase in hand and a smirk on his face. True to his word, he had joined John, though he complained endlessly about the academic hoops they both had to jump through. After a great deal of deliberation between them, John chose to take the *Tripos*: a rigorous degree program divided into two sections. This system was uniquely Cambridge, its structure designed to breed both depth and breadth of knowledge. Students could split their studies between two subjects, one feeding into the other, creating a hybrid intellectual curiosity. Bowlby began with the Natural Sciences Tripos, a path reserved for those with an appetite for challenge. This wasn't the easier humanities route; it was for students whose ambitions leaned towards medicine, science, and discovery.

As they began to flit between classes and dedicate themselves to their new life, their room quickly mushroomed into a mess. Books were piled on every surface; papers littered the floor. They argued over everything, from how best to memorize anatomical terms to whether Aristotle's theories held any real relevance.

But Cambridge wasn't easy, both to get into and to study in. It was the second-largest university in England at the time, home to around 5,200 students. But these numbers belied its exclusivity: only 5 percent of secondary school pupils from England between 1921 and 1924 would make it to university. John, like many of his peers, had been fortunate enough to be born into the class that formed the backbone of this institution: sons of clergymen, doctors, and professionals.

And even if this was a world of privilege, it was also one of exacting expectations, both from the faculty itself and from back home.

Thankfully, there were moments of levity, too. Late-night debates fueled by strong tea, or the time Donald, in a fit of boredom, attempted to translate Shakespeare into Latin, resulting in an unintentional comedic disaster. Yet much of their time was spent in studies.

Luckily for John Bowlby, the subjects fascinated him. Biology, a major part of the Natural Sciences Tripos, was especially captivating, and he spent long hours hunched over papers and peering into microscopes, navigating the complex corridors of evolutionary biology. Here, he would grapple with the ideas of Darwin, Mendel, and their intellectual descendants. Evolutionary biology was a subject of debates, of unanswered questions, of tantalizing possibilities that demanded a steady hand and an analytical mind.

He quickly found that medicine suited him. For all its rigor, it had a purpose that felt tangible. He liked the logic of it, the way each system in the body connected to another, a series of intricate mechanisms working in harmony. It reminded him, in a strange way, of the ship's engine room, where every part had its role, and failure in one could mean catastrophe for the whole. The line of methodical, practical, and logical thinking was deeply appealing to his slow, mature way of approaching the world. Quite naturally, the structure of the thought process behind medicine greatly seemed to echo his own way of seeing the world.

But what John would soon realize was how profoundly his experience at Trinity would be shaped by one man: E.D. Adrian. To most of the college, Adrian was an intellectually intriguing and passionate figure. To John, Adrian would become a mentor, a figure who opened the door to ideas that stretched far beyond the microscopes and slides of the biology lab.

Adrian was no ordinary tutor. Already a towering figure in the Faculty of Medicine, his experiments were known for their elegance, clarity, and rigor. In time, he would be made Lord Adrian for his contributions to science, but for now, he was simply Adrian, or Professor to his students. John was assigned to Adrian as part of the Natural Sciences program. There was a warmth and passion to him, a genuine curiosity about his students and their capacity to think. John quickly gravitated to him, and Adrian was more than happy about imparting much of his hard-earned wisdom.

"Science," he once told John during a late afternoon in the laboratory, "is the art of finding the unexpected in the familiar. If you approach it without curiosity, you may as well not approach it at all."

Under Adrian's guidance, John flourished. The professor had an uncanny ability to distill complex ideas into digestible fragments, sharpening his students' understanding without simplifying the material. He encouraged John to think critically, to question not just what he observed but why it mattered. The sessions often spilled beyond the lab, conversations continuing as they walked through the college's manicured gardens or sat in Adrian's study, surrounded by books that carried the scent of aged paper and dust.

What set Adrian apart as a mentor was his fascination with the uncharted territories of science. While many of his peers clung to the safety of well-trodden fields, Adrian gravitated towards the fringes, the areas where questions outnumbered answers. And one of those areas, as John would come to discover, was psychoanalysis. Adrian's interest in Freudian theory was not typical for a Cambridge professor of his day; Sigmund Freud's work, still controversial and often dismissed by the scientific establishment, was far removed from the world of microscopes and neurophysiology. But Adrian saw in it something revolutionary.

"Freud, the old boy," he once remarked to John as they walked along in the grounds, "didn't just give us theories about the mind. He gave us a way of connecting disciplines. Biology, psychology, sociology…why, they all meet under Freud's umbrella! Quite brilliant…"

This idea electrified John. He was, by nature, a thinker drawn to connections. His studies in evolutionary biology had taught him to see the interplay of organisms and environments, the delicate dance of adaptation and survival. Now, under Adrian's influence, he began to consider the mind as another kind of ecosystem, one governed by its own rules but deeply interconnected with the world around it. His mentor's enthusiasm for psychoanalysis was infectious, and John found himself fascinated with the idea of exploring Freud's works himself. And so, ever so subtly, the study of medicine, once a lodestar for his ambitions, began to feel less like an expansive horizon and more like a narrowing corridor. Psychology, with its tantalizing questions and uncharted terrain, began to whisper to him, urging him to reconsider the direction of his pursuits.

Professor Adrian, as ever, was quick to notice the way John Bowlby's questions had begun to lean toward the intersections of biology, behavior, and the human mind. One afternoon, the professor regarded Bowlby with a piercing gaze.

"Well, what have you been reading?" he asked.

John hesitated. "Well," he began. "Freud, mostly. And some papers on behaviorism."

Adrian nodded, as though he had expected the answer. "Ah, so you took me up on that... now there's a new frontier. Mark my words, the human mind is a mystery worth unraveling. Tell me, what did you make of Freud?"

What followed was not a lecture but a conversation, a spirited exchange that spilled over into the evening hours. Adrian's enthusiasm for Freudian theory was tempered by his critical eye; he lauded its ambition while challenging its occasional leaps of logic. Bowlby, for his part, found himself drawn to Adrian's ability to weave connections between seemingly disparate ideas, neural pathways and unconscious drives, physiological responses and emotional undercurrents. It was as if Adrian held a key to a locked door Bowlby had only recently discovered.

These conversations became a fixture of their mentorship. John began to spend more time in the presence of his mentor, and they debated the merits of psychoanalysis versus behaviorism, the role of heredity versus environment, and the ethical implications of experimental research on living beings. Adrian, with his characteristic precision, would often push Bowlby to articulate his thoughts more clearly, to refine his arguments until they could withstand scrutiny.

"You're not just studying some dusty book, young man," the Professor told him one day, "you're building the scaffolding for your own ideas. Be deliberate about it!"

He also began to recommend texts that he thought might resonate with Bowlby, not just the foundational works of psychology but also interdisciplinary studies that touched on anthropology, sociology, and even philosophy. And in many ways, as he studied, he began to look back, back into his own childhood, at who he was, how his childhood had molded and developed him. As he sat in the yellow light of his bedside lamp, devouring books on psychology, chewing thoughtfully on the end of a pencil, he found himself analyzing his own life as keenly as any case study on the yellowing pages of his books.

Yet even as his interest in the human mind deepened, John could feel the weight of his medical studies pressing down on him. There were lectures to attend, exams to prepare for, and clinical rotations that left him exhausted and uninspired. Medicine was demanding in its own right, but it lacked the spark that his meandering forays into psychology had ignited in him.

"It's remarkably dull at times," he confided to Donald one day in their shared room. Donald, for his part, looked up with interest; as usual, John's musings tended to come seemingly out of nowhere, after periods of prolonged silence.

"What is?" Donald inquired.

"This whole medicinal business," John said, waving his hand in vague exasperation. "Mind you, I would like to be of some help to the world…it's better than parading about the country, yes…"

"You're right about that."

"…But it's also not the only way to be of use," John continued, picking up one of Freud's thick, black-covered books. "There's whole sciences emerging these days, whole new fields opening up…"

"But none as steady as mortality," Donald said wryly. "Long as man walks the earth, he shall need a physician. It's a good future, Bowlby, and you're quite taken by that queer fellow."

John smiled. "Queer, perhaps, but right about many things."

"I should also like to be right about many things," Donald yawned as he settled back into his bed. Outside their little window, the sky was the color of dark, bruised purple. "We will have to memorize quite a bit if we're going to make the cut for the Tripos…"

"Hm," said John, agreeing even though his mind was seemingly leagues away…

***

By the summer of 1927, was Cambridge humming with its usual end-of-term frenzy: students cramming under the arched ceilings of ancient libraries, tutors pacing the courtyards with their hands clasped behind their backs, and a palpable energy that coursed through the stone walls as exams loomed like an unrelenting specter.

John Bowlby, now two years into his studies, was among the restless cohort preparing for the Natural Sciences Tripos Part I, a three-week gauntlet of written, oral, and practical examinations that demanded a mastery of anatomy, botany, zoology, and mineralogy. The weight of expectation was everywhere, not least in John's own mind; the Tripos was infamous for its rigor, and the whispers of students collapsing under its strain weren't entirely unfounded. For John, the idea of the Tripos came with the aftertaste of anxiety; he had, after all, spent much of the past two years wrestling with subjects that neither excited nor inspired him. Anatomy, though necessary, felt tedious in its memorization of every bone, muscle, and nerve. Zoology never quite interested him, and the study of rocks and plants seemed to him a study so far removed from his humanist ambitions as to feel purely superfluous.

The exams came much too quick, and lasted for far too long, three weeks of grueling tests that passed by in a slow slog of ink-stained fingers, headaches, and bleary-eyed mornings. The written portion was dense and relentless; question after question probed his understanding of topics from the microanatomy of amphibians to the taxonomy of flowering plants. The oral and practical sections were no less daunting, requiring absolute composure under the scrutinizing gaze of examiners. Yet, as the days wore on, something unexpected began to happen. Where he had anticipated stumbling, John found steadiness; where he had feared inadequacy, he discovered a surprising clarity. The knowledge he had accumulated over the past two years, however reluctantly, seemed to align itself at last, like puzzle pieces falling into place.

When the results were announced, John approached the board with a mix of dread and detachment, bracing for the mediocrity he had all but resigned himself to. He scanned the names and marks, his eyes flitting over rows of seconds and thirds, until they landed on a result he could scarcely believe: *first-class honors.*

For a moment, he simply stared, as if the words might rearrange themselves into something less improbable.

The surprise was not his alone. Letters soon arrived from his family, thick with congratulations. His father, who had never had the chance to attend university, was particularly proud, though his pride was expressed in his usual understated way. *"You've done us all a great credit, John,"* he wrote in a letter that John would keep for years.

And yet, beneath the surface of celebration, John wrestled with a quiet ambivalence.

The achievement, while undeniably gratifying, did little to resolve his lingering doubts about the path he was on. The Tripos had demanded diligence and discipline, qualities he did not lack, but it had not ignited his curiosity or stirred his imagination. If anything, the process had only deepened his suspicion that his interests lay elsewhere.

***

By his third year, John had decided to commit to the pull of psychology. Medicine was left behind, an unfinished sentence; in its place stood the Moral Sciences Tripos, a curriculum that offered philosophy and psychology in near-equal measure.

He found himself sitting under the guidance of Sir Frederic Bartlett, a towering figure in Cambridge psychology and, by then, the director of the university's renowned psychology laboratory. Bartlett was a man of purpose, his face a map of sharp lines. In class, his bald crown would gleam faintly as he stood upon the lectern, a fringe of wiry gray hairs clinging defiantly to the sides of his head. His brows, thick and dark, framed eyes that gleamed with intelligence, and he had a quick, impassioned way of talking that sometimes left his students in the dust, scrambling to keep up.

John had encountered Bartlett before, during a series of biology lectures in the Natural Sciences Tripos. Back then, Bartlett had seemed like an anomaly, a psychologist who talked about his subject with the precision and certainty of a chemist. Bartlett's insistence on grounding psychology in observation and introspection felt both rigorous and oddly liberating. It was a philosophy that emphasized the careful recording of responses, not just from external observation but from within one's own mind. Bartlett believed that people—participants, students, subjects, could offer valuable insights about their own reactions if they learned how to notice them properly.

"Very often," Bartlett said in the first lecture Bowlby took, "The most valuable information can be given in terms possible only to the person himself who responds."

His roundabout and flitting style of speech, however, made psychology feel only alive, immediate, and rooted for Bowlby. But as classes wore on, he began to feel a sense of ambivalence; the laboratories, where students trained in experiments on animals and human responses to stimuli, held little appeal to him. He had no interest in the cold detachment of animal testing, no matter how carefully the results were recorded or interpreted. There was something dreadfully antiseptic about it all.

"What use is it," he complained to Donald, "to know how rats navigate a maze if we cannot understand why children cry for their mothers?"

"Don't ask me," Donald replied, sounding amused. "Perhaps you should ask the rats."

To these joking barbs, John would roll his eyes and return to his classes. Despite his mild dislike for the lab, though, the questions Bartlett raised and the problems he pursued in his lectures lingered in his mind. At the very least, Bartlett's focus on real-life challenges, studied with as few artificial simplifications as the laboratory could allow, resonated in a way the repetitive experiments themselves did not.

The psychology laboratory at Cambridge had an almost mythical status; it had been the first in the Commonwealth and produced a staggering share of the history of British experimental psychology. But to Bowlby, the laboratory was less important than the broader principles it stood for. Even Bartlett himself rejected statistics as a *scientific makeshift*, focusing instead on qualitative observation, on the idiosyncrasies of human behavior that couldn't be captured in neat charts or tidy tables. While

Bowlby never fully embraced the lab work, he found himself drawn to the discipline's ambition, to make sense of human responses to their environments, to strip away the noise of life and understand what was truly happening beneath the surface.

It was this tension, a disinterest in the minutiae of experimental methods but a fascination with their implications, that kept John engaged. He could sit through the laboratory exercises, even find value in the precision they demanded, because he was already looking past them.

***

Outside of class, Bowlby continued to be active in Cambridge, which was a world of its own, cloistered yet restless, ancient yet insistently modern.

The students, including John, were all seized by a sort of brilliant, academic rush; they thought themselves revolutionaries in tweed, debating grand ideas in smoke-filled rooms while the bells of King's College Chapel echoed across cobblestone streets. This was a world with its own groups, teams, and organizations, and among these, two debating societies stood out: the legendary 'Apostles,' for the elite, and the lesser-known but no less spirited 'Magpie and Stump.'

John Bowlby, who was quite spirited himself these days, belonged to the latter. Unlike the Apostles, whose members, such as Lytton Strachey and Leonard Woolf, would go on to form the storied Bloomsbury Group, the Magpie and Stump existed in a kind of boisterous obscurity.

91

Its debates were less about reshaping the world and more about poking fun at it. The motions were often absurd, bordering on the satirical: "That this House is in favour of a tax on betting," or "That an underground railway in Cambridge would ruin its aesthetic."

The society met in a dimly lit room that smelled faintly of pipe smoke and damp wool. The walls were lined with books, a mix of dusty classics and newer works that hinted at the rapid pace of change in the world outside. It was here that John Bowlby first found his voice, standing awkwardly at the lectern as he argued, with the conviction of an overconfident undergraduate on topics that mattered quite little.

Whenever Donald came with him to these meetings, he would leave laughing with John.

"For a man who does not like to waste time," he would say with a grin, "You do passably well at it."

"When the occasion arises," John replied with a smile. "I try not to disappoint."

In the pages of Trinity Magazine, the Magpie and Stump's antics were chronicled with a mix of affection and disdain. Bowlby himself earned a brief mention in 1928: "Bugs and drugs. Don't teach your tutor to suck cooking eggs." The first part referred to his academic pursuits in biology and psychology, the second to his reputation as a know-it-all. After years of fighting with his brother, John still had developed a knack for standing up for himself, even if it meant making people bristle with his rebellious spirit.

"It's not my fault I have opinions, Donald," John would defend himself when the latter raised up the magazine with a raised eyebrow.

"Yes, I agree," Donald smiled wryly. "Only, no one asked you to *share* them quite so liberally. You forget, Bowlby, you *are* a student."

"As are the rest of them," John shrugged. "And I wouldn't apologize for being right. Would you?"

"Point made," Donald grinned.

The two had also decided to join the Shakespeare society together, and John had come to appreciate the evenings spent in the smoky lodgings where the meetings took place. They were half performance, half intellectual duel.

"You're completely missing the point," Donald said during one of their heated discussions. "Brutus isn't weak…he's human. He knows the cost of his actions. That's why he falters."

"And that," John replied, voice even, "is precisely what makes him weak. To know the cost and proceed anyway…surely that's not strength but blindness."

The others groaned in mock despair. One of them, a wiry young man named Alistair, tossed a pillow in John's direction. "You'd have made a dreadful conspirator, Bowlby. You think far too much."

To this, John would only smile. Though he seemed to take these meetings far too seriously, in truth, they were but a reprieve from the rigid world of science and structure, a chance to toy with ideas without the weight of consequence.

But that was before the strike, before 1926 turned their studies and essay-writing into something distant, almost frivolous. The nine-day strike began in Britain on May 4, 1926, the first, and only, general strike in the country's history, aiming to push back against the influence of coal mine owners. When the General Strike began, the world outside their Shakespeare Society meetings felt suddenly loud and urgent. The streets buzzed with tension, the clash of ideologies reverberating in the air. Inside, as they still read King Lear aloud, John took the role of Gloucester, his voice deep and steady as he uttered,

"As flies to wanton boys are we to the gods."

Yet even as they read, their thoughts were elsewhere; the strikes were not just politics, they were life rearranging itself, and they could not ignore the pull to step into the fray.

John and Donald volunteered, not out of grand ideological conviction but because it seemed, to them, the practical thing to do. They were sons of the Tory tradition; their fathers had instilled in them a belief in order, in the necessity of keeping the gears of society turning, even when the machine itself seemed to lurch and groan under the weight of its contradictions.

"I suppose we'll be conscripted into some tedious clerical work," Donald said on the morning they signed up. "Suppose we'll see."

But their Navy experience steered them in a different direction. Within days, they found themselves at the base of a hulking electricity-generating station, staring up at a tangle of pipes, turbines, and wires.

"Well," John said finally. "Not what I expected."

"Nor I. Foolishly enough, I thought we left this sort of thing behind when we shed our uniforms," Donald muttered.

Nonetheless, John fulfilled his obligation alongside Donald, who whistled under his breath when the hours dragged on too long. They spoke little but shared a sense of duty, however conflicted; their efforts were small in the grand scheme of things, but they felt necessary.

And yet, as the strike dragged on, John began to feel the weight of its complexity. He knew why the miners struck; he could not ignore the injustice of it, even as he tightened bolts and monitored gauges. The world was not as simple as his father's Tory convictions had suggested. Then, during all this, he received a letter from his brother Tony, who was at Oxford; it shared the perspective of the Labour government on the whole situation, and John had to reluctantly admit that it made some good points. He had no idea when Tony had fallen in with friends from the Labour party, but clearly they were having an effect on him, and indirectly, on John as well.

When the strike ended, life resumed, or so it seemed. The Shakespeare Society met again; the essays reappeared, the ink drying into familiar grooves. But there was a change in John; over time, he would grow closer to leftist ideas.

Yet politics and debate were not the only things that consumed John's time as a student, there was also the little matter of love.

It was here that John found his first girlfriend. He had not set out to charm anyone; he was not especially skilled in the arts of flirtation or persuasion. And yet, there she was, at a garden party on the riverbank near King's College, her hands resting lightly on the back of a wooden chair, her eyes flashing with something between curiosity and amusement. Tony, who had been visiting his brother, watched them together.

As the brothers shared a quiet moment, Tony looked at her and then back at John. "So. You and her?"

"I have been seeing her, yes," John said, with his usual, unflappable calm.

Tony studied John then, with fresh eyes. He was tall, but not strikingly so; his posture was confident but unpracticed. His voice, however, was the key: deliberate, measured, precise. It lent him an authority he didn't even seem aware of. Sometime in the past few years, John Bowlby had grown out of Tony's shadow and into his own man.

"Ah. Well done," Tony finally said, clapping John on the shoulder. "You're growing fast here, aren't you?"

John simply smiled.

It was only later that Tony admitted to himself that he resented John a little in that moment. He had always seen himself as the more capable, the one who should have been ahead. But John had something... an assuredness, a quiet self-sufficiency, that drew people in. It was a little maddening.

John, for his part, hardly spoke about her. He was neither boastful nor embarrassed, only vaguely amused by Tony's sudden interest in his affairs. The relationship played out in the margins of his life at Cambridge. There were walks through Trinity's courtyards, stolen hours in libraries where conversation was exchanged in whispers, long afternoons where they did nothing but sit and read in the sun-dappled cloisters. And when it ended, it ended without spectacle.

When Cambridge emptied for the holidays, John retreated, not to home, where familiarity pressed against him like an unwanted embrace, but to Wales, to the Lakes, to places where the air was sharp and the hills unspooled like stories waiting to be read. Any time he went, he went with Donald and a small group of friends, and their days had a steady rhythm: study first, then walk, then argue, then sleep. The walks were not for leisure; they were pilgrimages of thought. He liked the way his body ached afterward, the dull pull in his legs as he climbed, the clarity of the world from the ridges.

There was something about the isolation of the hills that made their discussions sharper, their debates more urgent. The world seemed far away, and yet they felt closer to understanding it. John carried a small notebook where he jotted down thoughts half-formed; he was searching for something, though he couldn't yet name it. At night, they sat in cramped rooms with single lamps burning, books sprawled open, pages dog-eared. Someone read aloud, Freud, Shakespeare, a letter from a political journal, and they argued as if it was all that mattered, because in those moments, it did. They fought over words, over ideas, over whether the world was best understood through reason or emotion.

In the summer of 1927, though, John decided to undertake a longer trip, this time into mainland Europe.

His destination was to be Hagen, Germany.

The Ruhr Valley, with its factories and rivers, was the lifeblood of Germany's recovery in the wake of the Great War, and Hagen sat at its heart. The city's buildings, some still bearing the scars of conflict, stood like weary sentinels; their facades were cracked, but their foundations held firm. It was a beautiful town, and even if it was wearied and fallen on hard times, its charm remained.

John Bowlby, however, travelled more for an academic interest than a scenic vacation. His aim was to learn the German language, for it seemed like an interesting thing to do; as far as he was concerned, the future belonged to those who could move between languages and borders.

To this end, he stayed with a family in Hagen, a house tucked into the folds of a quiet street, where German was spoken in quick, clipped syllables that felt like stones in his mouth. He wrote to his mother that his tongue found it difficult to shape their words, that the sounds felt foreign in his throat. He practiced in the mornings, sitting at the kitchen table with the family's teenage son, who tried to explain the peculiarities of the language with the patience of someone humoring a child.

And yet, John struggled.

He had always been good at breaking things down, at understanding structures, but German resisted him. The grammar twisted, the pronunciations slipped just out of reach, but still, he persisted. He read newspapers with a dictionary by his side, repeating headlines under his breath. He memorized phrases, tested them out at dinner, felt the weight of his own inadequacy when his hosts corrected him with careful smiles.

But even though its language eluded him, Germany itself fascinated him. He wandered the streets, listening to conversations he barely understood, watching the people move with a rhythm that felt different from home. Underneath the charm of a foreign land, though, he also saw the dark undercurrents of a land that still hadn't gotten over the Great War. He saw workers move with a mechanical precision, their faces etched with the weariness of a nation still nursing the wounds of war. The streets were a patchwork of cobblestones and tram tracks, and the air smelled of coal and damp earth. Children played in the shadow of the Hasper Talsperre, the dam that loomed over the city like a silent sentinel, while their parents traded stories with nostalgic undertones even John could grasp. The churches stood as they always had, their spires piercing the haze as their bells tolled.

And when he returned, his German was still poor, but he didn't mind, he was more taken by the sheer experience. For what John saw during his visit was a nation in flux, a place where the past was a heavy weight and the future an uncertain horizon.

Yet even he could not have imagined the horrors that would one day emerge from the weary German frontier.

**

And finally, John Bowlby graduated.

It was a graduation like any other; names were called, and each step toward the podium felt both momentous and fleeting. Some walked with measured grace, others with the unsteady giddiness of disbelief. The chancellor's grip was firm, the handshake brief, the diploma cool against sweating palms. A flash of applause, a moment of acknowledgment, and then it was over, another name, another future, another person stepping into the unknown.

John left Cambridge with the weight of second-class honors in Moral Sciences pressing against his shoulders; it was not failure, nor was it triumph. It was something in between. A quiet ambiguity. A shrug from the universe rather than a clear direction. The question that followed was simple yet maddening: What next?

Donald McGavin, on the other hand, moved forward with unblinking certainty. He packed his books and his purpose into a trunk and took the first available train to St. Bartholomew's Hospital. Clinical medicine was waiting, structured and defined, and Donald fit into it like a keystone in an arch. Three years of study, then the final examination; beyond that, a career that made sense, a profession that spoke its name in full sentences.

John envied that clarity. His own ambitions were blurred, as if he had wiped them with a damp cloth and smudged their edges. Cambridge had given him knowledge, a disciplined mind, but not direction; he had spent years reading about the nature of thought, the structure of ethics, the moral dilemmas that shaped societies. And now, when he looked at the road ahead, it forked in so many places that it felt less like a road and more like an unruly field, overgrown and waiting to be cut into something walkable.

He told himself he would look around, perhaps look more into psychology and psychoanalysis, the subjects that had consumed his last years in Cambridge.

Little did he know that he was fated to become one of the key figures of the field.

Chapter 6.

In The Field

It was 1928, and John Bowlby found himself being offered a position as a science teacher at St. Paul's, a prestigious boys' school in London.

To be clear, this was the kind of opportunity most graduates would have taken without question. It was a position that promised respect, stability, and a clear path forward. But John hesitated. The weight of the decision pressed on him, not as a burden, but as a question. What did he want? Not just for his career, but for himself, for the ideas that had begun to stir in him, restless and unformed.

He had always been drawn to the human condition, to the invisible threads that tied people together. Science, with its empirical rigor, had been his chosen lens, but his curiosity extended beyond the laboratory. His observations on human nature that had interested him so deeply in Cambridge, in Hagen, even back home, lingered in his mind, unresolved. St. Paul's, with its polished halls and rigid hierarchies, felt like a place where such questions might go unanswered, where the curriculum was a script and the students were expected to follow it without deviation.

So, when the offer from Dunhurst, the junior school of Bedales, came, it felt less like a second choice and more like a quiet revelation.

Instead, he found himself in an environment unlike anything he had ever known—Dunhurst, the junior school of Bedales, nestled in the Hampshire Downs. The air smelled of damp earth and woodsmoke; the grounds were vast and green, speckled with children moving freely, laughing and arguing, unburdened by the rigid structures of traditional education. This was not Rugby, nor Eton, nor any of the public schools that had long dictated what an English education should be.

Bedales had been founded in 1893 by J.H. Badley, a man who had spent years embedded in the very system he later rejected. He had seen the cold discipline, the obsession with Latin and Greek, the relentless drill of team sports, the way boys were pushed toward a singular vision of success. He wanted something different. Education, he believed, was not about conformity but about cultivating a life fully lived. Learning should be experiential, shaped by curiosity and self-discovery rather than fear and obedience. Bedales, which had become coeducational in 1898, a radical move in itself, was designed around these principles.

Dunhurst, where Bowlby would teach, was perhaps the purest expression of Badley's philosophy. The students were between six and twelve years old, their curriculum built on Montessori principles. Maria Montessori herself had given her approval to its methods: children learned through doing, through engagement with the world rather than passively absorbing lectures. Creativity mattered as much as arithmetic; spontaneity and happiness were considered fundamental to mental development. Discipline was not

103

imposed, it was shaped by the rhythm of daily life, by an environment that encouraged independence and self-regulation.

This was a far cry from the world Bowlby had known, from the structured confines of Trinity College and the expectations that had followed him since childhood. He was not just teaching; he was observing, absorbing, and watching how children learned when they were given freedom. He saw their minds stretch in ways that were unpredictable, their understanding shaped by play, by interaction, by an environment that treated them not as vessels to be filled but as individuals with their own pathways to discovery.

One of the first things that struck him was the way these children carried themselves, unburdened by the rigid posture and clipped obedience expected in the traditional schools. There was a lightness to them, a sense that they belonged not just within the walls of the school but to the world beyond it. They explored, questioned, tested limits not out of defiance but because that was how they made sense of things. He watched as they built structures from wood, experimented with colors and shapes, debated over books that would have been considered inappropriate for their age elsewhere. They were not afraid to ask questions, nor were they shamed for getting things wrong.

It was here, in the quiet observation of these children, that something began to take root in Bowlby's mind. He had come to Dunhurst not because he sought a career in education but because he was searching for something, an understanding of development, a way to see psychology not as an abstract field but as something alive, unfolding in real time. The children of Dunhurst became his first real case

104

studies, though he would not have called them that at the time.

He noted how individuality was treated not as an inconvenience but as a core principle. Each child was different, and that difference was not just acknowledged, it was nurtured. The teachers did not impose a singular method of learning but adapted, guiding each student in a way that made sense for them. There was an intuitive recognition that a child's mind could not be forced into a mold; it had to be given space to grow. He saw firsthand how children learned when they felt safe, when they were not driven by the fear of failure but by the joy of discovery. And he began to wonder...

What does this mean for the way people develop? he thought to himself.

The concept continued to intrigue him, and it blossomed into further questions. What did it mean for how attachments were formed, how personalities took shape, how emotional well-being was built not in adulthood but in these early, fragile years?

He was aware of what J.H. Badley had believed. That education should prepare children for life, not just for examinations. *Training of the living for living by living,* he had called it. Now, Bowlby began to see the truth in this. Learning was not separate from life; it was life. And in those early experiences at Dunhurst, he glimpsed the foundation of what would later become his groundbreaking work.

But at the time, it was not a theory.

Not yet... for now, it was just a *feeling.*

John Bowlby began his work in Dunhurst in the September of '28, and he was teaching Physics and Chemistry by November.

By the time he began his classes, he had already helped revitalize Dunhurst's old laboratory. The jars were neatly labeled, the old benches cleared, and the equipment arranged with a precision that bordered on reverence. John Bowlby, now *Professor* Bowlby, stood at the front of the room, facing a group of children.

"I am sure you are all wondering what we should be experimenting on," he said to them after introductions were out of the way, before smiling. "For my part, I was hoping you would all have some suggestions."

The fact was, he had no intention of lecturing at them like his own professors often had as a child; instead, he handed them the tools and let them loose. The experiments were simple, almost foolproof, designed to yield results that even the youngest among them could grasp. He watched as they bent over their work, their hands tentative at first, then growing more confident. There was a spark in their eyes, a flicker of understanding that he found deeply satisfying. This was science as exploration, not instruction.

Biology, however, presented a different challenge. The children couldn't dissect frogs or peer through microscopes at cells; the tools and the subjects were too complex, too distant from their lived experience. Bowlby knew he had to start closer to home. He began with the body…their bodies. He talked about the heart, the lungs, the

106

muscles that moved their arms and legs. He described the way blood flowed, the way breath entered and left the lungs. It was visceral, immediate, and it held their attention in a way that abstract concepts never could. From there, he expanded outward, drawing connections to the rest of the natural world.

In the evenings, as he sat in his quarters with a notebook open before him, he would jot down fragments of thought, questions without answers. The letters to his mother still continued, and he wrote not just to update her on his work, but to clarify things for himself. The act of putting pen to paper forced him to articulate what he was doing and why.

"Practically speaking," he wrote in the tail-end of November, *"they cannot experiment on anything which is at all interesting to them."*

He was not just teaching science; he was teaching curiosity, engagement, a way of seeing the world. The children, he realized, were not empty vessels to be filled with knowledge. They were explorers, and his job was to give them the tools to navigate the terrain.

The days at Dunhurst were long, but they were filled with moments of quiet revelation. Bowlby found himself drawn to the children in ways he hadn't expected. He noticed how some of them hesitated before diving into an experiment, their uncertainty written in the furrow of their brows. Others charged ahead, their enthusiasm unchecked by the possibility of failure. He began to see patterns in their behavior, subtle cues that hinted at deeper currents. A child who struggled to ask for help, another who lit up at the slightest encouragement. These observations lingered in his mind, not as data points, but as questions. What made them this way? What shaped their confidence, their fears, their ability to connect?

Outside the laboratory, Dunhurst was a place of contrasts. The school itself was progressive, a deliberate departure from the rigid traditions of its time. But the world beyond its gates was still shaped by those traditions, by the scars of war and the uneasy tensions of a society in flux. Bowlby was aware of this, though he rarely spoke of it. His focus was on the children, on the small, immediate world they inhabited. He wondered how much of it the children sensed, how much it shaped their lives in ways they couldn't yet articulate.

But he had little time to ponder on much; the job came with responsibilities, some of which he was completely unprepared for. One of these, as it turned out, was teaching gardening.

He had no business teaching gardening; he knew as much about soil and seeds as the boys did, which was to say, almost nothing. But the school had asked, and he had agreed, because the idea of learning alongside the children intrigued him. The first session was a mess of overturned watering cans and misplaced enthusiasm. The boys, zealous and impetuous, attacked the task with a kind of reckless energy that left the garden beds looking more like battlegrounds. John stood back, watching as they dug and planted with no regard for technique or tradition. But this was a state of affairs he saw no reason to change, and in fact, he was quite interested to see where it would lead.

By the third week, the garden began to take shape. The boys argued over whose turn it was to water the seedlings; they debated the merits of one plant over another.

Bowlby intervened only when necessary, his role reduced to that of a referee rather than a teacher. He found himself enjoying the afternoons, not for the gardening itself, but for the way it revealed the children's personalities. There was the boy who insisted on measuring each hole with scientific precision; the one who planted seeds at random, convinced that nature would sort it out; the quiet one who watched from the sidelines until he was sure of what to do. These small details stayed with him, adding to the growing mosaic of his understanding.

On weekends, he took the older boys on long walks through the countryside. The pace was brisk, the routes demanding, and the conversations sporadic but revealing. Once, he walked too fast and lost half the group; they found him waiting at the top of a hill, sheepish but amused. The boys teased him mercilessly, and he let them. There was an ease to these outings, a sense of camaraderie that felt different from the structured interactions of the classroom.

The lack of corporal punishment at Dunhurst had been another revelation. The school's progressive ethos meant that discipline was handled through dialogue and mutual respect, not fear. Bowlby had, at first, his doubts about this; he knew schoolchildren could be an unruly lot. But as it turned out, the children, for all their energy and occasional mischief, were fundamentally kind and eager to please. He found that a firm word or a pointed look was usually enough to redirect their behavior. This approach seemed quite effective to his eye, though he couldn't yet articulate why.

By the next year, the school offered him a new role: running games and filling gaps. It was a catch-all position designed for his particular brand versatility, and this would not have bothered him, only, it came with a nominal salary and no clear focus. Bowlby accepted, but not without reservations. He liked the children; he liked the work. But he was beginning to feel the limits of his role. Mrs. Fish, the headmistress, had made it clear that she valued his ability to connect with the younger students.

"You have a gift," she told him, though she didn't elaborate.

Bowlby appreciated the sentiment, but it wasn't enough. The sheer burden now on his shoulders instilled in him a greater realization of just how demanding the job actually was, far more so than he had imagined.

In his letters to his mother, he wrestled with these thoughts. *"It is impossible to estimate the scope & value of work in education,"* he wrote one cold December. *"Work which has been touched on by most geniuses, & has been taken for granted by all fools."*

His time here had taught him how much there was to learn about teaching, and it felt absurd to him now, this idea that someone could simply step into a classroom without first understanding the weight of what they were doing.

By the end of the term, he had made his decision. He would leave Dunhurst, not because he disliked the work, but because he needed something...*more.*

***

As he continued to look for a new job, John Bowlby had come to realize something: he had no patience for ordinary schools.

The rigid rows of desks, the droning lectures, the weary-eyed children reciting facts they neither understood nor cared about, it all seemed to him like a factory designed to produce obedient, unimaginative clerks. He increasingly wanted no part of it; what he wanted was something *different*.

To this end, he visited schools that existed on the margins of the educational world, places that the traditionalists scoffed at and the reformers spoke of in hushed admiration. Among them was Summerhill, a school run by A.S. Neill, a man who believed that children were, at their core, good. Neill's radical notion was that children should be given the freedom to learn at their own pace, to follow their curiosities rather than be force-fed a curriculum devised by men in offices far removed from childhood itself. It was an idea that struck a deep chord with him, and the more he saw of these so-called 'extraordinary schools,' the more he felt aligned with them.

After all, these were places where children were not shackled by the expectations of the adult world; they explored, they questioned, they made mistakes, and they learned from them. And the more he immersed himself in these environments, the more the idea of teaching in a conventional school became intolerable.

"I could never be that kind of teacher," he found himself writing to his mother on a crisp morning in the December of 1928. *"The old repressive schoolmaster*

awarding prizes, pumping in knowledge, and dealing out punishments would never suit me."

Education, after all, was not about filling a child's mind with information; it was about understanding children themselves. He believed that before a teacher could truly educate, he had to know who he was educating. Schools, as they were traditionally structured, seemed like the worst possible place to accomplish that. It was as if the entire system had been designed backwards: teachers treated children as problems to be solved rather than individuals to be understood.

At Summerhill, he watched children roam freely, choosing their own subjects, learning through play and conversation rather than strict lessons. He was fascinated by the way children responded when they were trusted, when they were given responsibility for their own education. But even this was not quite right to his mind. He admired its philosophy, but he remained a scientist at heart, drawn to careful observation and practical application. What he wanted was a school that combined freedom with structure, where children could explore but also be guided. He did not believe that all discipline was bad, only that it should not be imposed mindlessly.

And it was soon after, before the year even had ended, that John Bowlby found himself at Priory Gate, and if Dunhurst was where his mind had been freed, Priory Gate was where it would now be shaped.

Chapter 7.

Priory Gate

Priory Gate had been established nine years ago, then, in 1919, by a man named Theodore James Faithfull, a veterinary surgeon by profession. It was not a school in the traditional sense. It was more of an idea, an argument against everything Faithfull despised about ordinary schooling. The institution was small, deliberately so; never more than twenty-two children, a mix of boys and girls from ages three to eighteen, all considered difficult in one way or another. Some had been expelled from traditional schools. Others had refused, outright, to endure them. Many came from homes where discipline was doled out with a heavy hand, their so-called maladjustment traced back to domineering fathers or overattentive mothers. The prevailing view of the time classified such children as unstable, nervous, or, most commonly, maladjusted.

Not so here.

As John Bowlby looked around, what he saw did not look like a school in the conventional sense; it did not loom, did not impose. It sat, instead, on the Norfolk landscape like an afterthought, an old building repurposed for education, its

113

stone walls softened by moss and time. The wind moved through the trees at its borders, carrying the salt air from the coast; the students, some in untucked shirts, some in ragged jumpers, ran across the courtyard as if no one had ever told them to slow down.

He was met here by John Alford, a staff member whom Bowlby took an immediate liking to.

"Nice to meet you, Mr. Alford," Bowlby said, nodding as they shook hands.

"Pleasure's all mind," Alford smiled back. "Shall I give you a tour?"

Bowlby accepted his kind offer, and they walked through the school. After touring the school's small but lively grounds, they made way for the library. They walked past leather-bound volumes, dog-eared and underlined, stacked in precarious columns on tables and shelves. Next, the science lab, it smelled of old wood and chalk dust, its tables marked with chemical spills and students' initials carved into the surface. The classrooms, meanwhile, had windows that yawned open to let in the Norfolk sun, when it chose to appear; for now, in the winter, only the cold bled through the stone walls. The students wrapped their scarves tighter as they scribbled notes, looking up only briefly as Alford and Bowlby walked past.

Finally, John Bowlby found himself in Alford's office. He leaned forward in his chair in his usual, careful fashion, elbows resting on his knees as he watched Alford refill his pipe with deliberate care.

"So, tell me," Alford said, striking a match, "what made you come here? A teacher of your

114

qualifications…why, there's plenty of places that would hire a man such as you for quite a bit more than us. So…why Priory Gate?"

Bowlby exhaled, rubbing the back of his neck. "Because the alternatives are London boys' school with too many rules and too little thought. You are correct that they would likely hire me, but…I want more. I wish to *teach*, not simply force-feed facts."

Alford smiled, shaking the match until the flame disappeared into the dim light. "You sound like a man who's read too much and seen little…a true idealist."

"That's why I came here," Bowlby said unperturbed. "To see more."

Alford took a slow draw from his pipe. "Most men your age, with your background, go where the path is smooth. Yet you've chosen to wade through the weeds." He leaned forward. "What is your exact problem with other schools, if you do not mind me asking?"

Bowlby hesitated. "The way they are run, most of them, anyway, it's artificial. I don't trust a system that forces children into rows like factory workers and expects them all to learn the same way."

Alford chuckled. "You're not the first idealist to sit in that chair, you know. The world is full of men who think they can change things. Most of them find out they can't."

Bowlby met his gaze. "And you? Do you think change is possible?"

Alford tapped his pipe against the ashtray. "I think children don't need to be controlled as much as they need to be understood. That's why Priory Gate exists…to observe, to guide. Not to punish. Not to dictate." Alford studied him for a long moment, then leaned back. "What do *you* think makes a child?"

Bowlby frowned. "That's an odd question."

"Most people say a child is what he's taught. His discipline. His obedience. His grasp of Latin. I say a child is what he's allowed to be."

Bowlby nodded slowly. "And you let them be…what?"

"Curious," Alford said simply. "Let them play, let them question, let them fail without fear. Give them the room to figure things out for themselves. Otherwise, you're just another schoolmaster stuffing their heads with facts."

Bowlby's lips curled into a faint smile. "And stuffing heads with facts would never suit me."

Alford laughed, a deep, knowing chuckle. "No, I don't imagine it would." He reached for a stack of papers on his desk, rifling through them. "You know, when I first started here, people thought we were mad. No exams? No punishments? Just...learning? They called it dangerous. But here we are."

Bowlby looked around the room. The mismatched furniture, the haphazard stacks of books, the window that barely latched shut. It was not polished. It was not perfect. But it felt right.

"What will I be doing if I stay?" he asked.

Alford smiled wryly. "Teaching, if you must. But mostly, you'll be learning."

Bowlby smiled. That suited him just fine.

That night, the two of them talked a great deal about quite many things that interested them both: psychology, pedagogy, the nature of human learning, societal structures, literature...and as John Bowlby retired for the night, he knew that Priory Gate was the place for him.

***

Over the course of a year, the journey to and from Priory Gate would become a matter of habit. The road leading to the school was narrow, with hedgerows that snagged at the tires of passing carriages and automobiles alike. Priory Gate sat beyond a low stone wall, more of a boundary than a barrier. Its windows were large but sunken in their frames, the roof a patchwork of slate and ivy. More often than not, children would be sitting on the front steps, watching Bowlby's approach first with suspicion and then with familiarity.

To Bowlby's care came the total student population, of which there were 22, although they never seemed to be in one place for long. Some had come from homes where love was conditional; others from homes where love was absent altogether. They were not bad children, though they had been called that elsewhere. Maladjusted, the world said; *different*, was what Priory Gate understood them as.

John Alford had been the reason Bowlby had been won over, but it was the children who kept him there. He watched them keenly, curiously, and with interest. They were all in various states of rebuilding, their instincts for self-

117

preservation sharp and visible. A six-year-old with a tendency to punch anyone who touched him too suddenly; a ten-year-old who never spoke above a whisper; a girl of thirteen who had mastered the art of leaving a room without anyone noticing.

Alford's insistence in the moral strength of the school had won him over, but the unstructured nature of how things worked here shocked the ever-orderly John Bowlby. On his first day, he came in time for breakfast only to be completely disoriented. There was no rigid formation of benches or sharp discipline, no barked orders from a towering authority figure. Instead, children sat in loosely arranged clusters, some speaking in loud, rapid bursts, others silent, retreating into the safety of their porridge. A boy, perhaps nine, dunked a crust of bread into his bowl, letting it soak until it disintegrated. Across the room, a girl with a pale, sharp face peered up from her seat with something like suspicion before returning to her meal. The air smelled of damp wood and weak tea.

Faithfull, the headmaster, strolled in with the unhurried air of a man who had long since abandoned the notion of control. His face, weathered and cheerful, seemed strangely detached from the state of the school itself. There was a benevolent chaos about him; his liberal philosophy, Bowlby was beginning to suspect, relied more on a vague hope that if left alone, children might somehow sort themselves out.

"It's a lot," Faithfull admitted as he approached the chaos, his voice tinged with something between amusement and resignation. "But they thrive here, sir, thrive. We try to keep them happy, you see. Give them space. They need a place where they aren't being kicked around."

118

Bowlby nodded but remained unconvinced. He had spent a fair amount of time contemplating the inner workings of the human mind, the fragile scaffolding of emotional development; this was something different. As far as he was concerned, happiness was not the absence of authority, nor the unchecked freedom to drift without structure. These children needed more than shelter. They needed guidance, stability, something firm beneath their feet. But for now, he did not voice these thoughts.

At midmorning, he walked into what had been designated the "Woodling group" classroom, a space that seemed caught between intention and neglect. A few desks had been pushed against the walls; a sagging bookshelf housed an unpredictable collection of books, some with pages missing, some so obscure as to be entirely useless. The blackboard was streaked with forgotten lessons, the ghosts of past efforts that had faded before they could take hold.

His students arrived in loose trickles, some with curiosity, others with wariness. There were ten in total, aged eight to twelve, their expressions ranging from disinterest to mild amusement. A boy named Edwin slumped into his seat as if it pained him to be there. Beside him, a girl with a mess of auburn hair drummed her fingers against the wood of her desk, looking anywhere but at him.

Bowlby stood before them, considering how best to begin. Authority, he knew, would not be given freely; it would have to be earned.

"What do you want to learn?" he asked.

Silence. Some of them exchanged glances, skeptical. The girl, Margaret, he would later learn, narrowed her eyes. "Don't we have to learn what you tell us?"

Bowlby smiled. "Not exactly."

That got their attention.

He walked over to the bookshelf and pulled out a book at random, one with a missing cover. He flipped through the pages. "Science," he said. "Geography. Myths. Writing. History. We could start with any of them." He paused, closing the book. "Or we could start with something different."

Margaret crossed her arms. "Like what?"

"Like why your heart beats." He tapped a fist lightly against his chest. "Or why the wind blows. Or why your hands feel warm when you rub them together."

A few of them perked up. Edwin, slouched as he was, lifted his head just a fraction. The drumming of Margaret's fingers slowed.

Bowlby leaned against the desk, his voice measured. "You don't have to memorize facts. You don't have to copy notes. You just have to wonder about things, and then we'll figure them out."

A boy named Richard, sharp and restless, frowned. "How?"

"You'll experiment."

The room remained quiet for a beat, then: "Like in a lab?"

"Like in a lab," Bowlby said, nodding. "Only better."

Richard considered this, then shrugged. "Alright."

It was a start.

The lessons that followed were unlike anything the children had known before. Bowlby did not lecture. He did not stand at the front of the room and demand attention with a ruler's edge or a raised voice. Instead, he guided. He introduced questions and let them wrestle with answers. For the first time, they were not passive recipients of knowledge; they were explorers, investigators. And for the first time, Bowlby saw their faces change, the slouched wariness replaced by something livelier.

At the end of the day, as the students filtered out, Margaret lingered by the desk, her arms still crossed but her expression less guarded. "So tomorrow," she said, "are we going to do more experiments?"

Bowlby smiled. "Quite so."

She nodded and ran out.

With her gone, Bowlby sat at the desk, exhaling. He was still wondering what he had gotten himself into when Faithfull showed up, hands in his pockets.

"Well, I can see you got along well with the children," he said, quite glad.

"I should have thought you would be observing my class," Bowlby said, frowning slightly. "Since it is my first…"

"Teaching is not so hard," Faithfull said dismissively. "Why, half of England is full of schoolmasters. What matters more is that you should understand the child, Mr. Bowlby!"

"Quite," John said, a little unprepared.

"So, what do you think a child wants, Mr. Bowlby?" he asked John, raising his eyebrows.

But John, though he had some ideas of his own, knew Faithfull was much more excited about revealing his own beliefs. "I wouldn't know, sir. What do you believe?"

"I believe that the child is quite rational, yes," Faithfull said thoughtfully, "I believe that inside, he should like to have an organization that gives him security, but that frees him for creative activity."

"So, much like the rest of us, then?" Bowlby couldn't help himself from saying, to an amused chuckle from Faithfull.

"Why, yes, I suppose we are all children in that sense," he laughed. "Mr. Freud's theories come to mind, at that..."

Faithfull had much to say on the subject of Freud, on the New Psychology and psychoanalysis that was flourishing now, but this theoretical lecturing held little appeal for John Bowlby. Much more interesting was the fact that he had the ability to put these theories to a pedagogical test.

As a teacher, his job was to teach, but not in the way he had been taught. While some, like Margaret, warmed to him quickly, others refused to participate at first. They had spent too long in classrooms where knowledge had been something inflicted upon them. But Bowlby had patience; he knew that the trick was to make learning feel like an invitation, not an obligation. He set up foolproof experiments with results that were unmistakable; he brought in specimens for them to examine, touch, and dissect. Slowly, they engaged. Even the quietest ones found ways to express curiosity.

There were no punishments, but there were consequences. If a child threw a book across the room in frustration, no one shouted. Instead, he, Faithfull, or Alford would retrieve it, set it back on the table, and wait. The waiting was often enough. The children learned they were not fighting against enemies here; they were fighting against themselves. After a long day of classes, then, the evenings were a time of uneasy peace. Some children read; others roamed the grounds, their hands trailing along the stone walls, as if mapping the edges of their world. Some stood at windows, watching the Norfolk sky deepen to indigo, pressing their foreheads to the glass as if trying to see something just beyond reach.

What was immediately apparent to John Bowlby, however, was that the school could not continue to function in this way. Yet, he also knew that as a young and new teacher, he would need support if he was to try and improve Priory Gates.

Support, of course, returned in the shape of John Alford, who had been away on holiday around the time of Bowlby's joining. Now, Bowlby talked to him about his beliefs, and Alford nodded. He, too, saw with unnerving clarity the thing that everyone else refused to name: the school, as it stood, was teetering. And if nothing changed, if something wasn't built from the crumbling edges, it would collapse in on itself, leaving behind nothing but wasted days and wasted children.

The two of them found themselves sitting in the dusky light of the common room, surrounded by old books. The fire was burning low, barely more than embers, as Alford leaned forward. His hands clasped between his knees, and he spoke with the kind of urgency that suggested he had spent the entire holiday thinking about this very moment.

"You're right, of course. We need to rethink everything," he agreed. "If we want this school to work, it has to be more than an idea. It has to function. It has to be structured in a way that actually benefits the children, rather than simply satisfying some abstract, progressive philosophy."

Bowlby nodded, feeling, for the first time in days, something close to relief. "That's exactly it," he said. "There's a framework here, but nothing holding it together. If we don't develop the system properly, if we don't put real thought into what these children need, then it's just going to fall apart."

Alford exhaled sharply, almost a laugh but not quite. "Then we start making our plans. But the question is this: will the headmaster listen? And if he doesn't, how much could you and I do on our own?"

That was the question that lingered in Bowlby's mind as he took over the Woodling group. Ten children, aged eight to twelve. A cluster of sharp elbows and wide eyes, all in varying states of curiosity and defiance. Here, at least, he had something close to control; a free hand, as they had called it, though Bowlby knew that freedom in this sense came with its own burdens. He could shape their days however he liked: structure them, fill them with meaning, or let them drift aimlessly through lessons with no more substance than a passing breeze.

But he would not let them drift.

***

Lessons would take place indoors from September to May, and in those months, the school looked almost conventional. Students sat at desks, though they often rearranged them; teachers delivered lessons, though they were more facilitators than authorities. Bowlby, who had arrived young and eager, slipped easily into the rhythm of the place. He was not much older than the oldest boys, and to them, there was something disarming about him: his lack of severity, his curiosity about them as people rather than pupils. He was quickly well-liked.

Tony Bowlby, visiting once, was told by some of the girls that his brother was a "nice man"—which, if the accompanying blushes were anything to go by, meant that he was the target of at least a few schooltime crushes.

But it was in the summer months that Priory Gate revealed its true form. School went under canvas, quite literally, and the world became their classroom. The younger children camped on the grounds, by the sea, or in the New Forest; the older ones took to the roads, walking and cycling for days at a time. Nature was their tutor. It was the educator who did not lecture, did not dictate; it simply existed, and in existing, it taught them something about themselves. Bowlby arranged the walking and the camping; Faithfull arranged the food. The children were given control, which meant they were given responsibility. In Bowlby's view, this was how cooperation was formed, not through enforcement, but through necessity. If a tent collapsed, it had to be put up again. If the fire died, someone had to relight it. There was no punishment, no rebuke, just reality, requiring them to act.

125

Among the children, two made a particular impression on Bowlby.

The first was a small boy of seven who spent his days trailing Bowlby's every move. He was quiet, unobtrusive, and fiercely loyal, as though his own sense of stability was somehow tied to Bowlby's presence. The staff referred to him as Bowlby's "shadow," a name that stuck, not because it was humorous, but because it was true. The boy seemed to shrink when Bowlby was absent, to expand when he was near. He was a reminder of how children attach themselves, instinctively, desperately, to those they trust.

The second was a boy of sixteen, whose presence was less endearing but far more significant. He was emotionally closed, unreachable in a way that made him appear older than he was. He stole, not out of need, but out of compulsion. His history was complicated. Born illegitimate to wealthy parents, raised by a nurse who later left, sent away, expelled from Eton for theft, his story read like a case study in neglect. Priory Gate did not punish him; it attempted to understand him.

Bowlby's take on the boy was that his condition was not inherent, but caused. Experience shaped people, and his experiences had been brittle and broken.

Bowlby's main compatriot in the institute, however, remained Alford. He was a man of forty, with hands that were permanently smudged with ink; he had the distracted air of someone who was always on the verge of a great realization but could never quite get there. He was, officially, a volunteer at Priory Gate. Unofficially, he was a father who had simply followed his children into their schooling and stayed. Neither an academic nor a traditional teacher, he was instead something stranger, an artist who spoke in half-formed ideas, a war veteran who rarely mentioned the war, a philosopher without conclusions.

He and Bowlby would sit for hours in the cluttered, musty staff room, their conversations wandering from art to psychology, from childhood trauma to the absurdity of formal education.

"You can't build a mind with rules alone," he told Bowlby one evening, his pipe smoke curling against the ceiling. "Children aren't machines. You can't just feed them information and expect them to run smoothly."

Bowlby listened. He always listened.

It was through Alford that he first encountered the ideas of Homer Lane, a name that kept surfacing in their conversations like a whisper of something important. Lane, an American lay therapist, had run a radical school for delinquent children—the "Little Commonwealth." There, children governed themselves, meting out their own justice, forming their own rules. The premise was simple: a child, given love and responsibility, could heal himself.

Lane's writings fascinated Bowlby. He read Talks to Parents and Teachers in a single weekend, pacing his small room at Priory Gate, turning the pages like they contained a secret no one else had seen. The ideas were raw, brash, and completely at odds with traditional education. Lane argued that delinquency wasn't born of inherent evil or weakness but of deprivation; children became difficult when they were unloved, when they were disciplined instead of understood.

The implications were groundbreaking for John Bowlby. If Lane was right, then entire systems of education were built on false premises; if love was the antidote to crime, then the cane and the stern lecture were, at best, useless and, at worst, cruel. Bowlby brought these thoughts to Alford, who listened with the same quiet attentiveness that Bowlby himself had mastered.

"Of course he's right," Alford said finally, leaning back in his chair. "The trouble is, people don't like simple answers. They'd rather believe a child is bad than admit they failed him."

It was during one of these conversations that Bowlby found himself articulating his own ideas for the first time. He had always been drawn to psychology, but now the subject felt less like an interest and more like a responsibility. What if he could prove what Lane had only theorized? What if he could take those instincts, the belief that love and security shaped a child's future, and ground them in something empirical?

Priory Gate itself seemed to reinforce these ideas. The school, for all its faults and despite the fact that it was perpetually struggling, was still a haven for children who didn't fit elsewhere. Some were there because their parents believed in progressive education; others were there because no other school had wanted them. And yet, despite the disorder, despite the uncertainty, there was something undeniably human about the place. The children weren't subdued; they weren't broken into submission. They were unpredictable, alive.

Bowlby now started watching his own group more closely. He paid attention to the way they behaved when they were scolded versus when they were encouraged. He noticed which boys withdrew after a reprimand and which ones lashed out. He started seeing patterns, not just in their actions, but in their fears, their defenses, their desperate attempts to be seen. Later, he and Alford spent long hours dissecting these observations. Alford spoke about art as a window into the unconscious, how a child's sketches could reveal the things he couldn't say aloud. Bowlby, ever the scientist, pushed for something more concrete.

Could these observations be measured, he wondered. Could they be studied? And for a while, these questions seemed to keep a bigger one at bay: was John Bowlby wasting away at Priory Gate?

Faithfull's experimental venture was not, ironically, instilling any of his staff with much faith. As interesting as the theoretical framework was, the lax and happy-go-lucky nature of Priory Gate meant that not only was it endangering its own success as an institution, but it was also slowly turning into quicksand for John Bowlby's career. While he could explore and apply himself to his heart's content, he could not apply his findings, or work on them further, or even further his own theoretical groundings. And so, it seemed evident to John Alford that at some point, the young Bowlby needed to pursue new avenues.

The first time Alford brought it up to him, the two of them were sitting in the staff room, the fire low in the grate, the cold creeping in through the cracks in the windowpanes. It was the kind of damp that settled into the bones, the kind that made men rub their hands together, clap them against their thighs, keep their shoulders hunched. Alford, however, sat back in his chair, at ease in a way that Bowlby envied; it was the ease of a man who had lived long enough to know that comfort was fleeting and not worth chasing.

129

"Psychiatry," Alford said suddenly, as if the thought had just arrived, though Bowlby suspected it had been waiting in the wings for some time. "That's where you'll find the answers you're looking for. Or at least, it's where you'll find better questions."

Bowlby let the words settle. The fire crackled, spitting an ember onto the hearth. He nudged it back with the toe of his boot. "I never wanted to be a doctor," he said finally. "And, frankly, I have no patience for useless psychological experimentation."

Alford let out a small laugh, shaking his head. "My dear friend, psychiatry is not academic psychology, and it is certainly not about testing what sort of rewards a mouse or shrew might like. It is quite what you want: the applied study of the human mind."

Bowlby frowned. Priory Gate was flawed. He knew that even without Alford making that clear, but at least it was alive. Children ran through its halls, slammed doors, laughed, wept; it was a place of motion, of emotion. The field of psychology, at least after the classes he had attended on the subject, seemed sterile and almost boring.

Alford must have seen the hesitation on his face because he leaned forward, elbows on his knees. "Look," he said, "you want to understand how people work. You want to understand why some children thrive and others don't. You're not going to find that answer in a book of theory, and honestly, you're not going to find it here. And between us, I do not even know if the headmaster can keep this place running for the next year or two! You need to see the object of your curiosity, my young friend, *really* see it. And that means stepping into places that make you uncomfortable."

130

There was an urgency in his voice then, a tension that rarely surfaced. It wasn't a command, though; Alford never commanded. He suggested, he argued, he reasoned; he laid the world out like a set of puzzle pieces and left it to others to put them together.

Bowlby settled back and ran a hand through his hair. He thought about the children at Priory Gate: their anger, their fears, their sudden, inexplicable sadness. He thought about how little he understood, how much he wanted to understand. If Alford was right, and he often was, then psychiatry was the way forward.

"I'll think about it," he said.

Alford smiled, a flicker of something satisfied crossing his face. "That's all I ask."

And Bowlby *did* think about it. He thought about it as he watched the children at Priory Gate; as he sat with them in the quiet hours, listening to their stories, their fears; as he read Lane's work, tracing the connection between love and loss, security and survival. The pieces were there, scattered, waiting to be arranged into something coherent.

And then, one evening, he found himself in Alford's room again, the same fire burning low, the same chill in the air. He closed the door behind him and leaned against the frame.

"I'm going back to London," he said.

Alford looked up from his book. He didn't seem surprised. "Psychiatry?"

Bowlby nodded. "I'll complete my medical training as well, but...yes. Psychiatry, and psychotherapy if I can manage it."

Alford set the book aside, stretching his legs out in front of him. "I'll be honest with you, old boy; you might well hate psychiatry at first," he said. "The theoretical nature of some things, the rules..."

"I know I shall," John Bowlby said, sighing.

Alford chucked. "Right, *but*. If you can stomach it, you'll learn things you'd never find in books."

Bowlby already knew that. He knew that the world he was about to enter would be different from Priory Gate, different from the warmth and disorder and idealism. But it would also be closer to having a career of some sort, and more than that, a purpose, or a calling. As important as Priory Gate had been, Alford was right; there was no telling if Faithfull could even keep this strange, wonderful, terribly managed little miracle running. As Bowlby accepted that he soon would leave, he stayed a while longer with Alford. The fire burned between them, the night pressing in. They spoke of other things: the future, the past, the roads that led from one to the other. They talked of interesting things and uninteresting events, knowing that they might not meet again at all; and then, when the fire had burned to embers, when the cold had made its way into the room, John Bowlby stood.

"I meant to thank you," he said, looking at Alford with his serious eyes.

But Alford simply waved a hand, dismissive. "You'd have gotten there on your own."

Bowlby wasn't so sure. But he let it go.

He left Priory Gate not a week later, the wind biting at his face, the path ahead uncertain but no longer unclear. Faithfull had tried to keep him, but John Bowlby knew now that he had other places to be, and another path to follow.

Chapter 8.

Early Psychology

John Bowlby had never been one for dogma; it made him restless, like an ill-fitting coat worn in the heat of summer.

Even as a boy, he had recoiled from doctrine, from the unyielding rules of Latin grammar, from the rigid corridors of Edge's where everything had its place, its time, its expectation. Yet here he was, standing at the threshold of the British Psycho-Analytical Society, a place that, for all its claims to scientific rigor, bore an unsettling resemblance to a church, one with its own Pope, its own doctrine, and its own excommunication rites.

There were two main hubs of psychoanalytic training, the British Psychoanalytical Society and the Tavistock Clinic, and for all the former's flaws, it also had a sense of professional credibility to it that made it the best place for an enterprising psychiatrist to aspire to.

But the flip side was that the Society, for all its talk of exploration and unlocking the deepest recesses of the mind, was at its core an institution ruled by a single will: Ernest Jones.

Jones was a man who spoke with the absolute conviction of someone who had never doubted himself. He had been Freud's disciple, Freud's ambassador in London, and he wielded his authority with a precision that bordered on the ruthless. If one wished to be a psychoanalyst in Britain, one needed his approval. And approval, as Bowlby would soon learn, was not granted lightly; there were *rules*. Unspoken, perhaps, but rules nonetheless. One did not deviate too far from the accepted doctrine. One did not publicly admire Adler or Jung. One certainly did not collaborate with Tavistock, which Jones regarded as a dilution of psychoanalysis, a watering-down of what should be, in his view, a pure and exact science.

Bowlby found this both absurd and quite tiresome. Psychoanalysis, as a field, was meant to be about understanding human nature; and yet, the Society operated like a medieval guild, complete with gatekeepers and inquisitions.

But still, he stayed.

He stayed because he knew that beyond the bureaucracy, beyond the rigid hierarchies and the territorial squabbles, there was something worth learning. He had read Freud, but reading was not enough. He needed to see for himself how theory met practice, how ideas took shape in the consulting room. The only question that gnawed at him, the one he could never quite shake, was this:

Was it worth it?

Was it worth navigating the politics, the rigid expectations, the weight of an institution that seemed more invested in its own preservation than in genuine discovery?

The answer, perhaps, was that it had to be. Because to reject it outright would mean being cast adrift, left to work on the margins without recognition or support. And he had spent too long fighting to be taken seriously to throw it away now.

In the end, he was accepted only provisionally into this world governed by symbols and interpretations; after all, he was twenty-two, barely past the threshold of formal education, still shaping his own intellectual identity.

He was assigned to Joan Riviere, a woman of austere intelligence, whose presence alone seemed to reduce the temperature of any room. She had come to psychoanalysis from literature and art, translating Freud into English with a precision that bordered on reverence. The pages she had transcribed carried the weight of doctrine, yet she herself had the quiet, deliberate skepticism of someone who had once belonged to another intellectual tradition. She had been a friend and follower of Melanie Klein, a woman whose name was spoken with a mixture of reverence and unease, depending on the audience. Klein's theories, particularly on the psychoanalysis of children, had cleaved the British Psycho-Analytical Society into factions. The Tavistock clinicians whispered their disapproval of her methods; the Kleinians called it progress.

Bowlby watched the battle from a distance, curious but unconvinced. Klein believed that children as young as two could be analyzed as rigorously as adults, that their play was not just play but the very architecture of their unconscious life. She would crouch beside them, her presence at once comforting and forensic, extracting meaning from wooden blocks and stuffed animals with the precision of a surgeon. A doll buried beneath a stack of books

136

was not merely a doll forgotten but a representation of the repressed self, crushed beneath the weight of parental expectation. A toy soldier discarded in the corner was not simply lost but rejected, a symbol of an internalized aggression the child could not yet name.

It was fascinating; it was also maddening.

Bowlby had read Freud's Introductory Lectures at Cambridge, skimming them first with the idle curiosity of a student, then with the meticulous attention of a skeptic. Now, in London, his reading turned rigorous. It was not enough to accept psychoanalysis as a system of thought; he needed to test it. Yet each attempt to apply scientific scrutiny was met with discomfort, even resistance. His analyst, Mrs. Rivvy, as he later called her, was not altogether pleased with his attitude. She regarded his relentless questioning as a kind of arrogance, a refusal to take anything on trust. He remembered one of their sessions with particular clarity:

"You take nothing as given," she had said, sitting across from him, arms folded.

"I don't see why I should," he had replied.

She had sighed, almost imperceptibly. "And you assume, I suppose, that thought can be built from the ground up, without ever standing on the shoulders of those who came before?"

He had not answered immediately. He had thought of Cambridge, of the endless debates with his friends Evan Durbin and Henry Phelps Brown, economists by training, masters of intellectual dissection by nature. With them, there had been no room for blind acceptance. Every argument had to be justified "up to the hilt," as Bowlby put it later. It was an environment that demanded rigor, that treated ideas as hypotheses rather than doctrine.

That was not how things worked at the Institute.

Here, the Freudians and Kleinians argued over theory with the intensity of theologians debating scripture. Ernest Jones, the Society's founder, presided like a high priest. He had built the Society from the ground up, securing Freud's place in England, defending him with a fervor that bordered on religious devotion. He had fought off medical skeptics, fended off Jungians, and, in the process, had become something of an inquisitor himself. He determined who was allowed into the Society and who was cast into the wilderness. A psychoanalyst's reputation was not built on independent thought but on loyalty.

Bowlby chafed against it. He respected the discipline, respected its potential, but could not bring himself to accept its methods uncritically. And yet, he knew he had to learn the language before he could challenge it. Meanwhile, Riviere continued her work with him, guiding him through the intricate landscapes of the unconscious, though not without exasperation. She spoke of phantasy with the same certainty as a physicist spoke of gravity. To her, the inner world was as real, perhaps more real, than the external one. It was a conviction that unnerved him.

The intellectual climate of the Institute was suffocating at times. It was not a place where one could merely be interested in psychoanalysis; one had to believe in it. He noticed, too, how the battles within the Society shaped its members. Some, like Klein, thrived in the conflict. Others retreated into silence, wary of drawing the wrath of Jones and his circle. Riviere, despite her authority, often seemed caught between allegiances. She had once been loyal to Jones, but her alignment with Klein had complicated things.

All in all, John Bowlby was beginning to understand that if he was to make his way in this world, he would have to navigate it carefully. After all, there were those who wielded theory as an unassailable doctrine, a gospel of the mind's secret workings, and there were those, like him, who picked at it, turned it over, measured its weight, and asked if it held up to the scrutiny of reason. He had never been one to take things on faith.

At Cambridge, he had been shaped by argument. Two of his friends, Evan Durbin and Henry Phelps Brown, had been among the fiercest minds he had ever encountered. They were economists, men who saw human behavior through the cold arithmetic of incentive and scarcity, yet they were drawn, as he was, to the mysteries of the mind. It was in their company that Bowlby had learned a certain intellectual posture, one of relentless skepticism. There had been late nights, the air thick with pipe smoke, the clinking of glasses as one of them paused to refill a tumbler. Durbin, in particular, was a force to reckon with; he had a talent for finding the weak joints in any theory and pressing until it buckled. Phelps Brown, more measured but no less incisive, would listen, head tilted, before delivering a question so direct and so devastating that it demanded an answer or an admission of uncertainty. And so, Bowlby continued to carry the skeptic's spirit in him, even though it caused him to butt heads more than once with Riviere.

Yet, much to his own surprise, and despite his rigid intellectual stances, he was, nonetheless, in 1933, selected for further psychoanalytical training.

***

It was in this same year that John Bowlby finally got his medical degree in hand, alongside that familiar question…

What now?

His aim in psychiatry had been to work on the adolescent mind, but there was, however, another problem. For all his ambitions, he was also beginning to realize there was little certainty in the world of child psychiatry. In the '30s, it was not so much a discipline as a convergence of interests: psychiatry, psychoanalysis, criminology, social work, medical psychology, paediatrics, all of them circling the problem of the disturbed child without ever fully defining it. Clinical services were sparse, research was an afterthought, and the few texts that did exist barely acknowledged children as subjects worth serious study. The only recourse, then, was to begin working with adults. Experience of adult psychiatry was a must for him to be considered for a Commonwealth Fellowship, allowing him to move to the discipline of child psychiatry.

In a stroke of good fortune, the very next day after his graduation, he found work at the well-known Maudsley Hospital, where he would be initiated into the intricacies of adult psychiatry.

The Maudsley was a hospital of prestige, a bastion of intellectual ambition, and also a fortress of glass and brick, standing starkly on the southern side of the Thames. Inside, its corridors were long and yellowed with time, smelling of

140

carbolic soap and the peculiar sharpness of paper; case files stacked in precarious towers behind office doors, their contents pressed into brittle pages, whispering of madness and melancholia, war trauma and quiet despair. Outside, the city rumbled, omnibuses growling past, factory whistles shrieking their demands, the distant, relentless clang of the docks. But inside, within the Maudsley's high, windowed walls, psychiatry was dissected and reconstructed, stripped of its excesses, made into something clean, something scientific.

Presiding over the hospital was Edward Mapother, London's first professor of psychiatry, a man equally revered and resented in various circles.

Mapother had once been drawn to Freudian theory, had written papers on it, had perhaps even believed in its insights for a time. But belief, Bowlby was beginning to realize, was something of a dangerous indulgence in this field. In Mapother, it had slowly led to a disillusionment and a dismissal so complete it felt less like a critique and more like an erasure. Freud's ideas had been discarded as wholly inadequate, and the very culture of the Maudsley bore the imprint of this rejection. There was a clear, almost physical division in the city's intellectual landscape: north of the Thames, psychoanalysts; south of the river, Mapother's Maudsley, where analysis was met with skepticism, even scorn.

Bowlby quickly realized that his own training straddled a fault line. On one side were the psychoanalysts of the British Psycho-Analytical Society, with their insistence on the unconscious, on repressed desires, on the buried traumas of childhood dictating the course of adult life. Too many members of the Society still viewed critique not

141

as an intellectual necessity but as a betrayal. To challenge a concept was to undermine the master himself. There were times when it felt more like a church than a scientific body.

On the other side were the Maudsley psychiatrists, who demanded evidence, who saw analysis as a house of speculation built on unstable ground. This should have suited his skeptic spirit, and yet, Bowlby could not align himself fully with the Maudsley school either. For all its insistence on rigor, there was a narrowness to its thinking, an unwillingness to acknowledge the possibility that psychoanalysis, in some form, might hold value.

And so, he was caught between two poles, with one demanding faith, the other demanding skepticism. To exist in both worlds was to live in contradiction, but John Bowlby had never been one to seek false comfort.

While working at Maudsley, he came under the supervision of Aubrey Lewis, a man only a few years his senior but already a figure of authority. Lewis was sharp, unyielding, and skeptical to the point of hostility. A balding, well-dressed, somewhat stern man, Lewis had little to no patience for what he saw as the quasi-religious devotion of psychoanalytic institutions. To him, they were not schools of thought but sects, with their own scriptures, their own rituals, their own rigid hierarchies of obedience. And yet, for all his criticism, Lewis did not dismiss psychoanalysis outright as Mapother did. He acknowledged its potential, albeit cautiously, demanding that it prove itself in a way its more dogmatic followers seldom attempted.

Bowlby's relationship with him was, at times, contentious. They did not always agree, more often than not, they did not, but they debated, often for hours, in Lewis' office. The office was neat but maximalist, with bookshelves full of well-thumbed volumes. The window, cloudy with age, let in only a weak suggestion of daylight. Lewis would sit behind his desk, sleeves often rolled to the elbow, tapping a fountain pen against his knuckles. Across from him, John Bowlby would be settled in his seat with his usual, alert pose: back straight, hands resting carefully in his lap.

At one such occasion, Lewis found himself sighing. "You can't have it both ways, you know."

Bowlby tilted his head slightly. "Both ways?"

"You're training here, under me, under Mapother. You're in the business of evidence, of rigor. And yet, you spend your evenings across the river, indulging in, what shall we call it?—*theological debate* with the analysts." Lewis's eyes sharpened. "Do you believe in Freud, John?"

Bowlby did not hesitate. "I believe in questions. In ideas worth testing."

Lewis chuckled. "Testing. That's generous. They prefer revelation, prophecy. 'The child wants to kill the father, the infant desires the mother's breast'—does it not trouble you how neatly the answers arrive?"

"They *are* convenient at times, yes," Bowlby admitted, then folded his arms. "Yet, for all your disdain, you don't deny that some of their ideas have merit."

"I acknowledge they are... creative," Lewis admitted. "But creativity is not science. You want psychiatry to be medicine, not mythology. Wouldn't you rather work with data than dreams?"

143

"Dreams are data," Bowlby countered. "So are childhood experiences, patterns of attachment, early relationships. Dismissing psychoanalysis wholesale is as dogmatic as following it blindly."

Lewis sighed, rubbing his temple. "So you'll do what, then? Walk the tightrope between fact and the fantastical?"

"If that's what it takes."

"Well then," Lewis shook his head, "you've got an uphill climb ahead of you."

And yet, for all their disputes, it was Lewis who encouraged Bowlby to question, to examine, to demand better evidence from every side. That, at least, they could agree on. There was less of this sort of interplay with Mapother, whose office he found himself in one afternoon. The old man's hands were clasped behind his back as he looked out of his window, his expression as rigid as the starched collar of his shirt.

"Still playing at psychoanalyst?" he asked.

And it was true; the evenings still found John Bowlby north of the river, training with the psychoanalysts under Mrs. Rivvy's firm gaze. Here, too, he was never entirely at home, straddling the chasm between two worlds.

"I do find it an interesting field, sir," Bowlby replied after a brief pause, knowing that Mapother was no Lewis. Any back and forth was rarely the norm in their meetings.

"Interesting or not, the discipline is…quite frankly… tosh. Psychiatrists must be builders, Bowlby," Mapother said, turning away from the window and glancing at him.

"Not poets, not snake-charmers, and *certainly not* soothsayers."

Bowlby nodded, though he disagreed. It was possible, he thought, to find value in both approaches, but he kept these thoughts to himself for the most part, huddling away for later conversation with Lewis.

But it was with his patients that Bowlby felt the deepest certainty of his work. Still working as a clinical assistant at the hospital, he now began his research into personality types associated with psychotic and psychoneurotic breakdown. With this objective, he spent hours in quiet rooms, speaking with men and women whose minds had unraveled under the weight of their own histories. Some stared at the ceiling, answering in monosyllables; others wept as they spoke; some said nothing at all. He traced their suffering back through time, asking the same questions again and again: Who were they before the illness? When did the cracks begin to show?

Some patients spoke willingly; others resisted, their voices brittle, their memories uncertain. Their families filled in the gaps, hesitant mothers wringing their hands, fathers who sat stiff-backed in their chairs, recounting childhoods marked by silence or sudden absence. The details varied, but a pattern emerged: loss. Again and again, it was a loss. A mother who died when the child was five; a father lost to war, never to return; a sibling buried too soon.

He was beginning to see that mental illness was not always a matter of inherent weakness or faulty biology; it was sometimes the culmination of wounds left unhealed, of loss never properly mourned. When he saw his patients, John

Bowlby was beginning to see children who had grown into adults still waiting for someone to come back.

Mapother and Lewis would have cautioned him against making too much of such observations; correlation was not causation.

But Bowlby could not ignore what he saw.

His research continued, the case histories accumulating, the patterns becoming clearer. He noted the way early separation shaped the mind's ability to withstand stress; he saw how childhood bereavement left fractures that could resurface years later, disguised as breakdowns, anxieties, phobias.

He was moving toward something, even though he did not yet have the language for it, not yet.

But he knew this much: the past did not stay in the past. It lived in the mind, shaping its contours, determining its weaknesses, dictating its reactions. And if psychiatry was to mean anything at all, it would have to reckon with that truth.

***

And so, the days passed as John Bowlby found himself flitting between worlds, feeling misunderstood in both. With this added stress, it became ever more important to find time for himself, and so, even with his busy schedule, he found rare moments of leisure. It was during one of these brief intervals that John Bowlby found himself in a café, sitting across from one of his old Cambridge friends, Evan Durbin.

Spoons clinked against porcelain, chairs scraped against the floor, and voices overlapped in a jumble of conversation as Bowlby observed Durbin. With his dramatically receding hairline, he looked older than he was, but there was still a passionate sort of wisdom in Durbin's eyes, alongside the familiar practicality. Durbin had always carried himself well, with an air of intelligent certainty. Catching up, Bowlby had learned that Durbin had recently secured a lectureship at the London School of Economics, and he spoke of it with an air of satisfaction, though his real preoccupation, as always, was with politics, the larger machinery of society.

"London suits you," Bowlby said, stirring his tea absentmindedly.

Durbin waved a hand. "It's where the real work is done. Cambridge is an echo chamber, these brilliant minds congratulating themselves in cloistered halls. But teaching here is much more fulfilling, and truth be told, I quite enjoy it." He leaned forward slightly, his voice lowering in emphasis. "But I worry for you, John. You have no mind to keep studying?"

"Not in the academic sense," Bowlby replied somewhat guardedly. "My studies are more intellectual than anything…though I do have social welfare as a higher purpose, so I suppose I'm not entirely selfish." He smiled.

"Similarly to me, then," Durbin smiled back, then turned serious. "But listen: to be able to make any impact, you need the right credentials. And it's not like you must force yourself to endure the subject, it's a field you clearly belong to. You've got a mind for this." He took a sip of his coffee before continuing. "What you need is proper scientific footing. A doctorate... I know of a certain Professor Burt who would be interested in a bright student like you."

"Dr. Cyril Burt?"

"The very same," Durbin nodded, leaning back.

Bowlby leaned back in his chair. The name was familiar, of course. Cyril Burt was a respected figure in psychology, known for his research and ambition. His work on intelligence, on aptitude, on the very mechanics of the mind was quite well known in psychological circles.

"He's teaching back at University College," Durbin continued, "and I can attest to the fact that every lecturer needs good students. If you apply for a PhD there, you'll be under his wing in no time."

Bowlby toyed with the idea in his mind. He was disinterested in titles for their own sake, but this was different. Burt was no idle theorist, he had built institutions, laid the groundwork for child guidance centres, and introduced rigorous intelligence testing. He had shaped the conversation about mental illness, about education, about delinquency. And yet, he had also been a member of the London Psycho-Analytical Society; he had moved through both worlds, much like Bowlby himself was.

"I shall have a think on it," Bowlby finally said, thoughtfully.

"You should," Durbin said. "If you want to make a difference...this is how."

148

In the end, Bowlby decided that Durbin was right, he had nothing to lose and everything to gain from a PhD.

The first meeting with Cyril Burt took place in his office at University College London, a room lined with bookshelves. The air smelled of old paper and pipe smoke, the kind of academic musk that settled into the fabric of a room over decades. Burt sat at his desk, his presence commanding without being theatrical. He was a man of neat habits, his hair combed back precisely, his suit impeccably tailored. Perfectly circular glasses with thick black rims sat on his nose, giving him a particularly bookish impression. Yet behind his glasses, there was something in the sharpness of his gaze that suggested he suffered no fools.

"So, you're interested in a PhD," he said, steepling his fingers.

"I am," Bowlby nodded.

"Working at Maudsley…hm," he said, looking down at the letter Bowlby had sent to him ahead of the visit. "And yet, at the same time, you have been…what, dabbling in psychoanalysis?"

Bowlby hesitated, searching for the right answer. "I've been in training, yes. But I have my criticisms… for both schools, in fact."

Burt's expression remained neutral, though there was the faintest flicker of approval. "Good. A mind unchallenged by its own discipline is no mind at all." He looked back down at the letter briefly. "I've seen your work from Cambridge.

149

Intelligence, personality, development… these are your interests?"

"Yes."

Burt nodded. "Good. We're in the middle of a transformation in this field. Psychology is not philosophy; it is not mysticism… it is a science. It is numbers, patterns, statistics. We must study the mind as a physician studies the body… objectively, relentlessly. Do you understand?"

Bowlby met his gaze. "I do."

Burt studied him for a moment longer before pushing the paper aside. "I expect rigor. I expect clarity of thought. If you come here, there will be no room for sentimentalism."

Bowlby knew what he meant. The British Psycho-Analytical Society had its fair share of sentimentalists, those who saw childhood as an endless battlefield of repression and unmet desires, who placed too much faith in symbols and dreams. Bowlby had always suspected there was something more tangible, more measurable, beneath it all.

"Then I think I'm in the right place," he said.

Burt smiled slightly. "We'll see."

And just like that, John Bowlby was playing a balancing act of three parts instead of two.

The days quickly collapsed into each other, indistinct and relentless. Mornings began at Maudsley, where he moved between patients like a ghost; noting symptoms, tracing histories, watching the way grief coiled itself around a person's mind…then, by evening, he was off. He would rush out of the hospital, hailing a cab down the long streets, through London's dusk-stained corridors of soot and movement. Bowlby would now sit amongst the psychoanalysts, listening to the theories that circled like birds overhead, unconscious desires, maternal deprivation, and a host of topics so ephemeral that he couldn't quantify them if he tried. He argued when he could, questioned when he dared, but mostly, he learned.

And then came the nights, bent over books, scribbling notes, tracing Burt's calculations with weary, ink-smudged fingers. Classes were sporadic, but he attended them all, and as weeks passed, Bowlby grew to understand Cyril Burt. He quickly discovered that Burt was not merely an academic; he was a man of action, an architect of institutions. He had played a role in shaping child guidance centres, in advocating for intelligence testing in schools, and in establishing the National Institute of Industrial Psychology.

Ideologically, Cyril Burt's main area of interest was of maladjusted children. They fascinated him, not just the delinquent ones who stole or fought or defied, but also the backward ones, slow to grasp what others learned with ease, and the gifted ones, whose minds outpaced their bodies.

If John Bowlby could agree with Burt on only one thing, though, it would be with his belief that psychology was changing, it was moving away from speculation and toward measurement, away from theory and toward evidence. Yet, on the other hand, Bowlby knew that numbers alone could never tell the whole story. Mental health was not *just* about intelligence, or aptitude, or the statistical likelihood of success. As far as he was concerned, it was much more about attachment, about loss, about the wounds carried from childhood into adulthood. It was about the past,

151

about the way it carved itself into a person's mind, shaping every thought, every reaction, every fear.

He would learn from Burt, yes. But he would also keep questioning. Because if there was one thing he had learned from his time at Maudsley, from his arguments with Mrs. Rivvy, from his own patients, it was that no theory, no measurement, no single truth could ever explain the complexity of the human mind.

***

At the same time, his psychoanalysis training with the British Psycho-Analytical Society was progressing well…at least at first.

He attended lectures; he sat through seminars; he took notes that would shape his thinking for decades. Edward Glover's lectures dissected psychoanalytic theory with clinical precision, peeling away layers of thought like a surgeon at work. On technique, there was Ella Sharpe: direct, unpretentious, razor-sharp. Bowlby would later remember her with something close to admiration. She had common sense, and in a branch of study so often clouded by abstraction, common sense was not to be underestimated.

His own first cases in the eccentric discipline came under the supervision of Sharpe and another supervisor named Nina Searle. The contrast between them was striking. Searle was meticulous, rigid; he found himself more than once thinking of her as a prim old maid. Perhaps it was because they never quite understood each other; their conversations felt hollow, and they lacked any semblance of mutual understanding in the clinic.

Their first joint patient was a woman in her late thirties, her anxiety palpable, her grief tangled around her like a net. Her mother had died recently. The relationship had been suffocating, pathological; now, in its absence, she had unraveled. But Bowlby didn't see it then. Nor did Searle. They treated symptoms, not causes, and only later did Bowlby realize how much Searle had failed him as a guide and supervisor.

With Sharpe, though, things were different. Her way of working was simple, and depending on a singular idea: that patients were not puzzles to be solved. They were people, complicated and fragile and real. Like with Lewis at the Maudsley, Bowlby enjoyed his talks with her, though here they stuck more closely to the case at hand rather than a meandering exploration.

"You look for theories," she told him once. "You look for structures, frameworks, something orderly." She paused. "But what if the patience isn't orderly?"

Bowlby frowned. "I imagine you have an answer to that."

"I do," Sharpe said. "And the answer is this: *listen*. Not for patterns, not for the clever way to untangle the problem. Just listen to the patient as a person. If you do that, they might show you what they can't yet say."

Bowlby nodded. This piece of advice would stay with him perhaps the longest, because of how simple, actionable, and just...*human* it was.

By 1934, Bowlby was living with his friend Durbin and his wife, Marjorie. Meanwhile, much of his free time was spent in Bogey's, a sandwich bar he and Durbin had helped set up in the spring of '33. Built in a small corner of Bloomsbury, it was not the result of boredom or rebellion; he was no dilettante. Bogey's sprang from loyalty to Doris Austin, a former colleague from Priory Gate, who had designs to serve sandwiches to the city's drifting minds. Bowlby, never doctrinaire in his sympathies, listened; when sufficiently convinced, he acted.

He and Durbin found a location with good light and steady foot traffic, and gave Doris the reins. She curated the menu with quiet pride and more than a little flair. Within weeks, the place filled with a shifting cast of eccentrics and intellectuals; poets with mustard on their sleeves, critics sipping tea. One friend later claimed "everyone who was anyone" passed through.

But all was not well with John Bowlby himself. Even at Bogey's, he would sit alone, despite Durbin's prodding to go talk to the girls.

"Not today," he'd say tiredly, and you could tell this was a man with a lot on his mind.

It was around this time that he found himself unable to keep a steady girlfriend, and sometimes to even approach women. The causes were neither surprising nor simple. He had been educated in a world constructed by men for boys who would become more of the same. The schools were single-sex, the friendships intensely male; tenderness, when it appeared, had to wear a disguise. There were moments of connection, short, indistinct, even passionate, for a while. But they did not last. And to make matters worse. His work at the Maudsley, combined with the strict and brutal nature of his training at the Society, was taking a toll.

But it was in 1935 that things came to a head, for that was the year John Bowlby found himself caught in the undertow of professional politics within the Society.

There was no single moment of rupture, no outburst or public defiance that split him from the orthodoxy; rather, there was a slow accumulation of tensions, like filings to a magnet, until the sum of dissonances became impossible to ignore. At the center of this conflict was Bowlby's decision to begin treating a patient via the psychoanalytic method in the Maudsley, and thus, outside the bounds of what the Society's Training Committee had formally assigned him. It was a modest divergence in scale, but not in implication. He did not seek permission; he simply did the work, believing in its merit. The patient was not exceptional, at least not in the abstract, but the treatment represented something more dangerous: independence.

Edward Glover, a senior figure in the Society, reacted as if a boundary had been crossed that could not be uncrossed. He was a strongly Freudian figure, an orthodox psychoanalyst who had previously attacked Klein and would, in the future, go on to contend with Carl Jung as well.

To Glover, theory and protocol were not ideals to be interpreted, but walls to be defended. He wrote to Bowlby with the clipped precision of someone who had written too many such letters. The message was clear: those not yet formally qualified, especially those who, like Bowlby, remained candidates, were not to engage in analytic work outside their sanctioned assignments. The letter bore the gravitas of institutional reprimand; Glover reminded him of

155

duty, of discipline, of the fine print that binds the aspiring to the learned.

Bowlby, for his part, had used psychoanalytic techniques with several patients at the Maudsley, offering sessions less frequently than the traditional five days per week that full analysis demanded. He had not abandoned psychoanalysis; he was simply adapting it, responding, in his view, to real clinical need. But to Glover, and to the more orthodox members of the Training Committee, deviation was indistinguishable from defiance.

When questioned if this was wise, John Bowlby would only purse his lips, and the truth would be obvious: his job was to help the client, using whatever means he had access to. Nothing less, nothing more.

When Bowlby remained unconvinced by his reasoning, Glover doubled down.

"This Training Committee," he spoke heatedly in a meeting, "*Must not* allow the use of psychoanalytic methods by anyone not properly qualified, especially not in a diluted form that lacks the rigor… and, presumably, the control of daily treatment!"

"That is true, but he *is* in the profession of helping people," Sharpe defended him.

Glover looked at her, his lips a straight line. "He is a novice playing with the human mind," he said flatly. "Nothing more."

But veiled in the language of patient safety, Glover's insinuation was that Bowlby's innovations might do harm. Whether the harm in question was to the patient or to the Society's authority remained unstated.

Yet, despite all this, John Bowlby did not stop.

Even as this conflict escalated, another was still brewing. His relationship with Riviere was quickly deteriorating, and he could feel himself at risk of censure whenever in her presence.

In a private letter to the Committee, he confessed that he feared her judgment might influence the Committee's opinion of him. He wanted, quite simply, to switch analysts. While technically permissive of such changes, the Committee was less than happy with Bowlby's letter. In the curt reply Bowlby received, the Committee advised against his request.

Experience, Mr. Bowlby, shows that a shift of analysts at such a late stage is often detrimental. We should not wish that your training be unduly affected or otherwise harmed by a decision made on the basis of feelings alone; thus, we would request against such haste.

The implication was clear: *Stay where you are. Do not disrupt the order.*

Riviere herself did not take long to find out that John Bowlby was having second thoughts. In a moment, she seemed to turn into a dark oracle as she summoned him into her office, her expression stormy. As he quietly took a seat, she leaned forward, her voice carefully modulated as her eyes narrowed slightly.

"If you leave," she said quietly, "you will ruin yourself."

The sentence did not sound like an observation; it sounded more like a verdict. She paused just long enough before continuing.

"Do you think it is easy to deal with you?" she said, still with the same dangerous quiet. "Not every analyst can handle...*you*. You, with your skepticism, your constant rebukes, your penchant for *disobedience*..."

He listened coolly as she continued. Over the next thirty minutes, she used every tool at her disposal, be it emotional, psychological, or rhetorical, to dissuade Bowlby from leaving. She warned him that he risked sabotaging his career, even suggesting that no other analyst could contain his supposed "depressive position."

And as he sat opposite her with dark circles underneath his eyes and an unsmiling gaze, it was not hard to see why she might think he was depressed. But what had worn John Bowlby down was not a malaise or a depression; it was this ceaseless bickering, these invisible walls, the politics, the backbiting, the guilting.

The guilting was almost the worst.

Soon after Riviere had shaken him down, Susan Isaacs summoned Bowlby to speak with her. Much to his consternation and embarrassment, during their conversation, she broke into tears. She implored him not to leave Riviere, not to undo the fragile alliance of theory, training, and shared allegiance that tethered him to the Society.

And finally, moved and confused by this emotional appeal, Bowlby stayed.

In early 1936, Bowlby submitted a formal application to qualify as a psychoanalyst of adults. He had been in analysis for over six years and had treated patients under supervision for nearly four. He felt, quite reasonably, that he had earned the right to stand on his own.

Only, the Committee disagreed.

Glover, again the deliverer of bad news, wrote with his characteristically restrained disdain that the request revealed a kind of premature anxiety, a hunger for qualification not matched by analytic depth. This critique was nothing short of an intended blow to Bowlby's identity.

And so, for no good reason, it would take another year and a half before John Bowlby was approved.

Chapter 9.

War and Its Children

(Part I)

By the summer of 1937, his analysis with Riviere had stretched into its seventh year; he saw her nearly every day, a ritual that had become both burdensome and ineffectual. She remained unimpressed by his progress; he, in turn, began to doubt whether she had had any meaningful impact on his inner life. Still, at last, she relented.

He was granted his qualification.

Even Ernest Jones, then President of the British Psycho-Analytical Society, wrote to congratulate him. The letter was brief but telling: "I have some good idea of what hard struggle you have been through."

And it was true; 1937 had plenty of struggles. For one thing, that was the year Bogey shut down. Bowlby's friend Doris had run it; neither cook nor hostess, she was the pulse of the place itself: directing, deflecting, absorbing. A former schoolteacher with some nebulous ideas about food

160

and freedom, for four years she held that impossible thing together. Tea, sandwiches, arguments, flirtations. A bar, and not a bar; a haven, and never quite home.

Then in 1937, she left, and a new manager had to step in… capable, perhaps, in ledger but not in spirit. The atmosphere collapsed, and within months, the tables were bare; the door stopped opening. And what had once been the murmur of minds became, simply, silence.

Yet 1937 was also a year of breaking away from struggles, as, in fact, that was the year John Bowlby met Ursula Longstaff.

The meeting came through a friend, Rose, who was close to one of the seven Longstaff sisters, introduced Bowlby to the family. There was something almost accidental in the way they met; a holiday, a trip to Ireland, the soft squelch of wet peat underfoot, birds rising startled from the sedge, and a man, not quite looking for love, no, he would have said it was not that, but finding it nonetheless. Love, or the shape of something like it, caught sideways in a glance, in the way she walked ahead of him and didn't look back, in the mist clinging to her coat, the quiet defiance of it. A woman who would come to define his days, not loudly, not insistently, but with the slow accumulation of presence that becomes permanence.

The house they were staying at had low ceilings and a fire that refused to draw properly; the air was thick with woodsmoke and damp dogs and the faint smell of barley. She had come with her sisters, all of them tall and articulate and somehow half-removed from the world, as if raised not by hands but by theories of womanhood. He watched her. Not the eldest, nor the youngest, Ursula. There was a steadiness

161

to her that the others lacked; a way of listening that did not wait to speak. He did not know he was falling in love until he already had.

It rained almost every day. Not heavily, not with the drama of storms, but with the slow persistence that makes one stop noticing. The fields turned to soft paper; the guns grew heavier. And still they walked. The talk was always of dogs, birds, cartridges, but between the lines, between the hedge and the open field, he watched her move, her shoulders in that waxed coat, the way she paused at a gate and waited for no one. She seemed, then, like the kind of person who knew how to live alone and yet did not want to. And perhaps that was what he saw, or thought he saw.

Their days passed in a blur; rain at the windows, tea served without speaking, newspapers that no one read. There was a piano no one played. At first, he spoke to her of nothing; small things, casual remarks; had she read this, did she shoot often, what kind of dog was that? She answered just enough, trading smiles with him as they spoke.

And then one afternoon, late, they were left behind. The others had gone ahead, or back, or somewhere. They were in a clearing, the trees close in, and he said something trivial, perhaps foolish, and she laughed. It was a real laugh, sharp and sudden, like the crack of frost in still water. He had not known she could laugh like that. It was then, perhaps, that he fell in love…or rather, that's when the fall was made visible.

She was the third daughter, neither eldest nor youngest, neither overlooked nor exalted. What Bowlby saw in her, beyond the angular grace, the Longstaff lineage, the way she must have stood on the Irish grass that day, is not something he wrote about. But perhaps he saw what he lacked: a family where feelings were noticed, named, or at least not shamed.

Their courtship, as it turned out, would be an adventure; they would often attend balls and plays, also attended sometimes by her sisters as well as her brother Dick. The families, too, began to intermingle; both Tony and Mrs. Bowlby would meet her, and offer their tacit approvals to John to continue his courtship. It was a warming relationship; she would write to him already, establishing a correspondence that neither of them knew would last for decades. Of course, in these youthful days, she would write of the things that seem so vital to the young: ballet productions, foraging for mushrooms and berries on the wet, grey evenings, and little sketches of her days.

They ended up beside the restless sea on one of those heady days, the water iron-grey under a shawl of mist. Ursula found herself watching the waves as though they could give her some final assurance of permanence. The shore was raw with wind, gulls wheeling, their cries sharp against the silence that often stretched between her and John when they walked together. Yet she had grown used to this benevolent, gentle silence; indeed, she had come to suspect it was part of his charm, a thoughtful silence, not the empty kind her father's held when he retreated behind his newspaper, shutting out the room, shutting out her mother.

That silence was a bruise.

"It's bracing," she said, drawing her shawl closer, though she rather liked the sting of the cold on her cheeks. "The sea, I mean."

"Yes," John replied, after a pause. He carried a stick more for habit than need, tapping at the stones as they walked like he once had on his walks with his Grampy up in the Scottish glens. His eyes, intent and serious, seemed fixed on the line where the sea blurred into sky.

And she thought: how he sees things, not like other men, not like the loud and laughing suitors at her parents' dinners, who could not speak three words without leaning too heavily on her allowance. She wondered what John thought of her wealthy background, the security that came with her like an unseen dowry. No doubt her private income was not a hindrance, but as she looked at him, she knew she was not looking at a man who would marry merely for money.

"You know, John," she said after a while, "my parents… they go on with their quarrels. Mummy insists she cannot bear him any longer. Father talks of freedom, though it seems only freedom to be miserable apart. Still…"

She trailed off.

"Still?" he prompted gently.

"I cannot hold with it. Divorce. It seems to me… a kind of violence. A tearing." She stopped on the stones, the waves breathing in and out beside them. "If one marries, one marries for life. Do you agree?"

He turned toward her, his expression unreadable for a moment, as though her words had dropped into the pool of his thought and disturbed it. Then: "I do agree. I could not imagine otherwise."

Relief came, quick and almost childish, like the warmth of fire after cold air. She smiled, and they walked on. But beneath the relief, another thought stirred…what if, years from now, that vow bound too tightly, what if affection waned as it had between her parents? No; she pressed the thought down, smoothed it as she might smooth the folds of her dress.

"And a sensible number of children," John said as they walked beside the tide, smiling in askance.

"What, pray tell, would be a sensible number to you?" she asked, smiling despite her faint blush.

"Four," said John, all too quickly.

She laughed, startled. "Four? Why so certain?"

"Because it seems the right number. Not too many, not too few," he said with a nervous smile. "Sensible."

"Four children, and a marriage for life," Ursula echoed, before returning his smile. "A fair bargain."

They would not be a fairytale couple. But theirs would be a long story, and that is rarer.

***

Elsewhere in 1937, new struggles were beginning. Unknown to most, the world was tilting slowly, almost imperceptibly, towards the abyss.

Spain was already burning quietly, its civil war a rehearsal of ideologies more than armies. Japan moved through China like smoke, consuming villages, then cities, then histories, while the League of Nations muttered into

165

irrelevance. Chamberlain smiled; Mussolini preened; Hitler tested himself in westward expansion and found, to his pleasure, that no one shouted back.

In London, the newspapers bore the scent of foreboding, but it was laced with distance. There were editorials, of course, and debates; but there was also tennis, and lectures, and brisk spring walks along the Embankment. Meanwhile, John Bowlby, newly graduated from medical school, stood on the edge of a period of history. The dark tides gathering in Europe still seemed unreal, abstract, a distant geography of consequence.

After his arduous journey to graduate, Bowlby joined the British Psychoanalytic Society that year, only to clash with his former supervisor and Klein almost immediately. That same year, Klein had presented her paper on the psychogenesis of manic-depressive states. At the meeting called, the case the paper was predicated on was presented to the members, and John Bowlby read in silence. Klein argued that the child's superego developed far earlier than Freud had imagined, rooted not in social structures or later conflicts, but in the infant's first relationship with the breast. The mother, in her view, was not a person but a phantasmic object, good or bad, loved or hated, onto which the child projected its most primitive feelings.

Klein's vision was inward; it privileged fantasy over experience, psychic reality over lived life. Bowlby, always more empirical than mystical, found this difficult to accept. In the margins of the paper, he wrote:

The Role of Environment = 0

Klein had completely neglected the case contest. As the others got done with reading the paper and the discussion began, he spoke cautiously but pointedly.

"If I may," he said with a cough. "I, personally, have worked with depressed patients at the Maudsley who have recently experienced real, devastating losses... deaths, separations, material collapses and the like..."

"And?" Klein asked coolly. "What bearing would that have on this case?"

"My point is that in many cases, their grief cannot be explained solely by intrapsychic systems," he said, looking her back in the eye. "We are in the business of science... real life and the environment *have* to matter."

Of course, Klein and Riviere disagreed.

Only later did Bowlby realize that this divergence of view was more than a footnote, it was a fundamental incompatibility. The Kleinian world, with its elaborate internal architectures of love and hate, guilt and repair, had little use for the messier terrain of actual life. Bowlby, by contrast, was slowly beginning to realize that it was precisely in the interface between inner world and outer reality, between a child and the mother who fed him, neglected him, left him, that human development was shaped.

And though he would remain a member of the Society, though he would not formally break from its structure, Bowlby had already begun to chart a different course, one that would lead him away from the phantasms still held onto so dearly by the Freudians.

But by 1937, there was something else John Bowlby had been working on for the better part of a year: clinical child guidance.

The final year of his psychoanalytic training had not ended in mere completion, but in something far less predictable: selection. One of only three Commonwealth Fellowships in child psychiatry had been offered to him; he had applied the year before and failed. This time, the door opened, and he was granted a year of half-time training at the London Child Guidance Clinic in Canonbury, a borough not yet fashionable, filled with the uneasy friction of working-class life, clattering bicycles, narrow brick lanes, and a thousand domestic quarrels muffled behind curtains.

The idea of child guidance as a field was the extension of an American idea. In the early part of the century, across the ocean, Americans had begun to believe that a child's tantrum was not simply disobedience, and that a withdrawn child might be more than shy. Psychological methods had been applied not to illness in asylum walls, but to children on street corners, boys who stole apples, girls who cried too much, young bodies whose futures tilted perilously toward courts and prison gates.

By 1909, clinics had begun taking shape, first in the major cities, then trickling outward. What began as treatment for juvenile delinquency soon broadened its gaze; not only lawbreakers but daydreamers, not only violent children but timid ones, fell under its domain. England, never quick but rarely idle, watched; and by 1925, figures such as Cyril Burt spoke in prose both confident and odd, his book The Young Delinquent outlining a plan for psychological clinics across Britain.

Enter Mrs. St Loe Strachey, a magistrate, and a woman who walked not with rhetoric but with resolve. She had visited American clinics herself and had not forgotten what she saw. Returning to London, she became the hinge. She suggested to the Commonwealth Fund of America, still a curious entity to most, that a demonstration clinic might be born on English soil. Burt and Professor Percy Nunn followed through, summoning the minds of psychology, education, and bureaucracy to imagine something new. The result of these efforts was the Child Guidance Council; its chair, Burt, its members, men of hospitals and ink-stained lecture halls.

For the location, Canonbury was chosen.

The site for something *new*.

The London Child Guidance Clinic opened its doors in 1929. Not the first, not even second, the Jewish Health Board had already established a clinic in East London two years prior. But this one, in Canonbury, had the eyes of the state upon it.

It had the money. It had a *future*.

By the time John Bowlby arrived to it, the building stood without grandeur: grey-bricked, narrow-faced, and watching the street with a modest, weary expression, as though it had seen too much to ever speak plainly again. It was tucked into a quiet corner on Canonbury; no plaque boasted its purpose, only a discreet sign whose paint had begun to flake from the gentle abrasion of time and weather. Inside, the floors creaked in a language of their own; the rooms were narrow and high-ceilinged, breathing faintly of polish and old books, of lavender soap and pencil shavings.

169

John Bowlby walked into this place not yet fully formed, still young in many ways. Yet the place he entered was not loose in its purpose. The Clinic was more than rooms and waiting benches. It was a machine of three parts. The 'Holy Trinity', went thus: psychiatrist, psychiatric social worker, and educational psychologist.

No one stood above; no one served beneath. They operated as satellites around the child, each bearing different tools.

The psychiatrist's task was inward; to parse temperament, to observe not merely behaviour but its rhythms—how a child turned his eyes, whether his fists clenched or flinched. The psychiatric social worker stepped outward, visited homes, knocked gently on front doors, and sat quietly with mothers who confessed fears they had never said aloud. The educational psychologist, practical and unblinking, brought tests and pencils and measured, with brittle accuracy, what a child could or could not yet understand.

It was from this intersection of analysis, confession, and measurement that treatment emerged. No pills. No straps. No prescriptions on yellow paper. Instead, an attempt to understand. The assumption was radical for its time: that the child was not broken, but bruised. That punishment was not a remedy; that environment was not a backdrop but a stage on which the child's mind performed, misfired, or retreated. It was understood, now, that the majority of troubles in children arose not from poverty or disease, but from the absence or confusion of love.

Still, love could not be prescribed. So the Clinic set itself to study: not only what the child did, but what the child lived. Its goal was prevention. Not cure. It sought to locate small abnormalities, hairline cracks, and treat them before they widened into fractures of personality or outbursts of crime. Research was originally relegated to a lesser priority. Training was paramount. But in practice, the patients kept coming, and the service became central. Parents referred their children. Teachers wrote letters. Occasionally, a referral arrived not for a child, but as a quiet cry from an adult too ashamed to speak for themselves. These were not always simple cases of misbehaviour. Often, the child reflected the parent's unhealed wound, the family's unspoken fracture. Treatment plans had to be patchworked: some relied on talk, others on routine, on observation, on slight adjustments to the atmosphere in which the child lived. There was no singular dogma. Each method was tried with caution and hope.

And in this, Bowlby observed, participated, absorbed.

Each morning, as if by quiet ritual, Bowlby crossed the threshold of the London Child Guidance Clinic, the light of Canonbury pale and diffused by soot-darkened windows. The smell of the place was a mingling of chalk dust, boiled tea, and pencil graphite, and he arrived each day in a coat too clean for the streets he walked. A coat reserved, in truth, for battle. Dr. John Bowlby, with his curious blend of aloof gentility and quiet combustion, entered the London Child Guidance Clinic each morning like a man walking into a trench. Here, he would face children who kicked chairs, spat at doorframes, slashed drawings with pencils snapped in half. Children whose pain had grown teeth.

"Messy work," said a social worker to another, watching him pull on the coat like armor. "But he's quite

171

convinced, you know. Quite the Freudian. More Freudian than anything."

In these trenches, he would stay for hours; mornings wholly given over, and the afternoons partly so, until the business of his psychoanalytic training called him elsewhere. The rhythm of those days was half-clinical, half-philosophical; he moved through rooms where furniture was rearranged weekly but the anxieties remained the same, folded into files, into the slant of a parent's voice, into the twitch of a child's knee. Other psychiatrists-in-training haunted the corridors, though they came to learn from the Clinic's structure and left educated by its exceptions. And if there were teachers worth remembering, they were not the ones who wrote the textbooks or gave instructions from behind polished desks.

They were the psychiatric social workers, quick of foot, untheatrical, eyes alert like animals in a forest. Bowlby admired them for being exceptionally able, and others agreed. Michael Fordham, himself a psychiatrist, remarked that it was the social workers who truly ran the clinic in its early, stammering years.

William Moodie, the official Director, gave nothing to the psychiatrists in training, at least not in the way of instruction. He was part of the building, like a well-worn coat left on a hook; present, reliable, but not particularly illuminating. Noel Hunnybun, one of those formidable social workers, recalled, rather dryly, that Moodie never brought the psychiatrists into his consulting room. There were no dynamic discussions of behavior, no explication of motive or symptom; whatever was to be understood had to be learned outside his walls, by listening not to lectures but to the silence between a parent's words.

So Bowlby listened, to the soft clink of teacups during home visits, to the tremor in a father's reprimand, to the strange logic of a child caught between fear and loyalty. He understood that his true apprenticeship lay in the company of women who rarely appeared in published journals, Molly Lowden and Nance Fairbairn, two social workers whose influence spread quietly and definitively like ink through paper.

Lowden was Freudian; Fairbairn, Jungian.

They were not rivals. They were not even especially theoretical in manner. They simply worked. They knew when a mother's voice dropped into something resentful, when a child's silence thickened into defense, when a question should not be asked but left to simmer.

It was from these women that he first heard the idea that the roots of a child's trouble often twisted backwards into the soil of the parent's unresolved past. This was not a metaphor; it was a map. And once shown, Bowlby followed it with the precision of a cartographer. There were two cases he would remember later with clarity, not because they were exceptional but because they illustrated the principle exactly.

In one, a father was consumed with anxiety over his eight-year-old son's masturbation. The punishment was swift: the cold tap. The shame was colder still. Bowlby asked, gently, whether the father had experienced the same worry as a child.

At first, there were denials, and then:

"My father didn't talk about such things. Ever. But I..." He stopped and looked at his hands, as if surprised to find them there. "I used to worry about it. Obsess, really. I

173

thought something was wrong with me. My mother caught me once. She said it was filthy. That decent boys didn't do that. I remember hiding in the airing cupboard for hours. Sweating. Praying."

Bowlby did not interrupt. He had learned from Molly Lowden and Nance Fairbairn to wait, to let silence make the invitation.

The man continued, voice hoarse now. "Even now, I still… I still think about it. That it might have ruined me. I've never told anyone. Not even my wife."

"And now," Bowlby said gently, "you see your son doing what you once did, and all of that fear, *your own fear*, comes back."

The father nodded, eyes glistening, though he blinked fiercely. "I just want him to be...better than I was."

"He won't be," Bowlby said. "He'll be himself. But you can help him grow up unafraid."

In another case, a mother punished her toddler's jealousy of a newborn with excessive severity. However, at first, she did not recognize it as jealousy at all. She sat with her arms folded, her mouth a tight line, her knee bouncing.

"It's not jealousy," she told John. "It's bad behavior. She needs discipline. She screamed for an hour last night because I was nursing the baby."

"And what did you feel?" Bowlby asked.

The mother frowned. "I was tired."

"No, not tired. What did you feel, when she screamed?"

174

The woman looked at him sharply, then away. "Angry," she whispered. "I wanted to shake her. Just like my mother used to do to me when I cried after my brother was born."

There it was again… echoes in the dark rooms of the mind.

Later, Bowlby walked down the corridor of the Clinic, past the small therapy rooms where voices murmured behind frosted glass. He paused outside Molly Lowden's office. She looked up, saw his face.

"Anything to discuss?" she asked.

"It's as you said, ma'am," Bowlby nodded. "They speak about their children, but really… they're speaking about themselves."

Lowden smiled, a quiet, tired thing. "That's where it always begins."

She spoke from experience; after all, Lowden and Fairbairn met with such parents weekly. These were not side conversations or moral interventions. They were analytic sessions, plain and simple; not because they used the tools of Freud or Jung, but because they treated the adults not as authorities, but as patients who had once been children themselves. To Bowlby, this seemed the sanest, most humane thing psychiatry could do. He saw no reason why psychoanalytic insights should end at the child's elbow; the child, after all, had not created the air they breathed.

From that point on, Bowlby became not merely a practitioner but an advocate. The analytic lens, he believed, should widen. It must. To treat the child without considering the family was a kind of malpractice disguised as a method.

175

William Gillespie, a fellow Commonwealth recipient, had said it plainly: "You can't really just consider the child in isolation."

Child analysis had tried, valiantly and unsuccessfully, to draw borders where none existed.

The Clinic, for all its lack of glamour, was a crucible. People from disparate theoretical territories were forced to work together, not always harmoniously, but with a kind of resigned cooperation. The building became not a temple of doctrine, but a place where theory met bread crusts, lice, and domestic quarrels. And so Bowlby learned not from the hierarchy, but from the human ecosystem that the Clinic had accidentally built.

It was not just psychiatry, then, that he practiced. It was an observation made ethical; listening was made into a method. What he carried from those years was not just a sharper diagnostic sense, but a conviction: the child's trouble, properly understood, is rarely solitary. It is relational. It grows in households and history. And to uproot it, one must speak to the silence between generations.

In those years, analysis of a child was expected to be surgical: five sessions a week, as if emotional infection required constant draining. But not at the Clinic. There, a child was seen once a week, one hour to explain a life unraveling; one hour to unpick grief folded into habit. Fordham had said it first: "The Freudians thought it either had to be five times a week or not at all. They were wrong."

Bowlby saw them one by one. The girl who counted windows and the boy who refused to be praised. The girl who painted her hands black and called it punishment. And one day, quietly, without flourish, a boy of eight. His limbs were bird-thin, his gaze tight and recessed like a lion forced into a too-small cage. He stole buttons and never looked back. Praise and blame slid off him like raindrops down wax.

He was in isolation, Bowlby wrote to himself later, dispassionately, clinically, in that neutral voice reserved for the wounded. *Nine months. From eighteen months of age to two years and three months. No visitors allowed.*

No visitors. He might as well have written: no witnesses.

The boy didn't cry when struck. He didn't smile when hugged. He moved through the world as though memory had set fire to the bridge between feeling and doing. Then came the girl. Another ghost, another photograph half-developed. She, too, had lived through long separations, through hospital corridors and the clinical fluorescence of maternal absence. She, too, stole, lied, and disappeared in the middle of math.

Facing the cases back-to-back, his mind began to turn. Not toward theory in its amorphous grandeur, but toward something he had seen over and over, in his own life and in others:

Separation.

The knife between parent and child. He knew, suddenly, that that was the origin, the site of infection. Love withdrawn too early, too coldly, too completely. And as he walked the hallways, coat swinging around his calves, trailing his quiet obstinacy, he toyed with the beginnings of a thought that would one day become a *theory*.

By 1937, John Bowlby was also teaching again, this time at Morley College, that democratic outpost for the working minds of London.

"Psychology of Childhood and Adolescence," the course was called. An hour here, an hour there, trying to build a ladder between suffering and understanding. It was an educational extension for the working men and women, and they came with the dust of their labors still on their hands; they came from bakeries and train yards and bedrooms shared by five.

And Bowlby stood in front of them, unassuming, watchful, and said plainly, "We will talk about the causes of things in this course; the causes of nervous difficulties, of bad habits, of delinquency."

He never called such acts evil. He never referred to delinquent children as being beyond hope.

Rubbing his face from exhaustion, he would finish his shift and retreat to his office to ponder, to rest a little, and, lately, to write. He would sometimes watch the ink dry unevenly on the page, thick at the bottom of certain letters, before continuing to write. Around John Bowlby, the world was slowly heading towards the precipice of the Second Great War, but in a quiet office in London, filled with the scent of dust and that peculiar dampness that clung to paper like breath on glass, John Bowlby wrote of children.

He did not write of them as others had: as devils or angels, as vessels of promise or clay to be shaped by the hand of reason. No, he wrote of them as inherently irrational

178

beings. His first published article, titled *The Abnormally Aggressive Child*, appeared not in a clinical journal, not buried beneath layers of Freudian footnotes, but in The New Era in Home and School, a magazine shaped by the idealistic bellows of the New Education Fellowship.

But why there? Why then?

Because psychoanalysis, that dark velvet curtain drawn open by Freud and pulled askew by his disciples, had bled into the classrooms of the progressive schools. Teachers had begun to look at the tantrums of boys and the sullen silence of girls with new suspicion; behind each misstep, a mother, a wound, a memory. Because Bowlby had once wandered the grounds of Bedales, had once spoken in quiet tones to the educators at Priory Gate School, places where children climbed trees and were encouraged to cry; where one might overhear, in the lunchroom, a conversation about Oedipus or oral fixation between spoonfuls of lentils.

And now, John Bowlby, still young, though already buttoned up with duty and a kind of anxious neatness, had decided to explain something which seemed an unexplainable evil to the layman.

Aggression in children.

He began with a premise that curled like smoke through the pages: that hatred, born from jealousy, was not an aberration in childhood, but inevitable. Natural. And more so, it was sculptable; not in its existence, but in its expression.

"Whether jealous hatred persists or not," he wrote, *"depends very largely upon the way they are handled."*

179

He did not mean, necessarily, the way one lifts a child from the floor, or holds their hand across traffic. He meant handling in the way one might handle fire in a hearth or a delicate chemical reaction; with precision, restraint, and the wisdom not to be cruel in the face of wildness. For it is easy, too easy, to punish. Easier still to dismiss.

He named the faces of aggression like one might name the shades of a storm.

Destruction following despair.

It began not with rage, but hopelessness. A child who has done wrong, who feels unloved in the act of wrongness, might burn the whole house down, not because they desire the fire, but because the fire proves they do not care. They must not care. If they cared, they would die from it.

Aggression as a defense against retaliation.

Here, the child flinches not because they are struck, but because they expect to be. And so, like an animal curled in anticipation of the blow, they strike first. Bowlby knew this child. Perhaps he had seen him in the clinic, in a room with too few windows and toys with their heads missing. Perhaps he had once been him.

Aggression as provocation.

A curious kind of test. The child dares you to love them and expects you to fail. "Hate me," their silence says. "Hate me as I know you must." And when you do not, they scream, or bite, or break the glass on purpose, because if love is possible, it is too dangerous.

180

Then, too, there was the *scapegoat*. The other child, the weaker one, the one with a lisp or a stammer or shoes that didn't quite fit. Into this child is poured every fear, every failure. The guilty child is redeemed through cruelty. In the classroom, it looked like a punch during recess, or ink spilled on someone else's notebook.

These theories, neat as diagrams in their origin, were not abstractions for him. He had seen them move. Seen them cry and smear their tears with dirty hands. Seen the peculiar kind of silence that sits in the back of a child's throat when they realize they are unwanted, or worse... unseen. For John Bowlby, his conclusions were not phantasy or conjecture; they were living facts, born in experience and practice and observations where nothing was said but much was revealed.

And as John Bowlby continued to work on the minds of children, continued to work with trauma and loss and separation, he perhaps did not realize how much his work would be needed in the coming years...

***

By the year 1939, the wind of Europe was shifting, with clouds gathering over continents and minds. As John Bowlby, still young and watchful, was working on curing separation and hysteria in children, the schism of war that was re-opening in Europe would only make his work more needed.

One could not yet smell blood in the hedgerows, but the air was changing. Softly, at first. A radio crackled in a Warsaw kitchen; the voice on it, thin and metallic, spoke of meetings, of border violations, of Germany, always Germany. To understand the war, that is, the particular war which began in September of that year, though wars begin far before trumpets announce them, one must look not at a single event, but at the long, exhausted shadow that stretched from the previous century.

The Treaty of Versailles that ended the first Great War had sewn seeds that could never grow peace. It had gouged borders into landscapes like careless knife cuts and told a humiliated Germany to smile while bleeding. A republic rose from that wreckage, thin as lace, fragile as spun sugar. It cracked under inflation, it winced under debt.

And then came a man who spoke of greatness, of rebirth, of purity… words that stung and seduced and poisoned.

Adolf Hitler, Chancellor turned Führer, played the rhythms of fear like a violin. In 1933, he had begun his march, not yet in boots, but in promises. By 1938, he had already swallowed Austria whole. Then came the Sudetenland, the Munich Agreement, the lullaby of appeasement. Chamberlain, returning from Munich, flapped his paper like a magician, proclaiming peace for our time. Yet the ink on the paper had barely dried before tanks rumbled like distant thunder behind it.

And still the world turned. As John Bowlby hurried to the clinic in England, children played with hoops along village roads. In Paris, lovers met beneath chestnut trees. In Berlin, shopkeepers opened their shutters and wondered how many uniforms would pass their doors that day. The illusion held for a while.

But then, Poland.

182

Hitler wanted Danzig, a sliver of coastline, yes, but more: a symbol, a stepping stone, a provocation. Poland, proud and battered, stood firm. And with her, France and Britain, at last awake, at last reluctant to give another inch. On August 23rd, in the infamous Molotov–Ribbentrop Pact, Stalin and Hitler agreed to split Poland between them. The world was caught unawares. The pact was announced, but not the details; in parlors and embassies, the air thinned with suspicion. Still, many in England hoped, foolishly, that war could be sidestepped, ducked, bargained away like a late fee or an insult.

Then, dawn broke on the first of September. Tanks, grey as the sky above them, poured into Poland. Blitzkrieg, the lightning war. Roads cracked under their weight. Planes swept low over villages, dropping not messages but fire. Horse-mounted Polish cavalry, noble and doomed, charged against machines that could not be swayed by courage. True to the war's name, the German army moved fast, like a mechanical tide that surged eastward. Cities fell in hours, not days. Civilians fled, carts creaking behind them, babies swaddled in rags, the sound of boots never far behind.

On the third of September, Britain declared war. France followed within hours.

The air across Europe felt strange, thinner, as if the trees themselves were bracing. It had happened again. No one quite knew how, and yet everyone did. The old men on benches in Kent, the schoolteachers in Bordeaux, the factory girls in Lodz, all felt the dread of repetition. The world had learned nothing.

Even as the declarations rang out, Poland was carved like a roast. By the end of September, Warsaw was broken,

183

its buildings crumbled, its people stunned. The partition complete, Poland disappeared from the map once more.

There were speeches, of course. Grave men in chambers. Pledges and condemnations. But words, by then, had worn thin; the world was no destined, or perhaps condemned, to war.

***

Yet even if it was clear that the world was turning toward some irrevocable descent, on one cool February day, joy seemed to flare up again for John Bowlby: bright, brief, like the glow of gas lamps along a fogged street.

The bells of the church tolled faintly through the London air, muffled, as though by the heavy folds of late winter mist, damp and sodden upon the streets. John Bowlby, standing in the church, felt a rare prick of discomfort. His gloves were slightly too tight, his breath was quickening against the cool iron of the vestry door, and he felt the weight of his own body, his pulse in his temple, the sheer immediacy of the hour.

"Steady, John, steady," murmured Evan Durbin, clapping his friend's shoulder, the gesture brisk, affectionate, tinged with the camaraderie of youth not wholly dissolved by solemn occasion. Evan had been his companion through debates and late-night arguments, through the smoke-hazed rooms of Oxford; he, too, felt the thrill of something epochal, though in a different vein: the idea, the dream, the plan for the nation's betterment. And now he was best man, his tie neatly knotted, his brow alight with pride.

184

John half-smiled, as if caught between laughter and awe. "I shall need steadying, Evan. I feel as though I were walking not to the altar but to the bar of judgment."

"You'll stand all right," Evan replied brusquely. "You always have, when it mattered."

A hush fell then as the great door creaked, and the faint rustle of gowns and coats began. The pews filled quietly, as though all knew this ceremony was not one of pomp but of inward solemnity. Women drew off gloves, men coughed discreetly, hats were tilted, gloves folded. And Ursula came: at first a figure in the misted porch, then nearer, clearer, her veil catching the dull glimmer of the light. The simplicity of her dress seemed almost more radiant for the lack of ornament: pale silk, modest, unembellished, but suffused, as she walked, with an undeniable luminosity.

John, turning to watch her approach, felt as though the years contracted into one sharp point, piercing and brilliant.

She came up beside him and the vicar spoke; his words floated, then dissolved, reforming again, like smoke rings: *dearly beloved, we are gathered here...* The solemn cadences, repeated from centuries past, carried forward in this brief present moment. And as the vows were said, John's own voice rang strange to his ears, firmer, deeper than he had thought possible. Ursula's voice was lighter, but clear, crystalline, carrying perfectly through the nave.

"I will."

"I will."

It was done, then, in the instant the ring slid upon her finger, in the clasp of hand, in the silence that followed the words. A murmur passed through the congregation; a cough, a faint shifting of skirts, the creak of wood. And beneath it all a mixture of joy and dread, as though to step into happiness was also to trespass near its opposite, for who knew what the years would bring? Yet such doubts were natural as the mist, and just as easily dispelled by the warmth of laughter, clinking glasses, voices swelling in the hall where friends and family gathered. The gas lamps hissed faintly; outside, carriages rattled past; inside, the voices rose, buoyant.

"My dear John!" cried an acquaintance, plump, rosy, adjusting her brooch as she pressed his hand. "Such a day, such a day, and the bride so very radiant; why, the whole church was smiling with her!"

Ursula, beside him, smiled modestly.

Now, well-wishers and relatives came and went; the festivities were in full force.

"Evan!" John said, catching sight of his friend across the room. He smiled warmly as they embraced. "You've done me a service I shan't soon forget."

"Which one?" Durbin said with mock affront. "I've done you a number of services, if I so recall…"

John chuckled. "No, really. Standing there beside me…well, it steadied me as much as any prayer."

Evan, lifting his glass, grinned broadly. "Ach, you needed no steadying. You looked the picture of resolve, you realize? A suspicious might believe you'd rehearsed it all in debate."

186

John laughed again; only Durbin could elicit this much mirth from him in a go. "Perhaps I did. Still, the heart plays no rehearsed part."

Around them, talk ebbed and flowed: of lectures, of colleagues, of Oxford days remembered with nostalgia already tinged with distance. Of course, beneath it all was the subtle, unspoken awareness: Europe restless, the world precarious. Already some guests muttered about the state of Germany, the instability in markets. And yet, in this hall, the conversation returned again and again to the bride, the groom, the new beginning.

Later, when the crowd had thinned somewhat, John and Ursula found themselves in a quieter corner, where the window looked out upon a narrow street, wet with rain, reflecting the blurred lamps like so many trembling stars.

"It feels strange," Ursula said softly, drawing her shawl closer, "to be spoken of as though we were characters in a play, 'the bride, the groom.' As though we belonged to everyone here, and not only to ourselves."

"Yes," John answered, after a pause, gazing at her, the curve of her face half-lit by the gaslight. "And yet we are ourselves still. We are more ourselves, perhaps, than before."

She smiled faintly, her eyes lifting toward his. "Do you believe so?"

"I do," he said. "Though perhaps it is belief that makes it true."

Somewhere behind them, laughter rang out; Evan's voice, carrying above others, animated, insistent. One could imagine him in Parliament already, speaking of policy, of workers, of reform. John, watching his friend, felt a stir of

187

admiration tinged with foreboding: Evan was brilliant, yes, and fearless, but in a world such as this, who could know what dangers lay ahead? And yet…this moment, Ursula's hand upon his arm, the warmth of her gaze, was unassailable. For a moment, it seemed as if time itself had consented to pause, to allow them this island of peace before the storm known to most as life.

The hour grew late. The lamps burned low.

One by one, guests departed into the February mist, their voices receding into the muffled hush of night. The air smelt faintly of smoke, damp wool, the sharp tang of cold.

Standing together in the doorway, John and Ursula looked out upon the street, the rain now only a fine drizzle. As the motorcar arrived, they stepped out, into the mist, the cobblestones glistening beneath their feet. It was a given that war might come. Sorrows might come. But for this moment, February held them fast, radiant against the gray, bound together by words, vows, and the knowledge that, whatever the world decreed, happy days were ordained for them first.

***

As John Bowlby settled into the period known to most for marital bliss, the outer world did not quite allow him this happy carelessness. The news was ill and foreboding, and worst of all, as the war developed, the everyday battles did not die.

These were battles between mother and child, affection and withdrawal, security and fracture. It was in this atmosphere that John Bowlby realized he had a duty to write, not from abstraction, nor from Freudian reverie, but from a place of observational gravity, tethered to real rooms, real families, real wounds. In a chapter he contributed to a volume on child psychiatry under the aegis of the Child Guidance Council, Bowlby placed a cautious yet insistent wedge between himself and the legacy of Freud. He did not inherit his notions from the Society of Analysts with its ornate certainties; he stepped sideways instead, into the lesser-trod lane of detailed chronology, he asked when, precisely, symptoms began. He asked what kind of air filled the child's home, what kind of mother fretted over the milk, or the boots, or the cough that might be consumption but wasn't.

Whereas his psychoanalytic forebears entertained the idea of gain, illness, they said, bestowed a kind of refuge, a manipulated grace, Bowlby resisted. He did not believe in hysteria as currency, something exchanged for advantage. Instead, he saw fear, grief, dislocation. A mother dies; a father is shipped off; a hospital bed becomes the only geography of comfort. It is from these frictions, the sudden dislodging of what is known, that symptoms sprout.

Hysteria, to Bowlby, was not performance; it was residue.

His diagnosis did not end with the child. It seldom began there, either. The mother's own childhood, her silences, her learned fears, her patterns of love, were all-important, he realized. Some mothers, he noted, were too tender, addicted to caregiving, wishing to keep their children small and sickly. Others were brittle with anxiety, clasping affection like rations in wartime. And some, perhaps the loneliest, purchased love with a currency of overattentiveness.

Bowlby did not accuse, of course; his task was to observe.

In his paper, he warned against the seduction of separation as a cure. Remove the child, one might think, and you remove the problem. But the wound is not in proximity; it is in connection, or the lack of it. A child under eight, he insisted, should not be torn from the mother unless bruises or liquor stained the walls. Instead, the dyad must be healed; the pattern untied from both ends.

When treating such children, he got used to the slow, far-off sort of gaze one sees in cats, or old portraits. The mothers would sit beside them: gloved, rigid, often smelling faintly of powder and soot. Bowlby would observe them with the same alert sadness a botanist might feel for a withering vine.

The trouble, he knew, was not the tantrums, nor the silence. It is the absence of understanding. That space between them, filled with noise neither of them could hear.

The last thing they needed was even more space; this is why he did not believe in separating children from their parents—not as treatment, not as policy. The instinct to remove a child like a rotten tooth, he resisted that. Because what if the rot was not in the child, but in the root? He believed in the past. The child's troubles did not begin at six, nor the mother's with motherhood. That was the lie of timelines. Bowlby saw generations as rivers; emotional habits passed like sediment. His job was to trace floods back to their spring, and often the origin was separation.

With these realizations in mind, 1939 saw Bowlby publish a short, unsentimental article in *Mother and Child*, titled 'Substitute Homes'. The title, if anything, was a veil. For what Bowlby wrote was not an essay on substitute homes, it was an on-ground report of a quiet, ongoing catastrophe, the slow starvation of love in the youngest of human beings.

The children he wrote about were not loud. They were not necessarily violent. They did not cry or scream or break their toys. They did not look at you.

That, Bowlby believed, was the entire point.

"They do not care what others think of them," he wrote. It was an observation with the precision of a scalpel and the sorrow of a prayer. These children, he argued, had learned early... too early, that trust was a dangerous indulgence. The adults they had once adored, whose voices had been lullabies in their ears, had disappeared. A

And so the child, left behind, unlearned affection.

You could see it, Bowlby noted, if you knew where to look: the flatness of affect, the way a child might smile without warmth, touch without tenderness. It was not malice; it was a sort of armor. A defensive architecture built in silence and sorrow. These were not children of bad temperament or low intelligence. These were children whose hearts had once been open and were now, irrevocably, closed.

"They have no relationships at all," he said, "or only very superficial ones."

There was, he insisted, a pattern. Not a coincidence. In their histories, you would find it: prolonged separations,

191

always, from the maternal figure, whether by death, by institutionalization, or by the slow erosion of absence. Sometimes the child had been hospitalized. Sometimes placed in the care of strangers. Sometimes, it is merely ignored. But the result, Bowlby argued, was the same.

The mother, real or symbolic, had been the axis of their early world. And when that world cracked, they did not forget; they simply ceased to risk affection again.

"They believe," Bowlby wrote, "that the one person whom they really trusted has deserted and betrayed them."

And betrayal, in childhood, is not like adult betrayal. It does not become poetry or songs or even revenge. It becomes silence; it becomes withdrawal; it becomes a lifelong doubt that anyone, anywhere, might be safe to love.

And Bowlby saw something else, too, hidden beneath the layers of scientific prose: a child's monstrous capacity for guilt. Not rational guilt. The child, he said, believes himself to be the cause of the loss. If the mother has gone, it is because he has wished her gone.

"They feel," Bowlby wrote, "that they are being abandoned for their hardly acknowledged wishes."

Grief, horror, guilt: too much for a child's mind to metabolize. The consequences, he believed, could be permanent. Not necessarily visible. But permanent nonetheless. A life lived without depth of feeling, without trust. A life of mimicry, perhaps, even joy, even success, but joy tinged with something absent.

He was suspicious, he said, of the so-called "happy" adopted children.

"They suffer," he wrote, "from a sense of inner emptiness and gloom."

It wasn't a condemnation; it was a recognition, a bleak kind of honesty. Bowlby wasn't interested in demonizing institutions or foster parents. He was interested in facts. And what he had seen, what he kept seeing, was the simple and devastating truth that a child without a secure early bond was not just lonely, they were changed. Yet Bowlby was not entirely fatalistic. He had, perhaps out of professional duty, perhaps out of compassion, a list of measures. Things that might not cure the wound, but could prevent the cutting.

If, he said, a child had to be removed from their home, it should be done early, before the age of nine months, when attachment systems are still soft clay, not hardened wire. Earlier separations, though regrettable, were at least more malleable. The self had not yet formed its deepest imprints.

If a child must be hospitalized or institutionalized, Bowlby urged that one person, not a rotation of nurses, not a staff of twenty, be designated as the child's constant. A child could, perhaps, bear the loss of a mother. But to float among indifferent caregivers, never forming a tie at all, that he believed, was ruinous.

He was explicit: "The children have no opportunity of forming solid emotional ties to any one person. This, more than any other single thing, accounts, I believe, for the withdrawn impersonality of the institutional child."

He acknowledged that sometimes children had to be placed into foster care, but even here, he was skeptical. Foster homes, no matter how well-meaning, were a poor substitute for the organic chaos of a real family. Even a bad home, he suggested, provided a kind of emotional background noise, a continuity of love, or at least familiarity.

Children needed a past to stand on, even if uneven.

And he had sympathy for foster parents, too. "Their job is very difficult." Taking in a child scarred by early loss was a kind of spiritual rescue work, he implied. Noble, yes, but also nearly impossible. Still, he did not speak sentimentally. Bowlby's prose, like his thought, was clear, sharp, uncompromising.

But even as John Bowlby fought on the frontlines of one cause, he did not yet know he would soon be called into the trenches of another.

Chapter 10.

War and Its Children

(Part II)

Yet even as fate bore him towards the winds of war, there was one matter to be resolved first: his full membership into the British Psycho-Analytical Society.

In the long corridors of the Tavistock Clinic, the floors squeaked as he walked. The windows filtered the fog-grey light of a world poised between wars. Outside, car horns and the weary bells of trams announced themselves like faint arguments. Inside, men argued too; not with their voices, which were often decorous and polite, but with their theories, which bristled with envy and allegiance.

John Bowlby walked as if carrying an invisible burden on his back, one of observations, clinical fragments, and orphaned stories whispered through the cracked mouths of children who stole coins and disappeared from classrooms. There was no romance in their crimes; no glamour in their absence. What he found was something rawer, something unshaped and half-buried, as though their souls had curled in early on themselves and stayed there, brittle and dormant.

He was still only an associate in the British Psycho-Analytical Society, a member without a vote, a passenger on the fringe of an elite voyage. Since 1937, he had borne that title with a polite patience, but always with an eye turned inward, calculating; watching the mechanisms from beneath the surface, like a boy peering at gears through the cracks in the floorboards of a clockmaker's attic.

Now he had to present a paper.

He had chosen not to immerse himself solely in analytic sessions; no, he had gone further, out into the world, into the grit and grind of clinics, where children sat in wool coats that didn't fit, legs swinging, gazes hollow. He had looked at their records, walked their streets, visited their schools. He was less interested in phantasies so favored by the Kleinians than in facts. Or, at least, experiences; the felt and physical *real*.

These children who stole, who drifted like shadows across institutions and courtrooms, who couldn't, or wouldn't, attach…he had asked what had happened to them.

It wasn't the topic that he knew would disturb the older members; it was the method. Melitta Schmideberg had already warned him, with that mix of admiration and foreboding that people reserve for the stubborn and talented.

"You will be attacked," she said. "You must be defended."

Now, in the prim and peeling hall where the Society met, with its wood panels lacquered with years of civilized

196

disagreement, he stood before them. They wore spectacles, frowns, cufflinks; they clutched copies of The Standard Edition like hymnals.

And he began:

"I have gathered material concerning the personal backgrounds of deviant children over the course of three years…"

There was a moment of held breath, but he had come not to float among the accepted currents but to row, sharply and deliberately, against them. He stated, clearly, that the environment had profound, perhaps foundational, consequences for a child's mental development. He spoke of children whose relationships with others were shallow, disjointed, false; who smiled without warmth, touched without connection.

The audience, trained to seek conflict in phantasy, in the deep-sea terrain of the unconscious, shifted in their seats.

Among the sixteen children he identified as "affectionless," fourteen had experienced major separations from their mothers before the age of three. The numbers told a quiet, devastating truth. The pattern was stark, unignorable.

And yet, it was resisted.

The Kleinians, torchbearers of internal drama, objected. To them, Bowlby's work seemed blunt, anatomical, even mechanical. Where they sought the metaphorical knife in the child's dream, he sought the wound left by absence itself. For Bowlby, the absence was not symbolic. It was real. It was measurable. It mattered.

But not all turned their faces away.

Susan Isaacs supported him. Though she admired Klein, she sensed something in Bowlby's thesis that could not be dismissed. And behind her, others—Sharpe, Glover, Strachey, not entirely aligned, but intrigued enough to hold the line when opposition swelled.

"What is it," said Rickman, his voice both clinical and weary, "that qualifies a paper like this for full membership?"

Winnicott, seconding without warmth, echoed the doubt. Riviere nodded as well, looking at John coolly.

In the end, the Society almost barred his way... almost.

And yet, by votes cast under breath, he was elected a full member. In that moment, beneath the paint-flaked ceiling and the drawn faces of the old guard, he became something else: a figure at the fulcrum of a new mode of thought. Neither inside nor outside. Not a follower. Not quite a full rebel. But a man with a theory sharpening in his hands.

Not many were interested in the real experiences of children.

But some were.

Not many. But enough.

And it was through that slim crack in the polished wall of psychoanalytic doctrine that he stepped, carrying with him not only data and diagnoses, but the memory of children who had looked at him not with hatred, nor hope, but with the expressionless stare of those who have waited for something too long to believe it will ever arrive.

***

Meanwhile, a war was coming, and John Bowlby didn't know what to make of it.

It was a time of unease, and the streets of Oxford trembled not with noise, but with ideas—fierce ones, trembling and tall, shuffled in darkened lecture halls, inked into the margins of worn books. Among them, Bowlby sat in partial silence, his fingers splayed across the spine of a manuscript still wet with argument.

War and Democracy. The title alone breathed like a hot wind down the back of the neck.

His brother Tony had always been more socially elastic, floating into groups of thinkers the way coal dust settled on windowpanes, undeniable and permanent. Through Tony, Bowlby found himself at the margins of a cluster of young Labour economists. Their talk was hurried, not in tone but in necessity; they knew something was coming, and they knew it would not wait for intellectual pleasantries.

To his surprise, he'd met Durbin there, and each was surprised by the other's apparent turn towards labor policies. By 1938, they had already written a paper together: Personal Aggressiveness and War, a treatise or a dissection, depending on one's inclination. It began not with declarations but with questions; it did not so much build an argument as excavate one. Durbin held the shovel of sociology; Bowlby, the scalpel of evolutionary psychology.

In London, talk in those days had been fragmented. Prime Minister Chamberlain paced behind closed doors, fingers steepled in thought or prayer, it was difficult to tell. He had called the fears of war 'imagination'; and had suggested that the creeping dread was a mirage conjured by journalists and armchair prophets. The press, eager to believe in commerce more than conscience, had spun Hitler into something manageable, less monster than unpleasant business associate.

"Peace," they'd repeated, "is good for the market."

As if stock could cushion a blitzkrieg.

Yet Durbin, and Bowlby with him, had ceased to believe in polite fictions. The war was coming, and they'd both known it.

Some days, the talk in Labour circles fluttered with the ghosts of pacifism, once a sacred cow, now a pale ox being led gently toward slaughter. Others argued for collective security, a phrase as beautiful and brittle as church glass. There were even those who looked inward and downward, toward a war not across the Channel but within their own class, their own city, their own tea cups and rent slips. Communism became a mirror for the disgruntled. In these months, the Labour Party was less a party than a collection of factions stitched together by fear and idealism.

So when March 1939 came with iron boots and Hitler took Czechoslovakia, the doubters of the Labour movement, Durbin among them, turned. War would not be stopped with pamphlets. It would not hesitate for policy debates or the etiquette of appeasement. Force, though abhorrent, had become unavoidable.

Bowlby had always feared that war might interrupt his work, but now that it had broken out, he worked nonetheless. He wrote of primitive societies with the cold poetry of anthropology; he wrote of Western children with the warmth of recognition.

What was a nation, he asked, but a nursery with sharper teeth?

Then September arrived, not with fog but with locomotives. E-Day: the day the city emptied itself. First the schoolchildren, then the mothers holding infants like woven bags of flour, and then the blind, the pregnant, the fragile, all shepherded into trains that reeked of coal and cold hope. They moved like ghosts in reverse, away from the war instead of into it. In total, nearly 1.5 million people were displaced by the very idea of destruction.

As Bowlby walked past the trains on the station, he watched a boy with red socks and a tin lunch pail clamber into the carriage, looking back longingly at his parents as they bid him farewell. Tears wet his big, blue eyes…and then the carriage door shut.

More separation. More loss. John Bowlby shook his head sadly and kept walking.

As the first days of war sank into Britain, the monograph he had written with Durbin became less academic and more prophetic. Reviewers who had been skeptical now cited it. Politicians lifted lines without attribution. The idea that war was born in the breast of the individual rather than the belly of nations, that was an idea whose time had come, though it had not yet been welcomed.

As for John Bowlby and his fellow members of the British Psychoanalytical Society, the breaking out of war meant being called into active emergency medical services.

Accordingly, he was placed in a War Neurosis Centre in Maidstone, a town unsure whether to brace for the worst or not. The war had come to them more as a rumor than anything, and for a time, it loitered amongst them like an indecisive guest.

And like this, John Bowlby found himself standing at the window of the Centre, which had once been a school. The panes were warped by weather, and through them he could see a gardener in a too-large cap pretending to tend roses that had already died. The roses, like the soldiers they were meant to soothe, had been planted in the wrong soil.

The ministry seemed to expect that the war would bring an avalanche of broken minds here soon. The problem was, so far, the expected avalanche was a snowflake. Within a few days, restlessness began to claw at Bowlby; this relocation was keeping him from more valuable work, keeping him away from doing something about the evacuations and what they might do to children. Here, he continued to grow bitter at the dull inaction…and then, a terrible realization occurred to him.

That night, when he couldn't sleep, he wrote to his wife.

*It appears we are here to take any serious psychiatric case from the 'front line' hospitals, but must concentrate attention on the people who are of **national importance**. So we tell everyone we wish only the Admirals, Generals, and Cabinet Ministers.*

It was clear: if you were merely a man, you were not quite essential. The Centre, though empty, would not admit the ordinary. The corridors echoed with the sound of heels on linoleum and the peculiar silence of unused beds; an institutional quiet that had nothing to do with peace.

They were here to play hospital. That's what it felt like. Frustrated, he wrote again the next day:

Here, we are playing around doing absolutely nothing, he wrote in bitter ink.

Perhaps Ursula read the letter in the grey morning, the post laid neatly at her place on the table, hearing the children's chatter drifted in from the garden, and she had to read the same line twice before it settled. Perhaps she heard his frustration in the way the ink pressed heavier toward the end of each sentence, as if the nib itself bore the weight of his idleness. And perhaps she thought of the distance between them, even as she folded the letter carefully, smoothed the paper as though her hands could press out the discontent, and placed it beside the others in the drawer. Her reply would, as always, attempt to soothe her husband, even though she knew that John Bowlby would never be content doing nothing when he could be helping people.

Back at the Centre, this was precisely the cause of Bowlby's discontent. Around him, the halls were stocked with morphine, tranquilizers, tobacco, and endless sheets of intake forms that nobody filled out. The medical cabinets were arranged like shrines; waiting, watching. Time crawled through the wards and coiled up in the corners. In the mess hall, someone had painted a mural of King George looking vaguely constipated and noble. Bowlby sat with his tea and stared at it, thinking not of monarchs or battles but of the children. Of the little boy boarding the train, unsure where he would end up...

"Don't you think it's eerie?" said a nurse to him. "How quiet it is? I thought we were at war…"

"We are," Bowlby sighed. "Though I suspect we're on the wrong frontline."

***

So when a chance came to leave the Center behind and join the London Child Guidance Clinic in Cambridge, John Bowlby jumped at it with relief.

When he reached Cambridge, he found that the war seemed far more real here than in Maidstone. The air carried a careful, hesitant silence, interrupted only by the wheels of bicycles ticking over the cobbles and the occasional military lorry rattling like a misremembered memory down the High Street. It was October, and the leaves along the Cam had begun their slow surrender into ochre and wine. It was somber weather, but Bowlby felt better than he had in weeks. Only recently freed from the peculiar imprisonment of the EMS, the prospect of having something to work on again gladdened him. He was, after all, a man who had never enjoyed the farce of idleness.

I can't tell you how pleased I am to be a free man again! he wrote to Ursula, and he meant it.

The war had not yet left burns across England's skin, not in the way it eventually would; this was the early stage, the 'phoney war,' where fear lived in anticipation more than in aftermath. But the evacuation had already uprooted thousands. Cambridge had absorbed 6,700 children. Little feet now passed beneath the cloisters of King's and Trinity; their voices bounced against sandstone walls that once echoed Latin and politics.

John Bowlby was quietly horrified, and he knew he had to make his relocation count. Something had to be done...but what?

It was Susan Isaacs, Bowlby's colleague in psychoanalysis, who had the idea. She, together with Sybil Clement Brown, sensible, sharp, and quietly furious at the government's blind logistics, proposed a survey of these evacuees.

"Let's make a study of the dislocated," she had said, a teacup poised in one hand, her other raking through loose sheets of demographic forms. "We need them to see the numbers. We need them to see how *mad* this all is."

It made perfect sense to John Bowlby, and he agreed to the plan immediately. They called it the Cambridge Evacuation Survey, though Isaacs preferred to think of it as a confession extracted from the bones of bureaucracy.

For his part, Bowlby offered methods, a clinical structure for the interviews, a classification for the children. They tested those whose placements had failed, those rated "unsuccessful," as if childhood could be graded like a Latin paper. And then they compared them with the "controls," the children who had simply adapted or simply not complained. He had complaints about the research, though.

These complaints reached Ursula in the thin blue of evening, when the house was hushed and the kettle's last breath hung in the air. She held his letter at the corner, as though it might smudge; the ink was hurried, the slope of his hand betraying fatigue.

Too ambitious, too academic, he had written, clearly after an especially weary day.

She lingered on the phrase, hearing the tiredness beneath its neat script. In her mind, she saw him bent over a desk in some borrowed office, surrounded by half-sharpened pencils and the muffled tread of officials passing in corridors. She wondered if he realized how much of himself he was spending on these lists, these categories, these fragile interviews that claimed to measure adaptation as if it were a skill to be examined.

Yet, despite his complaints, his work continued. In time, a paper began to take form. The findings of the survey were not surprising, but they struck deep. The final numbers would tell their own story. By mid-November, only 3,650 of the original 6,700 evacuees remained in Cambridge. By the next summer, 1,624. It was not that the danger had passed; it was that the alternative had proven unbearable.

The primary cause for the return of children from evacuation was simply *love*, or rather, its absence. Homesick children, distraught mothers. Another cause: the foster homes themselves. Some too cold, too crowded, or simply too alien. And lastly, money: the banal undertow beneath all the decisions of war.

"Imagine charging parents to lose their children," Bowlby muttered, more to himself than to anyone else, walking home beneath a sky bruised with twilight.

Susan Isaacs's criticism of the government's evacuation plan was unsparing. Bowlby, too, had his fair share of criticisms, not only against the evacuations themselves, but also against the implementation of them. Why, he wondered, were trained social workers not used? Why was experience ignored in favour of volume? The system had failed, and child guidance practitioners had become the de facto janitors of policy: picking up the pieces, even as they watched children migrate away from their families like birds, drawing pictures of their parents in bomb shelters.

His only solace from one war was to fight in another. And so he wrote in the evenings, a kind of monastic repetition that, though ordinary in act, assumed a solemnity in wartime. The desk was small, pressed against a cold wall, and the ink froze sometimes before it dried, but still he wrote—his pen scratching like a key against wood, soft, steady, near invisible.

As October continued, the sky seemed to turn a pale, metallic blue. Sirens began to act up with alarming frequency. And with the children, shoelaces uneven, mouths agape with excitement or terror, holding stiff hands of adults they did not know, there was, as Bowlby later wrote, a quiet slaughter of the psyche, invisible as pale ash on snow. They were being sent away, without mothers, sometimes without names properly sewn into collars. It was called evacuation; it was called patriotic; it was called necessary.

But in the private theater of Bowlby's mind, it was something else.

It was a *rupture*.

He saw in it what most others did not: a dismembering of what he knew to be a *necessary tether*. This was a truth that bled through his fingertips when he wrote to his wife beneath candlelight.

People think I'm making a fuss about nothing, he scrawled. *But a child does not yet know that leaving is not the same as abandonment.*

He spoke that much from experience. And alarmed and worried by this terrible state of affairs, John Bowlby had no choice but to act.

It began with meetings, modest ones, across the soft dust of civil parlors where he met with Durbin, Parker, and other people of interest from the Fabian Research Bureau. Parker, a Labour MP with youth on his collar and dust on his shoes, was sympathetic. He had known the children of Wales, seen the coal-gutted landscapes where boys became men by the age of nine, and he nodded when Bowlby spoke.

"It's a terrible thing, the death of hope," Parker said, shaking his head. Bowlby could only nod in assent.

And as these discussions further ignited Durbin and Bowlby's zeal, a pamphlet soon followed, describing the psychological hazards of maternal separation. Yet it vanished soon like steam on glass; in later years, no copy ever survived. Perhaps it was written and shelved. Perhaps it vanished beneath the weight of war.

They tried The Times next. A letter, strong and urgent, signed by names that meant something: Susan Isaacs, child psychologist and freethinker; J.R. Rees, director of the Tavistock Clinic, whose eyes were said to flicker with a visionary intensity. They tried to speak plainly. That the minds of children, especially the very young, are still unbaked clay; and to remove a mother from that process was to dry the clay mid-form. But the letter, much to Bowlby's irritation, was sabotaged and did terribly. Perhaps this was because of crowded columns, indifferent editors…or it was a slow political curtain drawing itself closed, brushing aside his concern like one might shoo a moth from the hem of a uniform.

In either case, the fact was clear: an entire generation was about to bear the weight of separation, and no one seemed to care.

In his letters home, nearly daily, the disappointment dripped steadily. The war had become not only one of bombs and hunger, but of perception: what mattered and what did not. And the invisible wounds of children, when weighed against the visible threat the children may face in the city, lost weight altogether.

For Ursula's part, she read his words by the yellowed light of the sitting-room lamp in her mother's house. The air smelt faintly of coal dust; outside, the night pressed against the windows with a soft, unbroken dark.

A child sent to strangers may wonder, he had, *what crime he committed to deserve banishment.*

The war was becoming something stranger in his telling; not just the sound of bombs or the thinning of rations, but a contest over what could be seen and what could not. The visible dangers were counted and named; the invisible ones, the quiet undoing of a child's trust, were allowed to slip soundlessly through the days. She could relate more to the second than most; her own husband's absence, his preoccupation with this work, was itself a symptom of this war. She wished he would be here with his children, but perhaps felt guilt for such feelings; after all, with his work,

John Bowlby might well be the man who could help the lot of thousands of children in the country.

There was still one publication to go, however, one lifeline. In December, a letter appeared in the British Medical Journal. Bowlby was not the only author; he had enlisted E. Miller of the East London Child Guidance Clinic and Donald Winnicott, who, in Oxfordshire, walked among rows of displaced infants like a field surgeon of the soul. Winnicott understood. He had seen what happened when the tiny architecture of a child's world collapsed, not under fire, but under silence. No mother, no explanation. Only the echo of her absence.

The letter spoke plainly but not without urgency. Children under five should not be sent away alone; their removal might plant seeds that grew into a future national disaster, what they termed a *widespread psychological disorder*. They warned of juvenile delinquency, of boys turning feral in back alleys ten years hence, of girls unrooted in a world they would never quite trust again.

At the London Child Guidance Clinic, Bowlby had already seen it. A young thief, ten or perhaps eleven, whose earliest memory was of a suitcase too heavy for him, and a woman in a railway uniform saying, "Don't cry now, your mum's being brave." He stole because he didn't believe in permanence. He lied because he thought truth had moved away with the trains. He had learned, too early, that attachments fray; and that love, as experienced in childhood, could be revoked like ration cards.

Later, in the Fabian Society's report Evacuation Survey, Bowlby gave structure to his theory.

He divided the ages like strata: the adolescent, somewhat spared by their budding egos; the five-to-twelves, half-formed, prone to guilt; and the very young, fragile and impressionable, who would not forget the shock of absence, no matter how kindly the foster mother. It was not all tragedy; he did not claim so. But for those already insecure, already sensing the tremble of home life, the evacuation was not salvation…it was confirmation that love could be rescinded.

He did not dramatize, however; his prose was cool, scientific, and utterly logical.

The child who feels unwanted… will find it very difficult not to interpret his being sent away as his parents' desire to be rid of him.

And this was the crux. Not the bombs, not the countryside, not the milk in enamel pitchers. But the *why* that would never be answered. That a child might spend decades translating that silence into a language of crime, or melancholy, or rage. Most children, he allowed, were wanted. Most returned home intact. But even one mind undone by misinterpretation, one child sitting stiffly on a borrowed bed, thinking he had been given away like an unwanted parcel, was enough to matter. And in every case of emotional disturbance, Bowlby insisted, the root was the same: the child's belief that mother had disappeared forever.

It was the only logical and rational conclusion, and yet he faced resistance. Perhaps it was the era, with its brass buttons and ration books, its burgeoning air of Churchillian stoicism. Perhaps it was discomfort with the unquantifiable. The nation had grown used to counting deaths, budgets, and

211

calories. But how to count *absence?* How to weigh a child's silent misbelief that he was not wanted?

Still, he wrote, rewrote, sent letters, and solicited signatures. He watched politicians nod and move on. And in the evenings, he sat before his small desk and the cold ink again, even as those very politicians met in the halls of power, deciding what to do with millions of small, tender hearts beating inside small, tender bodies.

As far as they were concerned, separation was salvation. The cities were dangerous; the bombs would come, and London would not spare the child's ribcage, nor the hands that clutched a toy rabbit or a crust of bread. And so it was that thousands, even tens of thousands of children were packed like brown paper parcels, name tags swinging from their necks, and sent to strangers in the country.

After all, it was wartime…and wartime always made strangers of all.

But John Bowlby watched this exodus and, at the same time, in the clinic, saw its effects. He saw small faces warped by confusion, little hands too calm or too wild, eyes that flicked with suspicion when they should have simply been curious. He documented these cases as best he could, still trying to find ears willing to listen…

In a small room that smelled of paper and ink and the rain that always managed to find the windowsill, he wrote of the boy named Patrick, three and a half years old, who had become a machine of repeated motions, as if trying to stitch the past back into the present through routine. And of Beryl, four years old, who had turned to stone, sat where her mother left her and refused even food, as if by staying still, she might be found again, as if love worked like a lighthouse beam.

He told anyone who would listen, he met with MPs, wrote to journals, and finally sent frustrated letters to his wife when it all seemed useless.

They think I'm making a fuss about nothing, his latest letter to his wife bitterly said. And more than once, defeated, he considered dropping the whole affair.

And yet, he returned to it each day, the fight inside him bruised but unbeaten. Perhaps they could censure him, hide away his letters from publication, ignore his requests for an audience. But there were others, people in his field, who cared; there were others who understood what he was saying, saw the sense in his words. There were men like Winnicott, for instance, who stood beside Bowlby, writing to the British Medical Journal as he tried to describe with sober precision the damage done by absence. There were people like Isaacs and Brown and Durbin and Parker, and they continued to make themselves heard.

But in the end, as a practitioner of mental health under a crown that saw only the utility of his profession, John Bowlby was to find himself enmired even further into the war.

***

It was the spring of 1940 when the war yet again changed the lives of those men and women whose professions were now tugged violently into the machinery of Empire.

John Bowlby, whose temperament leaned more toward reflection than regimentation, again received a summons from the Emergency Medical Service. It was not unexpected. The inactivity of the first time had been trial enough; yet the circumstances of this second summons, he suspected, might be even worse. He packed methodically; he left a note for Ursula on the table by the windows. He boarded the northbound train to Fazakerley.

Fazakerley was a village by name, yet in temperament seemed more like a bruised appendage of Liverpool. It smelled of wet stone, petrol, and churned turf. The sky hung low, industrial grey smeared with coal ash; it bore down like a second skin. The soldiers came to the clinic not with broken limbs or visible wounds but with minds frayed from the inside, with neuroses borne of sirens and silence alike. Bowlby was to treat them…or rather, observe them.

The first shock was that Dr. Johnson, the senior physician and a neurologist of the old stripe, forbade the word "psychotherapy."

"There is no use," Johnson had said in the first meeting, flicking ash into a tin tray as if to punctuate each word with authority, "in encouraging…*malingering*. Talk makes the sickness worse. It anchors delusions."

Kenneth Soddy, Bowlby's friend and colleague from the Child Guidance Clinic, sat opposite, mouth closed tight in disbelief; Bowlby himself had to force himself to not talk back.

To Ursula, in a letter dated May 30, he wrote:

214

The thing one has to be very careful about is to avoid objecting openly to Johnson altho' he is... the man we object to both because he's a neurologist & because he is here so little that we have to do all the work.

But thankfully, Johnson was often absent, and in this absence, Bowlby and Soddy tried to apply their principles to the treatment: the Freudian tincture, the observational rigour of psychoanalysis, and the careful human handling that war so rarely permitted. It was a fool's errand. Their patients were treated as unreliable narrators of their own experience; the cure was to forget.

"Johnson is close-minded if he thinks therapy is of no use at all," Soddy said, shaking his head as they sat in the break room one day. "I'm not fully beholden to Mr. Freud either, but it's clear that there are positive effects from psychotherapy."

"Perhaps this is what Dr. Breuer faced when he first talked about his *talking cure*," Bowlby wryly replied.

"He'd rather see us go back to medieval norms, I think," Soddy said, disgruntled. *"Let the mad be locked up until restored to reason.* In this day and age!"

By July, the constant struggle with Johnson had frayed even Bowlby's ordinarily diplomatic edges. The tipping point was not a dramatic confrontation but a morning meeting where Johnson curtly refused to authorize therapy for a young man who, two days prior, had tried to drown himself in a rain barrel behind the officers' mess. That same week, both Bowlby and Soddy resigned and left without ceremony. Their departure registered little in the hospital ledger but marked a significant pivot in their professional lives.

It was at this point that J.R. Rees intervened. At this time running both the Tavistock Clinic and the Royal Army Medical Corps, Rees offered both men commissions. Rees did not believe in protocols for the sake of order; he believed in systems that bent to the intricacies of individual psychology. He had a vision: war not merely as physical annihilation but as psychic disintegration; and psychiatry as a scaffold, not a seal.

And seeing the chance to actually make a difference, John Bowlby accepted.

***

During this time, there was another development that, in different circumstances, might have been a more happy affair: Ursula Longstaff-Bowlby found herself in the hospital, having just given birth to her first child: Mary Hamilton Bowlby.

Ursula lay back among the stiff white pillows, her body sore still, little Mary Hamilton sleeping in the bassinet beside her. Outside, the thin rattle of cart wheels, a porter shouting to another, and always, always the muffled clatter of war in the distance. She had not expected, not quite, the loneliness. The walls were close and smelled faintly of carbolic, the sheets coarse; all that was tolerable. But the hours passed in drips, the clock at the far end of the ward clicking as though each second were a small rebuke. She had written to John the night before...no, the morning, when the nurse had gone, and she could slip the pencil under the sheet, cry her complaints as though they might be overheard. He was busy with his work, she knew; yet, he made his efforts to come once a week if he could, doing as much as was in his power to be present for his family.

He would come, she had been certain, this weekend.

Only, John did not come when he had promised.

A letter arrived instead: his remorseful apologies, news of the Clinic being overwhelmed, his duties redoubled by the war. She had read the words through a veil of tears, pressing the paper against her lips as though some warmth might linger there.

I am very unhappy, she had written back, eyes wet. *The feeding is going badly.... I get so tired by the evening that my milk goes. Visitors make me so tired, but I am so lonely and on edge with only seeing Nurse all day. Nurse says I must stay 2 ½ weeks or 3, but I can't stand this much more. If only I had Mummy. There is no one here to comfort me, and I get so worried about the feeding and everything....*

Please come soon.

But the nurse entered soon after, starched cap, hands brisk, all purpose and order, and Ursula felt herself collapse inward again. The infant stirred in her arms; Ursula gathered her against her chest, a tremulous pride quickening her. But the nurse clucked at her indulgence.

"Best not too much rocking, ma'am," she said, a smidge crossly. "You'll only spoil her."

"Can one spoil a baby?" Ursula asked. Her voice trembled with tired defiance. "When she cries, she cries as though her very soul were abandoned. Am I to let her suffer so?"

"Routine, Mrs. Bowlby," the nurse said with a kind of tender firmness. "Discipline, even from the start. That is how babies thrive."

Ursula pressed her lips together, unwilling to argue further; the woman was simply doing her job, she knew. But as she bent her head to Mary's silken crown, she thought…surely it was not discipline but tenderness that shapes a child.

And slowly, three weeks passed. The days swelled like dull waves, breaking upon the sameness of the ward, the chatter of other women, the nurse's measured tread

At last, the morning came when they were taken, she and the baby, to her mother's house beyond the city. She was not well enough yet to rise. She was confined still, and in her mother's house lay propped against embroidered pillows, her brother Dick checking up on her every few hours. She was most grateful for her mother's presence, and between the two of them and Nurse, who would still visit the house, she would manage to take care of little Mary.

On weekends, John might come, or he might not. Sometimes, on Saturday mornings, she would smooth her hair, dress in her pale blue frock, and wait by the window, listening for the sound of his step on the gravel. Sometimes the hours passed into dusk, and no step came. Then she would undress slowly, fold her frock with deliberate care, and lie down with her back turned against the room. But when he did come, ah how the air changed! Mary in her cot, Ursula lifting her eagerly to his arms. He would take the child gently, as though she were some rare specimen, and study her. His eyes softened then, his long fingers stroking the baby's cheek.

"She's growing bigger each time I see her," he said once, with quiet happiness. "And see her eyes! Her gaze is clearer, more direct."

"Yes," Ursula answered, watching him, the old ache for his presence rising in her. "She knows me now, I think. And when she cries, only I can soothe her."

He looked at her with that half-smile she remembered from the early days, before marriage, before war. Yet soon he was speaking again of his work: the children in London, frightened, maladjusted, their behaviour strange under the bombs. His voice grew absorbed, distant. She listened, nodding, but her hands, restless, clutched at Mary's small limbs as if to anchor herself.

"Must you always return so soon?" she whispered when at last he rose to go.

"I must," he said gently. "The war does not wait for us, Ursula."

And he was gone again.

Her letters to him after he would leave proceeded to invariably sadden him. They were heartbroken letters, and it is difficult to imagine the ache of reading them so far away.

When you left yesterday, I felt blank, and knew that nothing made up for not seeing you every day, she wrote in one of the tear-specked letters. *And last night I woke up and thought you were still there. Soon we shall be together again all the time.*

219

And as Ursula struggled with her new role as mother, growing into herself and struggling between her youthful desire for personal freedom and the new responsibilities her role demanded, John Bowlby found himself flitting from meeting to meeting, trying to make sense of a world that, it seemed to him, was going slowly mad.

***

It is important to note that by 1940, the chaos of Dunkirk had hollowed out the British command structure. The sea at the beaches of that ancient port had been gray and infinite as men scrambled like ants across the sands, half-swallowed by tide and smoke. Men pinned down by barrages of fire sat, bled, and waited, some in silence, some in prayer, for the ghostly silhouettes of allied ships to slide from the mist like old gods summoned by desperation.

Orders were shouted, rescinded, reshaped with every passing hour, brigadiers with trembling hands, colonels whose neat ledgers meant little now; the chain of command frayed like the cuffs of a soldier's coat after weeks in the field. More than ever, the British now needed to strengthen the chain of command.

In the halls of Whitehall, commanders convened and drafted memoranda over tea brewed too strong. Dunkirk had not merely been a logistical disaster, nor merely a miracle; it was a mirror held up to the face of command. The war, they realized, would not be won by maps alone but by mentally strong leadership in key positions…and for this, they would

220

need to again turn to the psychiatrists and those who studied the mind.

And it was so that in the aftermath of Dunkirk's fallout, John Bowlby found himself in the curious position of sifting through candidates for military leadership, not by previous rank or accolades, but by the far more fragile material of personality. He tested cadets, quietly, precisely. But the selection of these cadets was the problem; the army still leaned heavily on its brusque, brutalist tradition: a fifteen-minute interview, a handshake, a gut feeling from a senior officer.

Bowlby watched this dispassionately, like a surgeon observing a medieval barber. It was the very opposite of the rigor he had been trained in, but before he could say anything against it, he needed to do his research. They had their way of doing things, and he had his.

Nonetheless, the program at least seemed to accept and respect the place of psychiatrists and psychologists at the table of national duty. Over the next year, psychiatrists were brought in to devise new procedures: simulations, extended interviews, psychological profiles. Gordon Fitzpatrick had already come out with a paper on this egregious selection process, which was already ruffling feathers up the ladder. In the meantime, Bowlby continued to compile his own paper on the subject meticulously, finding evidence to corroborate his views.

At the same time, he worried for Ursula and their child. It was a cruel twist of fate that just as one war had parted his parents, so too had another parted him and his wife and child. Briefly, as much as it pained him, he considered a plan to send Ursula and Mary away from England for their safety. Now, with the war swelling somewhere beyond the horizon like a rising sea just out of sight, John Bowlby pressed his pen to paper. Writing letters to Ursula had become, for him, a ceremony, a tether to something solid and particular. He wrote not only to inform but to shape a reality neither of them could control.

One way or the other, the war will not be long. If we win, you come back. If we lose, perhaps I shall join you, it would be easier to get myself out alone than you two.

The phrasing was as direct as it was disquieting, and yet in that necessary economy was a remarkable clarity.

The prospect of separation, no, of desertion, even for safety's sake, sat poorly with him. But worse than that was the idea of Ursula and the child caught in the interior machinery of a Europe unraveling. The contingency he had in mind was Canada, where Ursula's family had, generations ago, acquired small but sufficient investments in the Dominion. A boarding house, some government bonds. Property. Something to stand on.

But events turned as they often did in those years, abruptly, bureaucratically. That summer, the British Treasury moved to freeze all overseas holdings. No pounds would cross the Atlantic. No investments would be accessed, no accounts opened, no wire transfers granted for women with children attempting to embark from Liverpool or Southampton with the pretext of independence. Dependence, it seemed, was not just a fact of marriage or finance, but of wartime policy.

And so, Ursula remained.

She did not go to Canada, and not because she lacked resolve. She would later insist in a letter that she would have left if permitted; that she had packed, even, her mother's comb and the child's tin rattle; that she had said goodbye to England, but the system had refused her exit. And so, she remained in England; she remained his partner, not just in the abstract sense of marriage, but also as a co-actor in a shared historical moment.

When he read her letter, John Bowlby sighed and shut his eyes, resisting an urge to curse a bureaucratic machinery that continued to fail. But at least, he would comfort himself; this meant that the separation between him and his child would not be as drastic as being in two different countries. And so he lowered his head, and did the only thing he could.

He worked.

***

In 1941, he finally published his study on the high failure rate of officer cadets in training and confirmed what those in the barracks already knew intuitively: the army's current selection method was bleeding morale and money alike. Those chosen often broke not from battle, but from the burden of the role.

The findings came at the same time as a small, significant conference. Present were General Sir Ronald Adam, Major General Andrew Thorne, and psychiatrists Ronald Hargreaves and Ferguson Rodger. The room they met in was paneled in an Edinburgh sort of wood, and they

223

sat around a table looking at the latest reports. Sir Ronald Adam sat with one hand curled over the other, his knuckles pale. He was a man of tall habit, precise mustache, and long thoughts. Hargreaves and Rodger, for their part, came bearing the hopes and worries of all their peers, knowing that something must be done. They sat in tense silence until the meeting was started.

The discussion on the selection process's flaws and merits went on at length. Finally, the result was this: the formation of the first experimental War Officer Selection Board, No. 1 WOSB, in Edinburgh, January 1942.

And so it was that, in February, Bowlby would join No. 1 WOSB in Edinburgh, which was covered then in a somber white blanket. The snow still fell then, half-hearted, over the narrow roofs of the city, and the wind curled through the castle stones like an old suspicion. He carried with him notes, and a quiet, firm belief: that a man's past would speak, if only the room were quiet enough. No. 1 WOSB was the first of its kind, a place where candidates were asked to solve puzzles, speak freely, work in teams, and fail, in front of watching eyes trained not on outcome, but on behavior.

Yet not all were convinced.

The soldiers nicknamed analysts like Bowlby "trick cyclists." To be assessed psychologically was, to many, to be dissected, stripped of the stoic armor that British manhood, particularly in war, had long cultivated. And then came Churchill. In December 1942, the Prime Minister himself, exhausted by reports of delay and dubious of what he saw as intellectual overreach, complained to the Lord President:

"It is very wrong to disturb large numbers of healthy, normal men and women by asking the kind of odd questions in which psychiatrists specialize."

He called for restraint. He called them camp-followers. He, too, wanted war to be run as mechanically as possible; he wanted quantity, and most of all, he wanted to maintain the stoic vigor of the British trooper. And yet, the WOSBs expanded, with only one reason to blame: they *worked*. Officers selected through psychologically grounded methods lasted. Their men trusted them. And as the war wore on, psychiatrists were becoming, in slow, uneven strokes, essential.

In the evenings, after long days of interviewing and tabulating, Bowlby sometimes walked the edges of the training grounds. Edinburgh air was different, cleaner, drier than Fazakerley. The war was always present but always elsewhere; its nearness was tonal, not visible. Often, he thought of Ursula.

In his few breaks, he wrote more frequently now, as though by documenting the transformation of army psychology, he could steady himself against the world that trembled. And in this, he had found a rhythm, half-medical, half-philosophical, that allowed the war to be more than bombs and borders. He had begun to map the soft terrain that governments overlooked: the human mind in crisis, the mind as a battlefield, and the strange, stubborn need, amid orders and uniforms, for understanding.

But there was plenty of work to be done, and time to himself was scarce. Thirty-two men arrived every three days, each with a suitcase, a uniform slightly too new or too worn, and a private fear they would never name aloud. They stood in corridors whose paint peeled in solemn lines, as though history itself had scraped at the plaster, and they waited. Some were sons of grocers, others sons of peers; a few had tasted combat and found it bitter, while most still bore the untouched sheen of theory.

"This way," said the corporal, barely glancing up, as he ushered them into the common room, a long chamber with scuffed parquet flooring and an enormous blackboard that bore no writing. In place of instruction, there would be participation. Observation. Performance. And always, the tick of the clipboard—the quiet, omnipresent measure of the man under stress.

It was Erich Trist who designed the exercises: leaderless group tasks of simplicity and hidden complexity. Build a bridge from three chairs and two planks; decide the most efficient way to rescue an imaginary wounded man from behind enemy lines. These were tests of leadership, and yet, leadership was not enough. There were psychiatric interviews too, at first for all, later only for the ambiguous. Bowlby sat quietly in these sessions, his voice low, nonjudgmental, and his pen always at the ready.

By the summer of 1942, the WOSB was relocated to the coarse green of the Hertfordshire countryside. The building itself had been a hunting lodge once, oak-beamed, with chimneys smoking faintly like the pipes of thoughtful men. Wall Hall was its official name; "Valhalla" was what the junior officers called it, half in jest, half in awe, as they tramped up its gravel paths with notebooks tucked under their arms. And inside, Bowlby and his peers went about the business of determining, in under sixty hours, who among these men would command.

What fascinated John Bowlby most was the practice of watching people become themselves under pressure; of discovering that leadership was not loudness, nor obedience always virtue; that a man who deferred today might save lives tomorrow, not by command, but by cohesion. And perhaps it was that *cohesion* that lived longest at Wall Hall. The sense that men could be shaped not by discipline alone, but by understanding; that character, elusive and contextual, was the true field of battle.

But then, in the evenings, his curiosity would turn to longing... longing for peace, for home, for his wife and child. Here, in this wartime spring, his loneliness resisted summarization. He missed her, not merely as a correspondent or a fellow parent, but as the one person capable of uplifting him. And as he sat to write to her, he found himself unexpectedly blank. In earlier letters, he had sketched in his days with economy: lectures given, reports filed, meals taken in institutional silence. But he couldn't keep that front up for long.

And so, without warning or elaborate construction, John Bowlby wrote, *How I wish you were here to cheer me up...*

***

It was by 1943, as London lay under a war-stained sky and rattled with the weight of men in uniform, that John Bowlby finally returned home. Ursula, who had been with her mother in the country, took Mary and joined him here, and after a while, the family was reunited.

But he had come here, again, on work. He had been transferred to the new Research and Training Centre for Officer Selection in Hampstead, which brought him back to London's crumbling heart; or, more specifically, to its intellectual arteries. And a return to London also meant that John Bowlby was free, at least partially, to pick up some long-neglected strands of research the war had kept him from. It also meant that he could take a more active part in his role as a member of the British Psycho-Analytical Society.

It was at one of the society's winter meetings that he encountered James Strachey, editor, translator of Freud, aristocrat of analysis. Strachey, grey of beard and deft with a kind of ironic detachment, mentioned casually that the International Journal of Psycho-Analysis had nothing scheduled for the upcoming volume.

"Nothing at all?" Bowlby asked.

"Not a word," Strachey replied, drawing on a cigarette, "unless you've something tucked away."

"I have been working on a rather long paper that might be suitable," Bowlby admitted.

"Ah," Strachey said, moderately surprised. "I should have thought the war effort should keep you busy."

"It does," Bowlby shrugged. "I've been working on it for quite a while...there's still work to do, but quite a bit's already done."

"Bring it in, then, man," Strachey counseled. "Now's the time."

And so John Bowlby went back home and dusted off his notes. He had written part of the paper already, before war duties swept him into the military's psychological scaffolding. Now, he took counsel from statisticians in the army and revised the paper carefully. What emerged, once submitted, was the now-famous paper on Forty-Four Juvenile Thieves, the study that would eventually earn him the moniker 'Ali-Bowlby and his Forty Thieves' among psychoanalytic wits who appreciated a good cognomen, if not subtlety.

Bowlby, shaped by years at Maudsley and University College Hospital, had never been content with abstract hypotheses. He employed statistical tests, case histories, character types. From a clinical standpoint, it was a triumph of form meeting inquiry: 44 children labeled thieves were studied in concert with 44 non-thieves, maladjusted, yes, but innocent of criminal act. Each child, thief or not, had passed through the corridors of the London Child Guidance Clinic between 1936 and 1939, those interwar years when Britain, fragile in its empire, was at least still confident in its institutions. The clinics promised salvation through talk, and Bowlby, in turn, promised clarity through pattern.

What emerged in the case histories was a taxonomy of emotional lives. He divided the children not merely by behavior but by character: the normal, the depressed, the circular, the hyperthymic, the affectionless, and the schizoid. The last three were of particular interest, but it was the affectionless who held his focus.

These children, he wrote, had no warmth, no affection. They were not defiant in the romanticized manner of literature's misunderstood urchins; rather, they were unreachable. They responded neither to kindness nor cruelty.

And more than a few of them, Bowlby noticed with clinical alarm, had lost their mothers in the crucial early years, or had been separated from them, sometimes for months, sometimes for good.

In this view, theft was not rebellion; it was substitution. The stolen object, whether food or toy, was a *symbol*, unconsciously sought. A biscuit pocketed, a pencil slipped silently into a coat...these were not acts of disobedience, but of longing. They were not crimes against property, but cries for presence. One could almost see the child pausing, breath held, not in fear of being caught, but in the silent hope that someone might notice, that someone might understand what had truly been taken from them long ago.

To understand this, one had to adopt a psychoanalytic lens but sharpened with empiricism. Freud's ghost hovered, yes, but Bowlby preferred to interrogate that ghost with a clipboard in hand. To him, each theft was a cipher, a displacement, a reaching out from absence. What was taken stood in place of something else; some maternal warmth, some lost constancy, some vanished figure who had once, perhaps, soothed a fevered forehead or sung nonsense songs while buttoning a small coat.

Among the affectionless thieves, 12 out of 14 had suffered early maternal separation. Among the controls? Only two. It was not a subtle pattern. His conclusion followed with the same inevitability as the war's daily casualty reports: early, prolonged separation from the mother or her substitute was indelibly related to delinquent character.

"Superego," Bowlby noted, "fails to develop without the affective bond."

Here was the crux. Without the mother, or her consistent substitute, the child could not internalize affection, and without affection, morality failed to take root. Not as a philosophical doctrine, but as an emotional experience.

He differentiated also between physical and perceived absence. It was not enough that the child's parents be cold, distant, or neurotic; that was common. Seventy to seventy-five percent of mothers in both groups, thieves and controls, displayed some form of neuroticism. But it was *absence* that mattered, and not any removal would do. The separation had to come after six months, once the child had begun to form attachments…and thus breaking what had just been made, so vulnerable and delicate.

Substitution was thus the resolution to the child's crisis: if the mother cannot be returned, then let her be echoed in anything that can be taken, anything that might briefly fill the void left behind by her absence.

And so Bowlby, walking through the gardens of Summerhill or sitting among the "maladjusted" at Priory Gate, saw not defiance but improvisation; children constructing their own tokens of love from the detritus left behind. He saw them, too, in the streets, London's forgotten waifs. They loitered near railings and soot-darkened shopfronts, their pockets full of nothing and their eyes large and hollow. In the drizzle-soaked dusk, these boys became names lost among files marked *Neglect, Larceny, Absent Father,* or lost in the shadows of systems that could not rehabilitate their sheer, impossible number.

231

He also understood that sociology, economy, and the ghost of war had altered the very architecture of childhood. Fathers were gone, or killed; mothers labored or trembled. The war had also laid bare England's contradictions. The state asked for sacrifice but gave little structure to shield the smallest from its costs. Families fractured; nurseries filled. Was there any surprise, then, that such children became thieves?

And yet, the prevailing institutions still clung to labels. *Delinquent*, they said; *maladjusted.* They became a sign of decaying morals to some, objects of pity, targets of rage, the face of crime.

But the crime was not theirs.

The crime had already happened.

He finalized his paper as the war continued, as bombers swooped down, as policy briefings rearranged the nation with memos and new maps for child welfare. Slowly, John Bowlby had begun to understand what war did to children. And it was not only the war itself, but the machinery it required, the institutions it reinforced, the hell of systems built for efficiency rather than care.

"You must understand," he said to a skeptical colleague at Priory Gate, "they are not protesting. They are making up for what we failed to give."

The colleague frowned. "So, sentimentality excuses delinquency now?"

Bowlby did not reply. He did not see sentimentality here; he saw the failure of systems, designed to rescue children and seeming to drain them instead. They offered food, shelter, sometimes even schooling, but not affection, not permanence. And without those, children drifted toward what adults called crime, but what Bowlby had come to recognize as improvisation.

And thus, they had become the group Bowlby named the Affectionless: those with hands that reached now only to take. They were not simply mischievous or unruly; they were marked, inscribed with a chronic truancy, a compulsion for remorseless offence.

All but one of these had wandered into serious trouble by a kind of psychological gravity. They did not rebel, for rebellion implies an object; something to resist, some tether to pull against. These children, Bowlby argued, were not merely troubled; they were the bearers of a devastating pattern. And what scared him was that more than half of the worst cases belonged to this group.

Now, when he wrote, there was a hint of his old, rebellious spirit woven through the scientific fabric of the paper. He implied it cautiously, but it was there nonetheless: he argued that the system, not just the mother, was responsible. Britain's institutions, the very war machine that sent mothers into nursing service or evacuation zones, could beget not only orphans of circumstance but also orphans of affection.

By the end of his paper, he made a call. Juvenile delinquency, he said, was not just a psychological matter, nor merely sociological or economic. It was a developmental disease, curable if caught early, perhaps incurable if left to harden past the age of eight. Nursery schools, infant welfare centers, networks of informed caretakers, these were not just niceties of a progressive state; they were, in Bowlby's reasoning, antidotes to future crimes.

The paper would be published in '44, and would circulate with unexpected velocity. It passed from psychiatrists to probation officers, across desks cluttered with case notes and tea rings, into the hands of Rees, who saw the intrinsic truth behind Bowlby's words.

"Doctor John Bowlby's fascinating paper," Rees wrote later, "is perhaps the best work that has yet been done in this country on the problem. It demonstrates the very great importance of this sense of deprivation of love in leading to delinquent conduct."

The praise was well-earned; after all, Bowlby had managed what few others had: to transmute observation into argument without losing the texture of the child's life. The paper did not simply describe "stealing"; it anatomized it, traced its roots backwards through time, not to genetics or class, but to the quieter cataclysms of being left behind. And perhaps the demand for his paper was born of a deep and disquieting recognition: that beneath the petty crimes of war-era children lay a history of unmet needs.

But of course, there were criticisms in time. They gathered slowly, like a tide that rose with the discipline's maturation, lapping at the edges of Bowlby's early work.

The reliance on memory was where the first fissures appeared. The study had asked children and their parents to recall events from the distant years of infancy and early childhood; the past, filtered through time, grief, pride, or shame, had to be rendered in words. How precise could those recollections have been? Memory, critics observed, was hardly a fixed ledger; it was a palimpsest, overwritten by the needs of the present. Parents might downplay neglect; a child might conflate separations; details might fade or rearrange themselves in the mind. What emerged could not be wholly trusted as data; yet Bowlby had treated these narratives as solid ground.

Researcher bias was next. Bowlby had been the architect and the builder; he devised the questions, conducted the interviews, interpreted the answers. His theory of maternal deprivation was already taking shape, and the study, consciously or not, seemed to bend toward confirming it. In later years, the charge of confirmation bias would become familiar in psychology; here, too, it found a foothold. Bowlby's interpretations, rich and persuasive, might have been less the objective mapping of evidence than the careful arrangement of it to support his design.

There was also the matter of what he had not seen or not looked for. The sample was small, drawn from a particular clinic in London; these forty-four young thieves could hardly stand as representatives of the vast and varied population of delinquent youth. Other influences, such as poverty, peer groups, education, etc., were noted only faintly or not at all. Critics argued that a study of thieves, by its nature, could not speak for those whose paths had been shaped by similar separations yet who had not turned to crime. The findings, therefore, were far from universal truth; the conclusions, critics said, were correlational at best. Early separation and delinquency had been shown to coexist, but the chain of causation was less certain.

So, could it be that both were the product of another factor entirely? Family conflict, social disadvantage, or inherited temperament…Bowlby had not proved otherwise, and for many, the leap from correlation to cause was too great.

Then came the ethical reckonings. In 1944, the protection of research participants had been a looser, more ambiguous matter. But from the vantage of later decades, the omissions were stark. Confidentiality had not been rigorously guarded; names and identifying details had appeared in publication. Consent was dubious. Could the young participants, some scarcely in adolescence, have understood what it meant to be part of a study whose findings would be bound to their histories and publicly discussed? And could their parents, in the urgency of seeking help, have weighed those implications? By the standards that evolved in later years, the safeguards were not there.

Next, many noted that maternal deprivation, in Bowlby's early formulation, seemed to act as the almost solitary explanation for juvenile delinquency. It was elegant in its simplicity; it was also, some argued, reductive. In fact, the scope of the study in general had been narrow. Its lens was fixed on the axis of mother and child, separation and loss; the peripheral conditions, the scaffolding of society in which those relationships unfolded, remained blurred. Later scholars would insist that no single thread could account for the tapestry of delinquency.

Yet for all the criticisms, the study's influence was undeniable. It had forced the question of early attachment into the foreground; it had made visible the emotional costs of loss in childhood; it had challenged the complacency of institutions that treated the separation of children from their primary caregivers as a neutral act. In fact, the paper's demand would grow so much in later years that by 1946, *Forty-Four Juvenile Thieves: Their Characters and Home-Life*, would be republished as a monograph.

236

But as he walked past waifs and saw the angry-eyed children in the clinics, John Bowlby worried for tomorrow. He worried for the children and about the war; he worried for his own child, for his wife. And day after day, he worried and he tried his best and he wrote…for what else was a man to do?

Chapter 11.

The Peacemaker

But as this struggle continued, John Bowlby was embroiled in another struggle, this time in the ever-volatile landscape of the British Psycho-Analytical Society, a body as fractured and freighted with ideology as the nation itself.

From 1943 onwards, as war was drawing longer shadows across the British Isles, the internal politics of society were in full swing. To speak of psychoanalysis in wartime England is to speak of fire beneath ash; the debates within the Society did not merely echo the disruptions of the war but were a mirror to them. The certainties of empire, gender, and parenthood were eroding; in the shadows of old paradigms, new thoughts were beginning to take root.

These were not ordinary academic disagreements. They were intellectual hostilities animated by personalities who had endured exiles, losses, and betrayals. The Society's meetings became warzones of velvet-padded rooms hiding sharpened tongues. A scathing remark by Ella Sharpe during this time makes the point with a scalpel: "If you are looking for ideal parents or an ideal band of brothers and sisters, then don't join the British Psycho-Analytical Society." Behind the closed doors of these debates, held while ration books thinned, fathers died abroad, and children were bundled onto trains with name-tags, two women defined the landscape:

Melanie Klein and Anna Freud.

Klein, a fiercely inventive émigré who returned to London in 1941 after evacuation, saw in the infant's early months a primal theater of aggression and guilt. For her, the child's internal life, ferocious, unconscious, and symbolic, was shaped long before speech. She argued that the superego emerged in the child not after the father's authority had been impressed during the Oedipal phase, but within the child's earliest relationship to the mother. "The Oedipus conflict sets in as early as the second half of the first year," she had written in 1932. In these early dramas, play was the performance and the interpretation of its stage. Her radical, imaginative, and unwavering approach was a reimagination, or even a rebirth of orthodox Freudianism.

Anna Freud, by contrast, worked from a place more grounded in what could be seen and nurtured. For her, the superego was not a self-generating apparatus but an echo of the external world; of parents, their prohibitions and permissions, of social order impressed from without. Children, she insisted, did not yet possess the developmental strength to self-analyze. They could not yet carry the weight of the internal judicial system Klein assigned them.

Klein's insistence that play equaled verbal association, that the child's game of blocks and dolls was, in effect, a coded confession, was at odds with Anna Freud's more structured and educational approach. Where Klein saw

239

primal scenes lurking behind every dollhouse, Anna Freud sought scaffolding: developmental readiness, family interviews, collaboration with schools. The difference was less aesthetic than philosophical: should the child be treated like a miniature adult or as someone growing, incomplete, whose ego needed support?

Though he agreed with both of them at different points, John Bowlby ultimately resisted taking sides. At the London Child Guidance Clinic, Bowlby had employed play therapy, a seeming endorsement of Klein's view. But in his writings and reflections, he placed increasing importance on working with parents, collecting detailed life histories, and attending to "reality factors." Whether by design or not, this was John Bowlby asserting an emerging third position: neither Anna Freud nor Melanie Klein, but a new framework built on observations that arose from the realization that England was facing a very real crisis of the mind.

***

But the country was facing more than just one kind of crisis.

As the war wore on, England's situation was rapidly worsening. It was not merely that bread was scarce or petrol prohibited; it was that life, as it had been previously construed, had been broken open. Ration books replaced dinner tables; fathers disappeared into uniforms; mothers learned to repair engines and manage accounts. It was a strange and brand new world in the making, and its birth would come in the throes of a dying past.

This was the very mood reflected in the Society as well, in part. The old order, in its tweeds and its Viennese certainties, appeared slightly ridiculous under the fluorescent lights of wartime pragmatism.

"We are all amateurs now," said one analyst, drily, after a meeting collapsed into shouting over Klein's superego thesis.

Bowlby, not certain enough yet to split off into a wholly new path, nevertheless saw the cracks. They were everywhere; in theory, in practice, in the city, in the nursery. The child, once the quiet subject of adult projections, was now making claims of its own. And Bowlby, unlike most of his colleagues, was listening.

Now, Bowlby's work, which had always been quietly radical, began to treat the child's attachment to the caregiver not as a metaphor but as a mechanism.

So when John Bowlby visited those fractious meetings of the Society and sat through tiresome squabbles over *constitutions* and *committee terms*, he sat through them because he knew something larger was at stake. It was not only the battle between Freudian purity or Kleinian deviation. It was a reckoning with the modern child, born into uncertainty and shaped by global catastrophe. Bowlby listened, watched, disagreed; but more than that, he observed the child as neither an abstraction nor a symbol, but a human being.

Nonetheless, the factionalism in the society was continuing to grow by the day, a fact that confounded John Bowlby.

As far as he was concerned, both women had become caricatures of their own rigor; mirror images of each other, as he would later say, each locked in the certainty of her own interpretation, each unable, or unwilling, to concede ground to the other. Now, into this impasse came a third group, almost by necessity rather than design:

The Independents.

Bowlby found a natural home among them, not because he lacked views, but because he refused dogma. He did not believe in purity; he believed in synthesis. James Strachey, the translator of Freud and a man not easily flattered by controversy, described the matter with cutting accuracy: "The trouble seems to me to be with extremism, on both sides... These attitudes on both sides are, of course, purely religious and the very antithesis of science."

Ultimately, the real quarrel was not whose theory best explained the child, but who would shape the future analysts; who would train them, influence them, and mold them in their image.

It was during these years that Bowlby's administrative talent, often overlooked in accounts that focus only on his intellectual evolution, emerged. This was noticed by one Sylvia Payne, one of the pioneers of psychoanalysis in the United Kingdom, sister to the Governor General of Ceylon, and a long-time part of the Society. This played a part when Sylvia Payne was elected President of the Society and named Bowlby as Training Secretary. This was a position so central that it immediately sparked protest. Klein and Riviere immediately objected: Bowlby was not a training analyst, and as per them, he lacked the qualifications. The position, they believed, demanded someone inside the clinical tradition.

But Payne, who understood that the Society could not afford another rupture, held her ground. Bowlby, she replied, was not only an excellent organizer (he had managed logistical and research operations both in child guidance and in the army) but he was trusted, and trust was, at this moment, a rarer currency than theoretical alignment.

Bowlby took the role not as a mediator, but as a designer. He knew it was futile to try to resolve the unresolvable; instead, he had to build an architecture within which differences could co-exist.

And so, he set to work.

He admired aspects of both traditions, but did not see them as irreconcilable positions; they were fragments of a larger system that Bowlby sensed, though it had yet to be fully articulated. His impulse was not to discard either perspective, but to relate them to observable development, to patterns not only evident in the analytic couch but in bomb shelters, orphanages, and hospitals. The war had democratized childhood trauma. One no longer needed theoretical elaboration to see it; one only needed eyes.

There was something English in his method: not a sense of confrontation, but accommodation. He avoided abstraction; he worked with the grain of institutions and took another look at both approaches. He saw how the Kleinians, for all their perceptive insights into early fantasy and guilt, remained curiously uninterested in the lived world of the child. He saw too how Anna Freud, with her firm anchoring in reality, often reduced complex emotional structures to matters of adaptation.

And soon, he was done.

At the end of his restructuring, he set forth a proposal. What he had designed, quite literally, was a system. Two training paths: Course A and Course B. The first adhered to the older pre-war methods of the British Society, rooted more closely in the continental tradition. The second incorporated the innovations favored by Anna Freud and her supporters, particularly with regard to child analysis. Both tracks would run in parallel; neither would have the authority to cancel the other.

It was, in a sense, a constitutional compromise, a kind of psychological federalism.

The agreement was reluctantly signed by all three leaders, Payne, Klein, and Anna Freud. That none of them were satisfied in full may well be the clearest indication of its success. As Bowlby recalled with faint amusement, he also implemented a reform that was as personal as it was structural: a four-year limit on the duration of training. No longer would candidates wander indefinitely through supervision and analysis; the process would be clear, bounded, and achievable. He had suffered enough delays and ambiguities; he would not pass those on.

There were many ironies in the arrangement. That Bowlby, who would later challenge some of psychoanalysis's most entrenched ideas, should have been the one to save its fragile internal pluralism; that Klein, so certain of her originality, should have needed a bureaucratic compromise to preserve her place; that Anna Freud, daughter of the founder, should have submitted, at least on paper, to an arrangement that made her one option among several.

244

And yet such ironies were inevitable, and arguably, were only the signs of a living discipline.

And of course, it was not a clean peace. The discussions ended with no scientific resolution. Positions remained entrenched. But there was, for the first time in years, a framework. And that framework, though imperfect and provisional, would have to be enough.

In the quiet after the meetings, in the long train rides between London and the countryside where children evacuated from the city were being studied, Bowlby began to think more clearly. His work was no longer only about theory; it was about systems of care. The psychological could no longer be extracted from the social. Training, theory, policy, all would need to be aligned if children were to be understood and helped.

Later in the 1940s, the Society would settle into its uneasy truce. Analysts would continue to train under their chosen paths. Students would still whisper about whose views were more modern, more scientific, more humane. But they would train, and they would practice.

And John Bowlby would carry the lessons of this venture not only into his research but into the institutions of postwar Britain.

Chapter 12.

After the War

By May, the war had been won in Europe; by September, the Pacific Theatre would also collapse under the weight of a nuclear blaze.

Europe breathed a sigh of shaky relief. The war had taken its toll; entire nations had been turned into itinerant societies as people moved not from city to city but from ruin to ruin, searching for a house, a cousin, a reason to stay. Berlin itself had become a kind of theatre of the absurd: Soviet tanks parked in the shadow of shattered cathedrals, even as children dug through trash for bread rations. In Paris, the liberation had already become memory, sweetened in retrospect, though the ration queues remained.

In England, the fall of the Axis was heralded with church bells pealing in scattered tones across English hillsides; with the uncoordinated singing of "Land of Hope and Glory" in pubs and streets where only weeks before the blackout had still been enforced. In London, people gathered without instruction. Trafalgar Square filled like a tide coming in. They climbed lamp-posts and kissed strangers; they lit bonfires from broken furniture, and for the first time in nearly six years, not a single person stopped them.

Victory in Europe, VE Day, was declared on May 8th, 1945, and Churchill, in that characteristic blend of gravel and ceremony, told the British people they had "come safely through the worst and most prolonged trial they have ever endured."

There had been victory, yes, but at immense cost. The men who returned from fighting often found themselves foreign in their own homes. Their children, raised in evacuation or in households dominated by mothers and aunts, regarded them with awkward awe or outright defiance. Marriage, long delayed or hastily undertaken, had frayed at the edges. Divorce rates spiked. And not all the wounds were visible.

For women, the end of the war was not liberation. It was a kind of demobilization of identity. During the war, they had been summoned into work: in factories, on farms, in offices, and underground stations. They had worn trousers, carried tools, and tasted a species of independence that had not been offered before, not without judgment, at least. But now, as soldiers returned, they were asked to relinquish those roles.

And meanwhile, the very idea of childhood had been irrevocably reshaped. Children had lived years apart from their parents; they had been reared by strangers, by councils, by the improvisational love of foster homes and institutional shelters. As John Bowlby had feared, the war had definitely taken its toll on an entire generation.

As for London...that great citadel of endurance emerged that May like a scarred witness. Its face was altered, with half-demolished streets, scorched parks, and gutted terraces. In Bethnal Green and Elephant and Castle, children still played among debris. They turned craters into dens; they knew which rubble piles yielded tin toys and which held shards too sharp for boots already worn to the welt.

England had survived the second Great War, even despite great losses. The age of bombs and rationing was ended; now, the time was ripe for an age of hammers and cranes.

Accordingly, reconstruction began before the celebration had even finished. There was too much to be done; roofs to be patched, railways re-laid, lives coaxed into coherence. The 1945 Labour government, under Attlee, now pushed forward policies that would reshape the very architecture of British life: the National Health Service, nationalized industries, and education reform. It was a kind of moral inheritance from the war, the idea that having endured together, the country must now care for itself collectively.

In September 1945, John Bowlby was invited to a weekend conference, one of those curious postwar gatherings in which political theorists, psychologists, civil servants, and skeptical ministers came together to ask not only what could be built from the ruins, but what should be. The conference, framed around "the psychological and sociological problems of modern socialism," was infused with the earnestness of a country trying to think anew. There were ministers present, like his old friend Durbin, and thinkers such as Mannheim, Cole, and Panken.

248

At this gathering, Bowlby presented a paper he called Psychology and Democracy. It was published the following year in The Political Quarterly, a left-leaning journal unafraid of challenging political orthodoxy. The paper was, in tone and method, uncharacteristic of the Bowlby who would later become synonymous with maternal deprivation. Here, his concerns lay not in nurseries or hospitals but in the very shape of political life. He referenced Kurt Lewin, whose American social psychology had, through wartime networks, found its way to Bowlby's desk via his colleague Eric Trist. Lewin's experimental studies of children's behaviour under autocratic, democratic, and laissez-faire group structures offered empirical grounding for a politics of care, discipline, and autonomy.

But now, a new project was calling for his attention, and this is how John Bowlby found himself travelling to central London, heading towards Tavistock Square.

***

In January of 1946, when the debris of war had generally been swept under the rug of London's new peacetime routines, John Bowlby stepped across the threshold of the Tavistock Clinic.

The Tavistock had been many things since its founding in 1920 by Hugh Crichton-Miller; first, a place for nervous disorders, mild eccentricities, and the psychological tremors of clergymen and middle-class housewives; later, under the duress of global conflict, a recruiting ground for army psychiatrists, who found themselves stationed in field

249

hospitals and barracks rather than drawing rooms. Before the war, psychoanalysts of the stricter sort had dismissed the Tavistock as a kind of well-meaning sideshow. The phrase "Parsons' clinic" had circulated with a sort of condescension.

But war had changed things.

Even as artillery had redefined the contours of Europe, so too did wartime service redraw the boundaries between psychology's competing houses. Now, analysts and psychiatrists work side by side. The Army Group, as they came to be known, was less a movement than a convergence: men and women from disparate branches of psychiatry drawn together under the collective demands of military necessity. The Tavistock had become their anchor.

John Bowlby, now, knew he had the opportunity to build something. With the Army Group and others like him, he knew there was a chance to do something...new.

"Who knows," he mentioned to his wife with a shrug. "Something might just come out of it."

And something did.

What had been a wartime improvisation became the nucleus of a postwar vision, and the world was watching with interest. The Rockefeller Foundation, with characteristic transatlantic foresight, took note. Dr. Alan Gregg, their medical adviser, visited in person. With him came a team of psychologists, ostensibly to study with them.

Alan Gregg was a man who had spent years in the medical division, helped develop the USA's model for medical research funding, and helped finance the development of sulfanilamide and penicillin. He was a

250

serious-looking man with faint eyebrows, a broad forehead, and a piercing gaze; as they shook hands, John Bowlby knew recognition from this man, this might be a big step not just for the clinic, but the discipline as a whole. Now, he observed their work, noted the range of talents, and, crucially, understood its potential.

At the end of this affair, Greggs put forth an offer: a £22,000 investment, distributed over three years beginning in February 1946, to develop a new model of preventive and social psychiatry. From this fund, a new branch of the institute was born: the Tavistock Institute of Human Relations.

It would now spearhead the Tavistock project's own, in-house restructuring drive, which they called *Operation Phoenix*. The metaphor was too apt to ignore: out of ruins, something reborn. What they were reconstructing would be the very meaning of mental health, of institutional care, of the relationship between private trouble and public condition.

And soon, this new limb of the institute was up and running.

Immediately, the new body would be tested in the crucible of post-war need. Requests immediately came in by the droves; industrial firms wanted help managing personnel, addressing morale, and increasing productivity. But at the center of the reorganization was the question of children: how to understand them, how to treat them, how to recognize what war had done to the most silently affected generation.

But here, conflict reemerged. This was not the ghost of the old Freud-Klein division, but a newer tension between tradition and innovation. The Children's Department of the Tavistock, though its origins went back to 1926, had operated with a degree of autonomy that now seemed untenable. The Interim Medical Committee, established to chart the postwar direction of the Clinic, found itself at odds with the old Children's Department.

Solutions needed to be found, but the Committee members saw no value in picking sides. What they wanted was a clinic for children that did not isolate but contextualized...and for this, they needed the right people.

In the end, three names were put forth.

There was Winnicott, beloved by some for his deep intuition, dismissed by others for his sometimes theatrical gentleness.

Evelyn Lucas: competent and established, but perhaps too entrenched already.

And then there was one John Bowlby: a man whose Army Group associations, organizational skill, and growing reputation in child guidance made him a natural candidate, even if no one would say so outright.

In the end, his skill, connections, and reputation were enough to win him the position.

For his part, John Bowlby accepted the post quietly, without ceremony; by January of 1946, he had begun his work at the head of the new Children's Department.

Outside the Clinic, Britain still wobbled on the threshold between austerity and hope. Ration books

252

lingered; housing was scarce; coal strikes threatened to undo fragile gains. But inside the Tavistock, the reconstruction was still taking place.

By the end of that year, another transition was upcoming. Rees, the wartime director who had guided the Tavistock through its army years and into this postwar form, offered his resignation. It was not forced; it was, in some sense, inevitable.

Rees had enabled the rise of a wave of brilliant minds; now it was time to step aside in their favor.

In July 1947, the succession was completed as Sutherland was elected Director. With this came a rise for John Bowlby as well, who became his deputy. From then, the Tavistock entered its second life. The psychoanalysts who had once sniffed at its Christian roots now found themselves working alongside its staff, drawn in by the Clinic's expanding remit and increasing prestige. The lines between disciplines blurred as social psychiatry, industrial consultancy, family therapy, and child development were now all spoken in the same corridors.

Bowlby, for his part, did not concern himself with flamboyant theoretical gestures. He was not a prophet; he was an investigator. He read widely, questioned methodically, and resisted doctrinal allegiance. He had grown impatient with the internal feuds that had paralyzed other institutions like the Society. What mattered to him now was clarity: how attachment formed, how it failed, what it meant for the future of a child if the first bonds were fractured.

So in those dense, transitional years when the shadow of victory lay awkwardly over a fraying empire,

253

John Bowlby would find himself walking deliberately through the long corridors of the Children's Department, deliberating on the future.

His first task, as he saw it, was to build a clinical service.

"A good clinical service," he remarked to his colleagues, "must be the foundation. Without it, neither training nor research means much."

He was convinced of this fact; after all, he had worked in places where ambition outpaced infrastructure, where theory floated above practice like steam above a kettle.

He would not allow it again. Not here.

The Tavistock, with its layered history and its recent reinvention under Operation Phoenix, lent itself to bold experiment. He recruited with precision, selecting individuals not for their credentials alone but for their alignment with his growing vision of child psychiatry. Among his first appointments was Esther Bick, a Polish-born psychologist immersed at the time in psychoanalytical training with the British Psycho-Analytical Society. Her manner was unassuming; her insight, fierce. She would later be known for her work in infant observation, but in those early days, she was simply one of the few who understood that a child's distress could not be separated from the web of relationships in which it was spun.

He also brought in Noel Hunnybun, a senior social worker he had known from the pre-war London Child Guidance Clinic. They shared a professional language shaped by years of dealing with the raw material of disrupted

254

childhoods. Hunnybun, after the war, had sought precisely such a setting, a place where analytic training could be applied, not archived. She wished for a place where her role would not be auxiliary but essential. The Tavistock would offer her nine years of precisely that.

By autumn of 1946, the Children's Department had opened its child guidance services.

In Parliament, the Labour government pressed forward with the architecture of the welfare state: housing acts, education reform, and the groundwork for the NHS. Children returned to school under the provisions of the 1944 Education Act, many for the first time with proper meals and regular instruction. And as the leaves along the Thames embankment turned brittle gold, the guidance services began in earnest.

That year alone, 313 new patients passed through the Department's doors, each one carrying in their small bodies the weight of absence, upheaval, uncertainty. Some were orphans in the literal sense; others had families intact in name but not in function. The war had loosened attachments, scrambled affections, and left many children adrift in homes that no longer knew how to be homes.

Of course, they were not alone in their efforts. Across Britain, the recommendations of the Curtis Committee were taking hold. Formed in the war's immediate aftermath to assess the condition and care of children removed from their homes, the Committee represented a national reckoning. Britain, having fought for civilization abroad, now turned inward to measure the civility of its own care systems. The 1946 Curtis Report, bolstered by the Education Act of 1944 and foreshadowing the Children Act of 1948, urged local authorities to assume active responsibility. Child guidance, once the work of a few determined practitioners, was to become a matter of the state.

Bowlby, like many others, gave evidence to the Committee. He was precise, almost clinical, in his phrasing, but beneath the testimony ran a steady current of conviction. He believed that mental health could not be tacked on after the fact. It had to begin early; it had to begin at home. Or, in the absence of home, it had to be constructed deliberately, through relationships strong enough to hold a child's developing sense of self.

There was, however, a problem.

There were not enough trained professionals. The postwar expansion in child care had outpaced supply. Thus, in parallel with clinical work, Bowlby began to organize training programmes for child psychiatrists, for educational psychologists, for social workers, and non-medical psychotherapists. Training, he knew, was more than an appendage to clinical service; it was inseparable from it.

This principle was embedded in the Tavistock doctrine: *no research without therapy, and no therapy without research.*

In a small room with dusty light and mismatched chairs, Bowlby outlined the method of child guidance that he had first absorbed at the London Child Guidance Clinic. "We begin," he would explain to new staff, "not with the child, but with the relationship in which the child is embedded." It was an inversion of the medical model; diagnosis was not a naming of symptoms, but a mapping of ties.

The procedure was as follows: first, a preparatory meeting with both parents. This was an essential step, as Bowlby insisted. Even in the many cases where only the mother arrived, the invitation to both mattered. It set the tone: this was not a question of the child alone, but of the relational field in which the child existed. Then came a second meeting with mother and child, in which the child's cognitive abilities were assessed by an educational psychologist while the mother was interviewed by a psychiatric social worker.

A week later, all parties would reconvene.

The parents, interviewed separately and together, would provide parallel narratives, confirming or contradicting. Meanwhile, the child was seen by a psychiatrist.

There was to be no rush to *prescribe*. No predetermined template. The idea was to gather enough of the child's ecology, the movements of affection and withdrawal, the positions held by different family members, the tone of domestic life, to begin to understand what had gone wrong, and where healing might begin.

"We stress in particular," Bowlby would write in a 1948 report, "the importance of the relationship of the child to his mother and the members of the family with whom he has to share her during the early years of life."

The words carried the weight of deep observation. From early relationships, he argued, came either the groundwork for emotional resilience or the fault lines along which future disorders would grow. If a child's first bonds were secure, the world could be approached with confidence; if those bonds were ruptured or confused, life

257

would be marked by a persistent unease, a difficulty in trusting others or oneself.

In the still-crumbling spaces of postwar London, this was not abstract theory. It was a daily reality. Children, adrift in new schools and temporary housing, in foster placements and institutional dormitories, carried into every encounter the shape of their earliest attachments, or their absence.

The work was exhausting. Bowlby held to high standards. He demanded rigour from his staff, not as a matter of prestige, but because he knew that inexact treatment could do harm. These children could not afford harm. They had already lived through enough of it. And still, in that department, among overburdened workers and the thick, slow machinery of state intervention, something grew: a practice that was empirical, intuitive, and above all, relational.

And unknown to many, it was to be a practice that would, over time, change how Britain thought about children and how it cared for them.

But it was also there, within the twin spheres of practice and study, that John Bowlby would encounter friction. The Tavistock, with its clusters of practitioners steeped in the language of Melanie Klein, did not uniformly welcome his views. Klein's influence still drifted through the halls; evocative, elliptical, abstract. There was poetry in her notion of the inner world of the child, a symphony of phantasy and projection. Bowlby, by contrast, stood squarely in the daylight: he believed in real mothers, real fathers, real absences that left real scars.

When he had brought on Esther Bick, he had believed that her psychoanalytic path would remain

Independent. "Michael Balint is her analyst," he had said to a colleague, half in assurance, half in hope. Balint, like Bowlby, stood apart from the Kleinians. But no sooner had she settled in than Bick shifted allegiance, drawn irrevocably into Klein's orbit. "She became," Bowlby would later say, not without a trace of disappointment, "one of Mrs. Klein's most devoted disciples." There was no malice in this reflection; only a kind of measured regret.

It was clear then, painfully clear, that if John Bowlby wanted to pursue his hypotheses, his structured, observation-based, environmentally grounded inquiries, he would have to establish a separate domain. Not an adjunct to therapy, but an autonomous research unit.

Clinical work and research had to become neighboring states: each with its own customs, each requiring a different passport. "Two distinct worlds," he would say later. "And when you are operating in the one world, it is proper to have one frame of reference; when you cross the road and operate in the other, quite another."

This idea, that epistemologies must be contextual, was his attempt at a practical solution to a tension that ran through the very fabric of postwar psychoanalysis.

***

By 1948, the Tavistock Clinic had come under the broad, bureaucratic wing of the National Health Service.

The NHS did not so much arrive as emerge from meetings in Whitehall, from memos passed between desks, from tired hands lifting teacups beside flickering gas fires. There had been hospitals before, certainly; wards manned by

259

pale nurses in long aprons, charity-funded, church-adjacent, overstretched. But this was different; this was systemic. It was structural. It was the State, no longer aloof, stooping to attend to the bruises and breaks of the body, the dim muddle of the mind.

And, inevitably, resistance came.

From doctors, from editors, from those who saw the State as an intruder in the sanctum of professional discretion. Yet the pressure of war had changed things; evacuation had exposed what had been concealed: rickets, lice, tubercular coughs in children barely five. There had been, in the camps and temporary schools and converted churches, a reckoning. The empire had stretched itself to the edge of ruin only to discover that the health of its citizens was not assured. And so the Ministry moved forth with determination. Aneurin Bevan, the architect, faced the glare of Parliament and the growl of the press, and did not retreat.

Finally, after a long struggle, hospitals were nationalized. For some, it felt like a theft; for others, like a beginning. In London, nurses unpacked fresh linens in hospitals now marked not by crests but by a new seal: the NHS. In Manchester, coal miners' children were seen by a doctor for the first time without charge. Everywhere, the ledger was being rewritten not by market rates or private need, but by a common assumption: that illness should not mean ruin; that health, at last, might be a right, not a reward.

And so, quietly, the State began to care.

In the case of Tavistock, the NHS now provided funds, but only sparingly; Bowlby's aspirations exceeded the budgets meted out to him. Still, he managed to make ends

260

meet through what must have been a formidable network of correspondents needed to secure a modest grant.

With this, he could begin.

The question he chose to pursue was one that had been with him for years, rooted perhaps in the orphanages he had visited during the war, or the temporary homes into which children were thrust during evacuations. The new cause was to be the old cause, one that had driven him for years now with the threat he knew it posed. It was a threat contained unassumingly within the one word he had thought about the most during the war:

Separation.

Separation as a measurable rupture: the tragedy of the child sundered from his mother or mother-figure in the early, formative years of life. It was a phenomenon, Bowlby argued, that had been overlooked precisely because it was so ordinary, so embedded in wartime and postwar life. And yet, its consequences, be they emotional, social, or pathological, seemed to him profound. And as a victim of separation as a child, it is no surprise why he thought so.

In practical terms, though, four reasons shaped his choice. First, separation was definable; it happened or it didn't. In a field awash with ambiguous variables, this clarity had methodological appeal. Second, it caused harm, often *profound* harm, on development. Third, it was, perhaps, preventable. Fourth, and most pointedly, it had been underestimated by the very community tasked with understanding children.

That neglect, John Bowlby believed, had to be redressed.

261

His hypothesis was this: a continuous, loving relationship with a mother or substitute during the first five years was a biological necessity. Its absence, the rupture, was pathological in its consequence.

To begin this inquiry, Bowlby needed hands and eyes. He appointed James Robertson as his first research assistant. Robertson had been a conscientious objector during the war; he and his wife Joyce had taken refuge at the Hampstead Nursery, run by Dorothy Burlingham and Anna Freud. Everyone, regardless of role, had to observe, to note, to document the daily lives of children. Observation was a discipline. Robertson had practiced it until it had become almost second nature.

In his work ethic, Bowlby found a kindred spirit. Robertson, unpolished in academia but rich in direct experience, became his implementer. Together they began to construct protocols for studying separation by watching children, moment by moment, in hospital wards and nurseries, across hours and days.

Their approach was, at first, met with skepticism. The idea that observable behavior in the aftermath of maternal separation could lead to enduring psychological disturbance was not widely accepted. The Kleinians, in particular, dismissed it as reductive; they saw pathology as blooming from within, shaped by internal phantasy, not external disruption. But Bowlby, methodically, continued. He formed an advisory committee, pulling together pediatricians, child psychiatrists, psychologists, nurses, and social workers in a rare confluence of disciplines. And in these weekly gatherings with coffee gone cold and papers scrawled over in pencil, the future of attachment theory quietly gestated.

They knew the research would be slow, and it would, above all, require fidelity to the minutia, to the observable, to the real. Bowlby had chosen a long, slow path, but he had chosen it clearly.

***

Yet in the years between war's end and the slow rise of institutional psychiatry, John Bowlby found himself split between a variety of causes other than the Tavistock project.

He rose late by the standards of his contemporaries, those gray-suited men of 1940s London who paced corridors before the morning mist had lifted; Bowlby began his workday around ten. But the hour at which he began his rounds at the Tavistock Clinic did little to protect the rest of his evenings. They were filled with committees, lectures, boards, and advisory councils that sprawled into twilight. Often, he returned after supper had cooled, shoes dusty with the day's obligations; sometimes, he left again shortly after dinner, as though the domestic space could only half-contain him.

Ursula eventually drew a line: three evenings a week, she said, and no more. He agreed, but even at home, John Bowlby remained half elsewhere.

He found himself writing in political journals, and for good reason. For John Bowlby, the line between public and private life was never absolute; psychological well-being, he believed, depended not only on mothers and homes but on policies, principles, and institutions. And yet, in the same months that he composed articles for these journals,

263

Bowlby also gave talks on the BBC. These were modest broadcasts, intended for parents more than professionals. They were published in 1948, and in them he addressed the delicate, often unspoken problems of the day: the return of a father from war, unrecognised by the child he had left behind; the tensions in homes reassembled under ceilings that had not been bombed but still bore cracks.

His tone was direct, explaining in his even rhythm the psychological bewilderment of children who had grown in absence. These talks were based, one suspects, not only on theory, but on the cases arriving at the Tavistock's Children's Department week after week.

Bowlby's professional life, then, was not a single channel. Alongside his work at the Clinic and his efforts with the research unit, he retained his position within the British Psycho-Analytical Society. From 1944 to 1948, he was a member of its Council; until 1947, he served as its Training Secretary. It was not a comfortable arrangement. He did not pursue analytic training in the traditional sense; he declined the opportunity to become a training analyst. But he gave lectures on child development to first-year students, and, perhaps more importantly, helped establish a dual-course structure that would allow for different theoretical allegiances to coexist without rupture.

There was, however, more than governance and theory to his routine. Once a week, on a weekday afternoon, Bowlby left the Tavistock and travelled across town to a Maternity and Child Welfare Centre. There, he met with groups of mothers attempting, as women have always done, to raise children in circumstances never quite stable. These were discussion groups; they met in clinic rooms over tea, among prams and coats. The idea was simple and radical: to create a space where mothers could articulate their feelings, learn from one another, and better understand the goals of child development.

He did not stop there. His voice, urgent and increasingly confident, was heard also in the inner rooms of government. He joined the Mental Health Standing Advisory Committee in 1949, which was a body convened under the new NHS to advise on mental health and disability policy. It was, in theory, a place of influence. In practice, it was often a place of friction; the fact was that Bowlby's earnest, unrelenting, and intellectual manner did not sit well with the civil servants. He was described in less than favorable terms, for he was in their eyes only an advanced theorist.

Still, he spoke. He argued for preventive psychiatry, for the integration of family care into mental health services, for better training of professionals working with children. He called, most notably, for a separate department of government devoted to children's welfare, a body that could coordinate efforts otherwise split between the Ministry of Health, the Ministry of Education, the Home Office, and the Board of Control.

Ultimately, nothing came of the suggestion, but it marked him as someone who did not simply observe the fragmentation of systems, but tried, however unsuccessfully, to stitch them together.

And while John Bowlby moved through clinics, lecture halls, and government panels, his wife Ursula was shaping words of her own. She wrote in *Nursery World* and *Childhood*, journals with a readership composed of young mothers, of women balancing the mystery of infant moods with the demands of wartime ration books and postwar exhaustion.

She had been working on a manual for new mothers; Bowlby read it eagerly, sent back comments, even suggested a title: *Broken Hearts and Broken Rules: A Book About Babies.*

In the end, however, the manuscript faltered on the threshold of publication. Preliminary reviews from acquaintances were unfavorable, and the book was seen too close to John Bowlby's own work. In the face of this, Ursula withdrew the book from publication.

It was true that her efforts were already fully demanded at home; after all, the late nights and constant work of her husband meant that she had to double her parenting responsibilities. This sustained absence also took a toll on Bowlby's family; his children struggled to make sense of a father only half-available to them.

"Is Daddy a burglar?" one of them once asked Ursula.

The question startled her. "Why ever would you ask that?"

"Well," the child said slowly. "He comes home after dark. And he doesn't tell us about his day."

Ursula couldn't help but laugh at this, but still, it was a fact that this was a household where the urgency of the father's vocation rarely allowed for bonding, idle conversation, or shared hobbies.

John's brother, Tony, would often wonder at the particular tone in Bowlby's interaction with the children. He dismissed them, jokingly and perhaps unconsciously, with family nicknames that reduced them, rendered them manageable. Juliet Hopkins, a longtime associate, thought he failed to introduce them to the things that mattered to him outside his clinical world: pictures, ideas, the delicate arts of appreciation. He took them on holidays, yes, long ones; but the substance of the father-child relationship, she suspected, remained ceremonial.

These holidays followed a predictable pattern. The Bowlbys visited the maternal homes; there were summer weeks spent in the shadow of Bowlby's mother and Ursula's mother, grandmothers whose presence recalled earlier generations of child-rearing philosophies.

But in the summer of '48, when Bowlby was in his early forties, there waited an event that would occur with tragic suddenness. While on holiday, he discovered that his closest friend, Evan Durbin, had drowned while on holiday himself. He died after having rescued two children from the water.

The shock was unforgiving.

How could Evan Durbin be dead?

He had been more than just a companion; Durbin had been Bowlby's lodger, housemate, wedding best man, fellow thinker. They had shared both space and sensibility; theirs was a friendship rooted in a history, a purpose, and long conversations carried late into the night. It was a friendship that had weathered war, austerity, academic divergence, and political disappointment.

Durbin had been living, speaking, writing, acting...and then, quite suddenly, he was gone.

267

Bowlby, vacationing nearby, was summoned into the aftermath of the catastrophe that had stunned all who knew Durbin. He did what he knew best how to do: organize, take responsibility, fill the gaps left by the departed. Together with Durbin's parliamentary colleagues, he set up a trust fund to support the education of the children who had just lost their father. It was done swiftly, effectively, with the sort of measured, distant compassion that characterized Bowlby's professional life.

Ursula would later write that the loss of Durbin was the greatest personal blow of Bowlby's life. There had been other losses, but Durbin's death was of another order.

What would he do now?

The short answer, of course, was to return to work; that was his only real way of dealing with grief. It was all waiting for him: the meetings at the British Psycho-Analytical Society, the manuscripts, training programs, advisory councils…and of course, the Tavistock.

And as he got ready for his day by nine, sleepless since the early hours of dawn, John Bowlby reflected perhaps on the frailty of life, or the pain of grief, or the constancy of death as a final separation. Perhaps he thought of all of these things or none of them as he looked out of his window at the grey London morning, and perhaps he shook his thoughts away as he grabbed his coat, his leather bag, and hurried out of the door.

***

Meanwhile, during the first eighteen months of the Tavistock research unit, Bowlby and Robertson found themselves deep in the field.

James Robertson's early days were consumed by quiet, slow pilot studies conducted in clinics and hospitals, sanatoriums, and fever wards. These were not glamorous places. The floors smelled of disinfectant; the air was heavy with procedural silence and coughs. Coughing as he adjusted his squarish, thick-rimmed spectacles, he observed with a pen in hand as infants were parted from their mothers for reasons deemed medically necessary. He tried, painstakingly, to distinguish between what pain was caused by the illness, what by the arrival of a sibling, what by the sheer act of being alone.

But the data resisted clarity. In children experiencing short separations, variables were tangled like roots beneath soil; the effects of fevers and new babies muddied the waters. And so the field of inquiry shifted toward the children sent away for months, into institutions of healing that healed one thing and bruised another. Tuberculosis sanatoriums offered one such population…but, even so, complications abounded. These were not places of emotional neutrality; they were institutions, and institutions are thick with forces: regiment, fear, detachment, and sometimes cruelty. Still, seven children from an early pilot study were kept under observation. This observation took place not in a laboratory, but in visits, letters, and teacher reports. Over three years, they accumulated a collection of human observations: drawings, behaviors, absences, odd flashes of joy.

By 1951, the primary work had taken shape as the Sanatorium Follow-Up. Thirty-six children, all patients before their fourth birthdays, were compared to one hundred and eight controls; the differences were neither catastrophic nor subtle. They were enduring. Ex-sanatorium children daydreamed more; they worked less steadily; they withdrew, struggled to connect, hovered at the margins of the classroom, unsure of the teacher's gaze. The correlations sharpened around age and duration: those separated under the age of two, or for longer than six months, or on more than one occasion, showed the deepest marks.

Yet even these findings, robust as they were, did not fully explain the texture of the child's mind during and after separation.

One of the main ways to further the research was suggested by members of the London Advisory Committee, who requested them to further look on whether young children in hospitals should be visited by parents. So was born the Hospital Visiting Project No. 1. Six hospitals were chosen. They had already begun to tinker with visitation policies; they permitted mothers to visit, sometimes for hours, sometimes daily. Robertson was dispatched with no script beyond his own sensitivity; he was instructed to watch and record.

Accordingly, he observed children standing motionless in cribs, their eyes scanning for a familiar face that would not appear. He saw the way a nurse's hand, however gentle, could not imitate the touch of a mother. Some children wailed; others fell silent, resigned, perhaps, or self-protecting. The staff, well-meaning and brisk, resisted the observations. They had grown used to these absences; they had to, or they could not do their work. The researcher, however, could not unsee what he had seen.

Meanwhile, Bowlby pushed the research further. He knew they must catalogue not only the long-term impact, but the shape of the moment: the initial rupture, the slow adaptation, the reunion, and what lingers afterward. Thus was laid the design for Current Studies No. 2: a map of separation, step by step. What does a child do, in the first hour, when the mother leaves? How does the face change after three days? How does reunion play out? Clinging, indifference, confusion? What comes next?

Two variables guided the inquiry: the child's age at separation and the quality of the previous bond. It was a clinical truth, Bowlby believed, that not all separations were equal; a secure bond may buffer, but a fragile one may collapse entirely under strain. These observations, however precise, encountered a deep methodological problem: how to integrate the rigor of scientific design with the sprawling, textured, human world of the clinic. To study a child, one must see not only symptoms but circumstances; to quantify emotion, one must first recognize its forms.

The researchers knew what they lacked. There were gaps in understanding, in method, in theory. But in place of certainty, they had focus.

The short-term effects were unmistakable, at least. What they did not yet know, though, was how long they lasted; what scars they leave; what paths they divert. His concern was not abstract; there was a lot of ignorance around the subject, as Bowlby found in his 1951 report. Here and there, there was a chink of hope; but for most of the time, the investigator had to fumble in an ignorance born of tradition: crystallized assumptions that children were resilient by default, that maternal presence was comforting but not essential. These assumptions were structural; they shaped policy, practice, even architecture.

By the summer of 1951, the team extended the Sanatorium Follow-Up to sixty children, with 180 controls, and began interviewing parents. They worked quietly, doggedly. The NHS provided just enough to sustain the project, so Bowlby had to find grants where he could.

But around this time, his attentions were also focused on another task other than the Tavistock: a report for the WHO. And as he worked on this report, John Bowlby unknowingly found himself at the cusp of theory.

Chapter 13.

The Theory

The first invitation had arrived earlier in December 1949 and had carried a kind of bureaucratic purpose, but beneath its official language, Bowlby had recognized a rare opportunity.

Ronald Hargreaves, who had known him in wartime through the corridors of military psychiatry, now reached out from the Mental Health Section of the World Health Organization. Hargreaves remembered the articles on juvenile thieves, those sharp, unflinching examinations of disordered childhood, and while Bowlby had declined a previous request to report on juvenile delinquency, he had said, almost in passing, that if anything came up about children, more broadly, he might be interested.

Now, something had come up.

The United Nations Social Commission had decided to study the needs of homeless children. Hargreaves, quick to sense a gap between policy and psychological understanding, moved to involve the WHO. He asked

Bowlby to examine the psychiatric dimensions of child homelessness: a task that was both diplomatic and diagnostic, calling for a wide-ranging survey of knowledge and practice. Bowlby accepted. Writing to Ursula, he called the position very much to his liking; after all, it would allow him to construct a scientific report on the nature and causes of psychological damage in children deprived of homes.

This was exactly what he was looking to work on. In many ways, he saw in it an extension of the separation research already underway at the Tavistock; Hargreaves, too, had praised that work as one of the most significant undertakings in the postwar mental health field.

The research comprised three interlocking questions: the adverse psychological effects of homelessness; the causes and prevention of that condition; and the therapeutic handling of children already displaced. These were familiar issues, ones reaching into institutions, foster homes, adoption procedures, and the training of personnel. It was a hard task, but one he knew he was already in the middle of.

In January, he began.

He would visit Europe first. A young Swiss psychologist was appointed to assist with abstracting literature.

Europe in these years existed in a kind of exhausted twilight, neither entirely past the war nor fully stuck in it. Across the continent, boundaries had shifted on maps and in minds alike. Nations had reconstituted themselves, often awkwardly; others had vanished in all but memory. Yet here too, a reconstruction was in progress. In factories refitted for civilian goods, engineers talked of peacetime efficiencies. There was talk, in small rooms and smoke-filled council

274

halls, of unity: economic, political, spiritual. The first flickers of what would become the European Coal and Steel Community were beginning to flare, drafted by men who knew too well the price of competition in iron and fire.

Bowlby travelled across this war-beleaguered continent for six weeks, moving from city to city, collecting impressions, notes, and references. In France, he met Roudinesco; in Sweden, unnamed colleagues with quiet urgency; in the Netherlands, a network of child guidance workers with whom he discovered an unexpected kinship.

There, he found Eugenia Lekkerkerker, who had returned from the United States carrying the seeds of the child guidance movement. Soon after her visit, social workers and psychiatrists from the Netherlands, with Nel Tibout among them, made their own pilgrimage across the Atlantic to study the clinics. From those studies, the first Dutch child guidance clinic was born. It was an idea passed hand to hand, place to place, as ideas often are in the ruins and reconstructions of war.

Nel Tibout had met Bowlby before at the SEPEG in 1947, in Paris, a conference of mourners and planners for the war's youngest victims. They spoke again in Amsterdam that year at a psychoanalytic meeting, where Bowlby presented his thoughts on juvenile delinquency to a room that still bore the stiffness of recovery.

In the years since, she, along with De Leeuw and Frijling, had been studying children whose parents had been deported in the early 1940s. The children had been raised in foster homes, some stable, some scattered. What they found repeated the Tavistock's findings: multiple changes of home wore at the child's defenses, left them withdrawn, clinging, sociable in the brittle, surface way of those trained to expect abandonment. Some adjusted after one move; others, less secure to begin with, fell apart. A good early relationship helped; a poor one did not.

Though their studies had been done independently, the conclusions paralleled Bowlby's own. The symmetry of the research affirmed his convictions, not as dogma but as a pattern.

Then to America.

The country had, within the five years since the end of the war, transformed itself into something new. Industry had become institutional. Prosperity, though uneven, had become part of the national vocabulary; the G.I. Bill filtered young men into colleges in numbers never imagined by their fathers. Reforming itself on assembly lines and in air-conditioned offices, the country was on its way to wholesale mechanization and middle-class ascent.

John Bowlby would stay here for five weeks, and make contact with persons of interest to the report. He met with Goldfarb, Spitz, Bender, and Senn. Of them all, Goldfarb stood out as the most lucid, the most empirically driven. But all in all, John Bowlby felt a sense of disappointment in what he found.

"No systematic research," he wrote, shaking his head.

It was a shame, but the structures that had seemed so vibrant to him from a distance had decayed. The adult psychiatrists, he noted, still showed a perplexing indifference to the nuances of the mother-child bond; among child guidance workers, though, there was a solid, shared

276

understanding. All across Britain, Europe, and America, he observed, there was a surprising consensus on the conditions of the homeless child.

He also came to realize that the methods used at the Tavistock, especially the inclusion of fathers, the joint interviews, were distinct.

"No one else does it," he wrote with a mix of pride and dismay. Their work, though consistent in its findings with others', was methodologically set apart.

Ultimately, what emerged from this journey was, in some ways, a synthesis. Bowlby became the hinge between scattered efforts, connecting Dutch clinic workers to French researchers, American psychologists to British analysts. He read the literature, recorded the testimonies, and slowly, deliberately, assembled a picture of the homeless child's psyche, its fractures, its compensations, its recoveries and failures to recover.

The work consumed the first months of 1950; it became, for a time, the gravitational center of Bowlby's thoughts. The letters to his wife, to colleagues, to Hunnybun were filled with details and frustrations, observations and small triumphs. What struck him most, again and again, was the fragility of the child's inner world when stability was withdrawn. The mechanisms of care, so often treated as logistical, administrative, became in his writing psychological necessities. The child needed a constant figure, not merely a roof.

In writing the report, Bowlby was attempting more than documentation. He was proposing, however cautiously, a new common sense: that a child's emotional needs should be seen as medical, that the arrangement of foster care should be guided by developmental science, that the loss of a parent was not simply sad but neurologically consequential: these were ideas not yet absorbed into public policy.

But Bowlby believed, always, that ideas could move institutions if expressed clearly enough.

***

In the high summer of 1950, after months of travel, interviews, and concentrated reading, Bowlby returned to London with a mind dense with notes and impressions. The corridors of Tavistock, familiar after the bristling pace of the WHO tour, became the stage upon which he gathered his thoughts. He began to write as a man compelled by duty, sketching the psychological geography of childhood onto international policy.

The resulting report, *Maternal Care and Mental Health*, was completed in 1951.

The structure of the report was simple: two parts, each demanding in its own way. The first catalogued the consequences of maternal deprivation; the second advanced a sequence of proposals on how to avoid, or at least mitigate, the damage that followed when a child's tie to a primary caregiver was interrupted. Bowlby wrote with the urgency of one who knows the bureaucracy of care is slow-moving, resistant, prone to delay. He did not write for theorists alone. This was for policymakers, nurses, civil servants, heads of orphanages; all those with the power to close or open the door between a child and his parent.

278

At the heart of Bowlby's thesis stood a single, insistent idea: that the mental health of a child rests upon the presence of a warm, intimate, continuous relationship with a mother, or a permanent mother-substitute, in which both parties find satisfaction and enjoyment.

He defined the child without such a relationship, be he in a hospital ward, a foster home, or his own family, as *maternally deprived.*

The evidence for this claim came from several directions. There were direct observational studies, carefully recorded scenes from hospitals and institutions. There were retrospective analyses of adults with psychological illness, their childhoods mined for patterns. There were longitudinal studies, following children who had undergone early separation, mapping the path from first disruption to future difficulty.

Among the pages, the conclusion that emerged was that prolonged deprivation could have grave, far-reaching effects on the child's development. The absence of mother-love, in infancy or early childhood, did not merely delay growth but warped it. The child deprived of secure attachment, Bowlby argued, struggled to develop a functioning ego or superego. Without the stabilizing gaze of a consistent caregiver, the inner structure of conscience, of self-regulation, failed to cohere. Some children withdrew; others adapted in ways that masked their wounds, superficial sociability, compulsive stealing, early promiscuity.

It was not, in Bowlby's account, that they lacked the desire for love. Rather, the desire remained intact while the capacity to form trustful bonds collapsed under the weight of anxiety and rage. The child's withdrawal, he wrote, was a defence, an unconscious attempt to shield the self from the agony of longing for one who could not be relied upon to stay.

To avoid the intense depression they experience as a result of hating the person they most dearly love, he explained, *they may retreat from human contact altogether.*

Despite the breadth of research cited, Bowlby was candid about the limits of knowledge. There were, he noted, crucial questions that remained unanswered; most pressingly, how long deprivation could be tolerated before irreparable damage occurred, and whether that damage could be undone if care was restored. He sensed a vicious cycle: the deprived child, left untreated, grew into the parent who could not properly care for his or her own children.

Unless the pattern was interrupted, the damage would be passed on.

He named three types of families as especially prone to producing deprived children.

There were families in which no stable home group was ever formed: cases of illegitimacy, abandonment, or institutional care from birth. There were families that remained physically intact but failed to function, with environments of neglect, silence, or chronic emotional absence. And finally, there were families disrupted by death, divorce, or separation, their support structures collapsing in the aftermath.

Yet, in all cases, the outcome was not predetermined. Much, he emphasized, depended on whether other relationships could fill the gap. A relative, a neighbor, a teacher, even a foster mother might become a source of stability if the bond formed early enough, deeply enough.

Adoption, too, received attention. If a child had to be adopted, Bowlby argued, it should be done swiftly. Delay magnified the risk. Early adoption in skilled hands, he concluded, though the data remained thin, could provide nearly the same chance of a happy home life as that afforded to a child raised by his birth parents.

And what of group care?

On this, Bowlby was unambiguous. If temporary removal from the home was necessary, foster care was preferable to institutional placement. A group setting with rotating staff and fluctuating peers lacked the essential ingredient of constancy. It was this, not resources or decor, that formed the true foundation of a child's psychological life.

But *Maternal Care and Mental Health* did not just offer analysis. In it, John Bowlby had outlined a program.

Child welfare and family welfare were, Bowlby insisted, two sides of the same coin. One could not be planned without the other. The professions involved in their delivery, from social workers, to psychiatrists, to educators, had to be trained with rigour. And there would be, he believed, no great public health victories in mental health without sustained, systematic research.

"There will be no triumphs," he wrote, "to compare with diphtheria immunization or malaria control unless we devote to preventive psychiatry the same seriousness, the same infrastructure."

He admitted, near the end, that the evidence remained partial. But, he warned, the absence of certainty must not lead to inaction.

To await certainty is to await eternity.

In this brief sentence, the urgency of John Bowlby's thinking was laid bare. If a society waited until all doubt had been removed before it protected its children, the children would have grown, suffered, and repeated the cycle.

There were criticisms, of course; a body of critics disagreed not simply with his emphasis on the mother but with the assertion that maternal love was essential to a child's normal functioning. The very idea, to them, smacked of determinism. Could a child's future be shaped so definitively by one relationship? Was parenting to be condensed to the cultivation of emotional continuity?

There were other critiques too, less moral and more technical. Bowlby, they said, had failed to distinguish between privation and deprivation. To attribute all symptoms to the absence of maternal care was to simplify a system of harms.

Yet, whatever the resistance, his name had entered public discourse. Recognition, in turn, brought funding. It was easier now to secure grants, and with support from the International Children's Centre, Bowlby assembled a research team at the Tavistock. Its consequences also rippled outward, and Hargreaves quickly became a supporter of this separation research. He would now use his influence to connect Bowlby's unit to a Technical Working Group of the International Children's Centre. The group included paediatricians and psychiatrists from various countries. They met biannually to review the Tavistock's work and a parallel French study under Jenny Roudinesco.

For Bowlby, the WHO consultancy marked a turning point. He had travelled, spoken, listened, and synthesized. He had read widely, more deeply than he had before. And he had, at last, set his ideas into the durable form of public policy. Years later, he would recall those months as formative, not merely for what he had produced, but for how he had changed. "First of all, I got to know a lot of people," he said; "secondly, I had a chance to read up the literature which I had not been able to do before, and thirdly, to put my ideas together on paper."

By the next year, *Maternal Care and Mental Health* had been translated into fourteen languages, read by policymakers and practitioners across continents, and, in its English paperback form, purchased in four hundred thousand copies. A year later, *Child Care and the Growth of Love*, published in the familiar, democratic yellow-and-white cover of Penguin Books, reached a different sort of reader: nurses, midwives, mothers, social workers, and people for whom such a book might be kept on a bedside table, consulted in the hours after dusk, or dog-eared by the sink between chores.

Among the earliest and most consequential of his appointments was Mary Ainsworth, a Canadian psychologist trained in rigorous method, thoughtful in theory, and most crucially, willing to look beyond dogma.

She arrived in the autumn of 1950 and quickly immersed herself in the literature Bowlby had drawn upon for his WHO report. Through long discussions with John Bowlby over case notes and published studies at the

Tavistock, she found Bowlby's open, non-doctrinaire approach to be intellectually liberating.

Her first contribution came in the form of a detailed review chapter in Child Care and the Growth of Love, but the most enduring fruit of her time at the Tavistock would be methodological. Observing Robertson's meticulous documentation of children's reactions to separation, she began to sense the power of direct, unfiltered observation. She then decided that whenever she could start a project, it would be a study of this sort: direct observation in the natural environment.

That resolve travelled with her into the future. After leaving the Tavistock in 1953, Ainsworth traveled to Uganda, where she undertook a longitudinal observational study of mother-infant attachment. Among the dusty roads and village compounds, she took to measuring what had so often been intuited or described anecdotally: the shape and texture of a child's emotional bond. She did not analyze the Uganda data immediately. Instead, the records sat, layered with time, until she resumed work on them while teaching clinical psychology at Johns Hopkins University in the United States.

There, in the quieter intervals between lectures and supervisory rounds, Ainsworth developed a scale for evaluating maternal sensitivity to infant signals. The data yielded subtle but statistically significant correlations. Infants were grouped according to the quality of their attachment: securely attached babies cried less; insecurely attached ones cried more, or in stranger ways; a third group, not yet attached, showed no differential behavior in response to the mother.

And importantly, the analysis showed that maternal responsiveness, though commonly treated as intuitive or unmeasurable, could in fact be recorded, rated, and studied.

***

Meanwhile, from the 1950s onward, John Bowlby was beginning to expand his talents into an intellectual territory that few in psychoanalysis put much stock in: ethology.

Ethology had emerged as the science that concerned itself with the patient observation of animals in their natural habitats, tracing each movement and ritual to uncover intrinsic instincts. It insisted that one must watch a creature where it truly belonged: among the grass, beneath the trees, on the threshold of its burrow. The ethologists believed that behavior was a structured pattern shaped by evolution, and each behavior had its own instinctual purpose.

When Bowlby encountered ethology, he had recognized in it a discipline as meticulous as it was radical, offering the promise of evidence where psychoanalysis offered speculation. Indeed, it was ethology that would grant him a language for his own nascent theory: *imprinting, fixed-action patterns, innate releasing mechanisms.* And indeed, such naturalistic observation interested him the way animal experimentation in a lab never had.

And so, when his thoughts had begun to pivot with new insistence towards the animal studies that seemed to promise a purer way of understanding attachment, he reached out to a man named Robert Hinde.

285

Hinde, who had devoted himself to the study of rhesus monkeys, was a figure of firm composure. Though just shy of thirty, he was already a man who had seen plenty out of life; he had seen action in the Second World War, and it had affected him in ways it would take a long time to articulate. But what was immediately apparent was that he was done with the business of war and death; increasingly more of a pacifist, after he stepped away from the RAF in 1946, he entered St. John's College at Cambridge and turned his attention to chemistry, physiology, and, importantly, zoology.

In short, he dedicated himself to *life*.

In time, Hinde would become a leading ethologist, and he and John Bowlby took an immediate liking to each other, reserved and hard-working men as they were. Under Hinde's *generous and stern guidance*, in Bowlby's words, he would come to see ethology not as an eccentric sideline to psychoanalysis but as an essential corrective to its ambiguities.

In his afternoons with Hinde, Bowlby would sit in the small office, among the papers that documented each permutation of the monkeys' separations and reunions; he'd read with a slow, deliberate attention, pausing sometimes to trace a line with his finger. Hinde's work fascinated him. The data was astonishingly detailed: the frequency of a mother's glance toward her infant; the duration of a young monkey's clinging after a period of absence; the degree of agitation that could not be calmed by any food or token.

And in these bare notations, he recognised what he was looking for: the living bond between parent and child.

Of course, Bowlby was a cautious and thorough man; he was aware that such knowledge was not to be adopted on a human model wholesale but sifted, weighed, and translated into the human register. One could not, after all, suppose that an infant's heart was the same as a rhesus monkey's, though the basic grammar of attachment, he suspected, was shared.

And so he took these findings, thanked Hinde for his time, and showed them to his own research team. But it is a universal truth that the mind of a group does not always move in step with the intuitions of an individual.

As such, John Bowlby discovered that the response to this link was surprisingly lukewarm.

As far as he was concerned, Hinde's studies were producing such clear signals, traces of a pattern so coherent it seemed almost inevitable. But the rest of his people remained unconvinced, meeting him with a kind of polite skepticism. He could understand it, in part; after all, the empirical papers they published in those years, exploring the effects of separation on young children, bore little sign of the ethological ideas which had come to preoccupy him.

Even Mary Ainsworth, whom he admired without reservation, maintained a certain distance from the more radical implications of his thinking.

"But the link, Ms. Ainsworth," he found himself trying to convince her, "is there! Look yourself."

She sighed, then spoke up. "Mr. Bowlby, it seems plain to me that a baby's devotion to its mother is rooted in the satisfaction of needs. I agree on the principle of attachment, but there must surely be some *need* behind it?"

Yet John Bowlby felt that such a conception failed to grasp the full measure of what he had glimpsed in the ethological literature: the possibility that attachment was not derivative but intrinsic, an organising force distinct from yet as primary as hunger itself.

So he continued on his own.

He corresponded now with Niko Tinbergen, whose studies of animal instinct exposed the layered choreography of instinctive behavior. Tinbergen's observations offered Bowlby another interesting contrast to the ambiguities of psychoanalytic speculation. When Tinbergen described the ritual dances of the stickleback fish or the precise arc of a gull's defensive posturing, he demonstrated that behaviour could be both innate and adapted, universal and particular. Bowlby admired the sobriety with which Tinbergen catalogued the fixity and plasticity of instinctive action, the delicate interplay between genetic programming and environmental circumstance.

And after a few meetings, he befriended Tinbergen as well; for John Bowlby had an uncanny ability to attract minds of remarkable force and delicacy, people who were willing to offer their hard-won expertise into his keeping.

He then read Lorenz's account of goslings imprinting on the first animate figure they encountered; he considered, as he turned the pages, the conviction of the newly hatched birds who followed a human figure across the grass. It was Lorenz's conviction that behavior had an evolutionary signature, and this was an argument that freed Bowlby to imagine human attachment as something more enduring than mere hunger-satisfaction cycles.

288

This immersion in ethology was having an effect; indeed, it had transformed Bowlby's conceptual frame. He had come to see that the psychoanalytic emphasis on oral gratification, the idea that attachment was merely a byproduct of feeding, could not account for the durable longing for closeness. Ethological research, with its insistence on direct observation, was showing him that the need for secure contact had *its own architecture*.

What followed was this realization: attachment was not an accidental byproduct but an evolved adaptation, an instinct that safeguarded the vulnerable young.

Out of these readings, Bowlby developed a hypothesis that would refute the consensus of his colleagues. He proposed that attachment was biologically grounded. a species-specific behavioural system shaped to promote survival. The child's tendency to orient toward the caregiver, to cry at separation, to greet with delight upon reunion…these were functional patterns, not sentimental excesses. And so, the way Tinbergen had charted the fixed action patterns of animals and Hinde had catalogued the subtleties of social communication in primates, Bowlby set out to show that human emotional development, too, could be mapped.

His ambition was simple, now: to construct a theory of attachment that could stand on its own two feet, rigorous enough to be falsifiable, but flexible enough to accommodate individual difference.

***

The work advanced by small increments.

In each conversation with Hinde, in every discussion with Ainsworth, there was the slow accrual of understanding. He came to see that the study of attachment would require a new language, one precise enough to do justice to the subtleties of behaviour, yet capacious enough to account for the irreducible individuality of each child's experience.

So he worked, he wrote, and as the city of London began to anxiously stir with the fervour of modernity, John Bowlby assembled his first formal statement of attachment theory. It had been a process, a slow accrual, a sediment of thought that had been forming through decades of encounters, from the quiet rooms of the Tavistock to conversations with ethologists, psychoanalysts, and developmental psychologists alike.

And at last, he was done…

…Or at least done with assembling something worth presentation. The papers would be presented before the British Psychoanalytic Society, which in itself was like juggling with knives. Trained to interpret human longing and injury through the elaborate hieroglyphs of drive theory and transference, these men and women would take quite a lot to be convinced.

It would, ultimately, take three papers over the next few years to present this theory.

There was "The Nature of the Child's Tie to His Mother," delivered in 1958; followed by "Separation Anxiety," in 1959; and then "Grief and Mourning in Infancy and Early Childhood," completed in 1960. Together, these papers would form a blueprint of attachment theory, assembled from ethological observations, long conversations, and a lifetime of conviction that the relationship between a child and mother was more than a 'hunger drive' or something secondary to the demands of libido.

Now came the task of saying this to a room still full of Freudians.

With the inevitable opposition already in mind, Bowlby came to present the first of these papers. This paper would thus have the unenviable task of dismantling common explanations for the infant's tie to the mother.

He presented the paper with his usual deference, reviewing and then setting aside the prevailing psychoanalytic doctrine that need satisfaction was the true engine behind a child's affection. Bowlby had, of course, taken inspiration from Freud's suggestion that mature sexuality comprised an amalgam of instinctual fragments. But he turned that idea toward infancy, proposing that the observable attachment behaviours of a 12-month-old, such as clinging, smiling, crying, and following, were more than an extension of hunger and thirst. Each response, he believed, matured along its own timetable, and by the end of the first year, fused into an attachment to the mother or mother-substitute.

Clinging and following, Bowlby argued, had evolved to ensure proximity; they were safeguards against the perils that had always menaced the immature young of the species. It was now that he drew upon the ethological concepts that Tinbergen had described in *The Study of Instinct:* 'sign stimuli' and 'social releasers' that activated and terminated

291

behaviour in predictable ways. To illustrate this, Bowlby gave the example of a baby's cry, which summoned the mother, and the baby's smile, which sustained her presence.

And he had come prepared. His argument was buttressed by the developmental investigations of Piaget, the minutes of the Psychobiology of the Child study group convened by Ronald Hargreaves at the WHO, and the long accumulation of observations he had made as the facilitator of a weekly circle for young mothers. When Bowlby presented these ideas to the Psychoanalytic Society, he encountered reactions that were neither wholly hostile nor entirely receptive. It was an uneasy thing for them to view Bowlby's attempts at a new theory, one that could splinter the school; however, it was a theory that did not so much fly in the face of psychoanalysis as it seemed to expand it. And so, there were few grounds to outright dismiss it.

Anna Freud herself had been absent from the meeting, but heard of it soon after. Undoubtedly, it did not please her.

In a letter, she expressed her unease regarding the matter: "Dr. Bowlby is too valuable a person to get lost to psychoanalysis." As far as she was concerned, John Bowlby's new theory could well turn into a riptide, pulling him from the shelter of orthodox interpretation.

In some ways, it was a prescient recognition.

The second of Bowlby's papers was presented in 1959, when he again found himself in the chalky hush of the lecture room, poised before the wary attentiveness of analysts.

This second paper was entitled *Separation Anxiety*, and it attempted the curious feat of trying to transcend the architecture of the nascent attachment theory and press its argument further into territory most psychoanalysts preferred to consider the sole province of internal fantasy.

Bowlby built his case upon observations gathered by James Robertson, whose descriptions of children in hospital had always struck him. For Robertson had seen children seated on their narrow cots, their faces open in grief when their mothers disappeared, then closed over by degrees until only a watchful blankness remained. Robertson's work, published in 1953, had delineated three phases of separation response: protest, which appeared as urgent weeping or agitated calling; despair, which stilled the limbs and hollowed the expression; and detachment, when the child, withdrawn into a protective composure, turned away even if the mother returned.

These phases fascinated Bowlby; they reminded him of Harlow's studies of infant monkeys whose clinging to cloth surrogates showed a hunger deeper than that of the stomach. He also drew upon Heinicke's fieldwork and the grim clarity of Zimmermann's data, all of it showing that the loss of the attachment figure could not be explained by the crude mechanism of mere *drive frustration*.

Squaring his shoulders, John Bowlby had made a stand; he had declared that it is not merely hunger or inconvenience that ignites fear, but rather the simultaneous activation of two ancient patterns: the urge to flee from danger and the yearning to return to the attachment figure, who alone made the world coherent. And when neither flight nor reunion was possible, only anxiety and abandonment remained the child's lot.

293

This explanation, which went far heavier on ethological references this time, unsettled his colleagues. Some accused Bowlby of discarding the mental life of the infant altogether, of reducing experience to mere observable acts. Indeed, in one passage he had written, with a peculiar mixture of tenderness and detachment, "to have a deep attachment for a person…is to have taken them as the terminating object of our instinctual responses."

It was a sentence that directly contradicted the psychoanalytic narrative, and it earned him suspicion. And the controversy only grew when Bowlby continued to challenge that overbearing father-figure of psychology itself: *Sigmund Freud.*

For John Bowlby had now challenged Freud's assertion that excessive mother-love, or 'overgratification', could pose a danger to the child's growth. Bowlby instead argued that what sometimes appeared to be overindulgence was in truth a mother's unconscious attempt to compensate for her own ambivalence or buried hostility. From these hidden conflicts, he believed, came the repeated threats of abandonment that could fracture a child's trust and give rise to chronic separation anxiety. If the infant showed no anxiety at all when the mother departed, it did not follow that he was mature; more likely, it signaled a defensive withdrawal. It was independence masking dread.

Needless to say, feathers were ruffled, and John Bowlby was increasingly seen as an outlier to orthodoxy. It was a fact that was neither here nor there for him; what mattered, as far as he was concerned, was the truth he believed he had stumbled onto.

And the rupture that had begun would culminate in a separation of its own with the presentation of his third and most controversial paper to date: *Grief and Mourning in Infancy and Early Childhood.*

For context, Anna Freud, whose stature in society was immense, had long contended that bereaved infants lacked sufficient ego development to mourn; she maintained they experienced nothing more than transient anxiety if a suitable substitute appeared.

Yet John Bowlby, assembled again before the increasingly hostile glances of his peers, now presented observations that directly defied this claim. He cited Marris's research, which revealed that grief, with its harsh alternation of longing and despair, emerged whenever the attachment system was activated and no comfort came. Mourning, he said, was neither deferred nor postponed; it began at once, folding the infant into a struggle whose outcome shaped all later loves.

Here too, he suggested that if replacements arrived too frequently, the child's capacity to form a lasting bond would gradually *erode.*

By now, the meeting was electric with disapproval. One analyst, half in jest and half in rancour, muttered, "Bowlby? Give me Barrabas."

By the time the paper appeared in *Psychoanalytic Study of the Child*, it was accompanied, to Bowlby's surprise, by rejoinders from Anna Freud, Max Schur, and René Spitz, each voicing both respect for his thoroughness and irritation at his conclusions. Spitz, whose own work on hospitalism had once seemed allied with Bowlby's, ended his critique with a rebuke: "When submitting new theories we should not violate the principle of parsimony in science...becloud the observational facts, are oversimplified, and make no contribution to the better understanding of observed phenomena."

It was inevitable that these attacks bruised him, but John Bowlby did not recant. Nonetheless, he saw now that his views would no longer be tolerable to the psychoanalyst's world. And after hearing enough rebuke and thinking over his decision, he ultimately decided to continue his membership in the Society.

But never again would he bring his work there for debate.

***

In the early 1960s, Ainsworth launched the Baltimore Study, an ambitious project that would carry her reputation into the very centre of developmental psychology. Working with colleagues at Johns Hopkins, she studied infants and mothers in their homes, watching not only the overt behaviours, feeding, cradling, distraction, but also the tonalities of response: did the mother notice her child's cues? Did she act promptly, consistently, with attunement or indifference?

Then, at twelve months, each infant was brought with their mother into a laboratory for what would become a landmark in psychological research: the *Strange Situation*.

The laboratory would be furnished with simple objects of everyday life: a soft rug, a scattering of brightly painted wooden toys, and a pair of chairs against the wall. It was an environment designed to replicate: familiar enough to soothe a child, unfamiliar enough to provoke curiosity and, eventually, distress.

The experiment itself was deceptively simple in design, consisting of just 21 minutes in which infants, between the ages of nine and thirty months, would be gently ushered through a series of separations and reunions with their mothers. Yet this procedure was designed to reveal profound truths about how children could bond with their caregivers, and by extension, how they would one day engage with the world beyond them.

The first step was always gentle. A mother would carry her child into the observation room, guided by an experimenter who explained only the practicalities: the mother and infant would spend a little time together while the child was free to play. The rooms were uniformly arranged: a scattering of toys across the rug, with blocks, a doll, a few small cars, and seating where the caregiver could settle. A one-way mirror stretched across one wall, behind which researchers quietly scribbled notes, their pens scratching against paper. For the infant, this entry marked the first moment of transition. A new place, but anchored by the presence of a familiar figure.

Some clutched tightly to their mothers' necks, hesitant to be set down. Others squirmed free immediately, toddling toward the toys with squeals of delight. These first minutes set the tone: here, researchers measured the child's willingness to explore when a trusted caregiver was nearby.

Once the mother was seated, the instructions were clear: she was to remain present, but not to initiate interaction with the child. It was the infant's choice to explore. In some cases, children ranged boldly across the room, stacking blocks or pushing toy cars along the carpet, glancing back occasionally to ensure their mother was still there. These infants seemed to draw invisible strength from her quiet presence, reassured enough to take risks in an unfamiliar space. Others remained close, orbiting tightly around the mother's chair. A few refused to leave her lap at all, eyes fixed anxiously on the doorway, as though sensing what was to come.

Behind the mirror, Ainsworth and her colleagues recorded how often the child glanced back, how quickly they returned for reassurance, how long they remained absorbed in play.

And then, familiarity ended.

For the next step introduced *the stranger*.

The door opened, and an unfamiliar adult would enter: usually a woman, often soft-spoken, chosen for her ability to adapt her demeanor to the child's cues. She greeted the mother politely before turning her attention toward the infant, first from a respectful distance, then with gentle overtures: a smile, a comment about the toys, perhaps extending a hand. For some children, curiosity won out. They approached with cautious interest, offering a toy or a glance upward. For others, anxiety surged; faces crumpled, and they retreated to their mother's lap, clinging tightly. A few seemed indifferent, carrying on their play as though the stranger were no more than a piece of furniture.

This moment revealed the child's threshold for "stranger anxiety," that universal signal of developmental progress. By their first birthday, most infants distinguished sharply between familiar and unfamiliar faces, a skill that once had life-or-death consequences in ancestral environments.

Yet perhaps the true heart of the Strange Situation came with separation. The mother, after a brief cue, rose from her chair and left the room conspicuously, the door clicking shut behind her. For the infant, this was no small departure. In a strange place, confronted by a stranger, the secure base of safety had vanished. Reactions varied with striking clarity. Some children erupted in cries, crawling or stumbling desperately toward the door, as though sheer force of will might summon their caregiver back. Others fell silent, eyes wide, their bodies stiff with distress but unable to express it outwardly. Still others turned from the door, ignoring both absence and stranger, as though denying the loss could erase it.

The stranger, by design, adjusted her behavior to the infant's needs. She might offer comfort, a toy, or a quiet presence. But she could never fully replace the parent, and it was in this gap between the comfort offered and the comfort desired that the essence of attachment as proposed by John Bowlby could be seen.

Of course, moments later, the door would open again. Now, the mother returned and she greeted her child warmly, and attempted to soothe them. Some infants, secure in their attachment, reached eagerly for their mothers, accepting comfort quickly and resuming exploration once reassured. Their protest at separation had been genuine, but their trust in her return was equally strong. Others reacted with ambivalence. They clung desperately, resisting any attempt to be put down, yet at the same time arching their backs or striking out in anger, as though furious at having been left at all. And finally, others still barely acknowledged the return. They avoided eye contact, turned their attention to the toys, or seemed more interested in the stranger.

And Ainsworth and her team took their notes.

Of course, the procedure could not be complete after one cycle. Following the brief reunion, the mother would leave once more, this time, leaving the infant entirely alone. For a child scarcely more than a year old, few stresses were greater. The room, so recently filled with familiar presence, now echoed with emptiness. Some sat frozen, whimpering softly; others collapsed into tears that filled the observation chamber.

After a minute, the stranger re-entered, again attempting to comfort the child. Her success was partial at best.

It was not her presence that the child craved.

Finally, the mother returned a second time. This last reunion provided the clearest window into the child's attachment strategy: whether they rushed forward with relief, clung with ambivalence, or turned away in avoidance.

These behaviors, she discovered, reflected the quality of the infant's earlier experiences. Those who had encountered consistent, emotionally available caregiving showed secure attachment; those who had experienced unresponsiveness or inconsistency fell into avoidant or ambivalent categories. Three categories were first devised, which were later expanded into four.

Firstly, the Secure children; these explored readily, protested when their mothers left, welcomed them back warmly, and soon returned to play. Their caregivers had been consistently responsive, teaching them that the world was safe when explored from a secure base. Meanwhile, anxious-avoidant children showed little overt distress at separation and ignored or avoided their mothers at reunion. Yet physiological measures later revealed elevated stress. Their avoidance was a defense, born from caregivers who often rebuffed or ignored bids for comfort.

The third type Ainsworth noted were anxious-ambivalent/resistant children, who clung desperately and were inconsolable at separation. They also reacted with anger or resistance at reunion. Their caregivers had been inconsistent, sometimes responsive, sometimes not, leaving the child uncertain and anxious about availability.

And finally, the disorganized/disoriented. This group was added later by Main and Hesse, and displayed contradictory or chaotic behaviors: approaching with head averted, freezing mid-movement, or collapsing in despair. Often these children had experienced frightening or abusive caregiving, leaving them without a coherent strategy to seek safety.

And just like that, one of the landmark studies of child psychology had been completed…and John Bowlby saw its significance immediately.

He had long believed in the primacy of the child-mother bond; now Ainsworth provided a method to test it. He wrote later with unambiguous admiration: "Her work... has led attachment theory to be widely regarded as probably the best supported theory of socioemotional development yet available."

And what had begun as a postwar investigation into maternal deprivation launched under the aegis of the WHO had now evolved into a full-bodied theory, with observational roots, developmental scaffolding, and clinical relevance.

Chapter 14.

Attachment, Separation, Loss

The 1960s had arrived, trailing its skirts of upheaval and promise, and the century had paused to inhale before releasing an exhalation of change. In London, narrow streets were newly bright with painted shop signs and the jangle of transistor radios; the old certainties of Empire and deference retreated, replaced by the suspicion that political and domestic life could, perhaps, be contrived afresh.

John Bowlby still occupied his office at the Tavistock Clinic with an intensity that seemed to defy the era's loosened seams. Here, in a building that held the smell of polished floors and ink on rationed paper, he arranged his observations like specimens pinned beneath glass. While others delighted in novelty for its own sake, he pressed on with the conviction that the child's first bond was the quiet axis around which all later experience must revolve.

Beyond the windows, the city shifted in rhythm with the times. Mothers carried infants wrapped in bright acrylic blankets, prams jostling along pavements where shopgirls in miniskirts and old men in tweed mingled without astonishment. Questions about the family's shape, about women's ambitions and children's needs, passed from the salons to the newspapers.

It was into this atmosphere, half buoyant, half unmoored, that Mary Ainsworth returns again in full force to John Bowlby's story. She had begun her analysis of the findings from the Uganda project, and now was invited by Bowlby to show her findings at the Tavistock Study Group before an audience whose composition possessed a curious variety; some were drawn from the rigorous chambers of ethology, others still were psychoanalysis, and others preferred the statistical clarity of learning theory.

The meetings convened by Bowlby bore no resemblance to the hushed, ritualistic assemblies of the British Psychoanalytic Society, where dissent often arrived wrapped in deference and disclaimers. Instead, these gatherings assumed the air of an expedition, each participant setting out from their own discipline's shoreline and drifting toward a common continent of discovery.

And so in 1963, Ainsworth's data on Uganda, nicknamed the 'Ganda Data', was shared.

She spoke to those assembled about the Ganda mothers who carried their infants bound to their hips in strips of bright cloth; of the infants who unfolded their limbs and reached, with slow and deliberate hands, toward the breast or the proffered finger. She described the measured way in which she had recorded each approach, each murmur, each gaze that lingered upon the mother's face before straying across the compound. Her listeners, among them Genevieve Appell and Miriam David, found in her observations an echo

304

of their own questions about how attachment took its shape in the earliest months.

Around the table, Henry Ricciuti and Harriet Rheingold considered whether the African infants' patterns could be mapped upon the familiar Western expectations of dependency and autonomy. Jacob Gewirtz, inclined by habit to frame every finding in terms of reinforcement and contingency, inquired whether Ainsworth's data might yet be rendered as a schedule of rewards. In a corner, Peter Wolff, whose own studies of newborn states of consciousness carried the flavour of physiology, leaned forward to puzzle over the relationship between arousal and the seeking of proximity.

The animal researchers listened with their own attentiveness; their presence at the meetings was another sign of Bowlby's increased Ethological ties and ever-firmer conviction that boundaries between disciplines were often imaginary. Harry Harlow offered his view that human infants showed the same hunger for contact comfort as rhesus monkeys. Robert Hinde, meanwhile, considered whether the mother's sensitivity was akin to the species-typical responsiveness he had catalogued in birds. Others present included names like Jay Rosenblatt and Thelma Rowell.

These discussions, dense with argument and recollection, convened beneath the ceiling of a Tavistock meeting room. John Bowlby himself presided with a quiet kind of watchfulness; he had an unmistakable satisfaction in witnessing the convergence of so many strains of inquiry. He had always suspected that the true shape of attachment would be discerned only when investigators ceased to guard their disciplinary fortresses and allowed their assumptions to be tested in the light of observation.

Indeed, it was this conviction that compelled him to invite such a diverse assembly into the clinic; he understood that progress required a willingness to endure discomfort, to permit one's cherished theories to be revised or discarded altogether. Whether it was the ethologists with their faith in instinct, the psychoanalysts with their maps of inner life, or the behaviorists with their tabulations of reinforcement schedules, each brought a fragment of insight that, when joined, might approach the reality of the infant's experience.

And so, in the evenings, as the last cups of tea cooled on the windowsills, Ainsworth would retreat to her notes, refining her categories. Already, she could see that what she had observed among the Ganda mothers bore a significance that extended beyond any single culture. The infants who had been met with prompt, consistent responses possessed a quiet confidence in their explorations; those whose mothers were less attuned showed a wary ambivalence or a tentative reluctance to depart from the mother's side.

These early patterns, she suspected, were not trivial variations but the first outlines of what would later be termed secure, avoidant, and ambivalent attachment. Yet in 1963, she held her conclusions lightly, aware that too great a certainty risked closing inquiry before it had matured.

The gatherings themselves proved quite fruitful: four volumes of proceedings eventually emerged under the title *Determinants of Infant Behaviour*, edited by Brian Foss. Each volume bore the imprint of these conversations: papers layered with citations, responses from colleagues who agreed or objected, and the occasional interpolated remark that revealed how much was still unsettled.

Bowlby read these pages with the satisfaction of one whose ideas had taken root beyond his own hands.

Of course, the volumes did not resolve every question. They did not bring a final agreement between those who held that attachment was an instinctual system shaped by natural selection and those who preferred to understand it as a learned dependency. But they created a record of a moment when disparate disciplines drew together around the undeniable reality of the infant's bond.

From time to time, Ainsworth would recall these meetings in later years, remarking how they felt both provisional and historic, as though they were constructing a bridge whose further span was still hidden by fog. Some of the names gathered there, Harlow, Hinde, Papousek, would in time become canonical. Others would recede, their contributions folded quietly into the greater works of their age.

Yet in the small hours of the afternoon, as one voice yielded to another, there was a sense of a shared recognition: that to understand the earliest attachments was to understand the architecture of the self. The infants in Ainsworth's Ugandan study, lying in the crook of their mothers' arms or venturing a few hesitant steps away, had become, through the slow accumulation of description and debate, figures of scientific consequence.

Bowlby knew that ideas, once loosed into the world, seldom travelled in straight lines; they encountered resistance, found unexpected allies, and were reshaped by the circumstances of their reception.

Yet he trusted that in time, the evidence would persuade more surely than any polemic.

307

Around this same time, he had set himself the task of putting his theories of attachment to the written page. He did not anticipate that this effort, begun in a spirit of confident curiosity, would swell into a trilogy; it had seemed, in those first months of study, that the questions he posed would submit to a single volume. Yet as he traced the contour of each argument, he discovered that he was trespassing across a territory once tilled by Freud, a territory seeded with concepts of instinct and drive that no longer seemed sufficient.

In *Attachment*, the first volume of this enlarging project, Bowlby found himself in the middle of an account of motivation whose ambition exceeded any prior attempt to reconcile ethology and psychoanalysis. He began by situating the human infant within a phylogenetic panorama, one in which each species, each fragile organism, must devise its own means of survival. Some creatures, he noted, relied on reflexive actions, which was to say those fixed patterns of behavior that repeated themselves without variance whenever a particular stimulus appeared. Others, especially the more complex, had developed the capacity for a goal-corrected regulation, so that every pursuit could be adjusted mid-course; a raptor dipping a wing to shadow the path of its prey, a primate altering its cry in response to the shifting signals of its group.

The language he borrowed for this description belonged less to Freud than to a generation of researchers who had found in cybernetics a fresh vocabulary for purposive action.

In the model of plan hierarchies, advanced by Miller, Galanter, and Pribram, he recognized a way to depict the organization of behavior that did not require recourse to the opaque reservoirs of *psychic energy*. Instead, an organism could be imagined as possessing a repertoire of *strategies*, subgoals nested within larger aims, each susceptible to refinement through feedback.

This conception implied that behavior, even when rooted in instinct, had plasticity; it could be shaped by experience, by the peculiarities of a given environment, provided those circumstances did not veer too far from what Bowlby termed the environment of 'evolutionary adaptedness'. It was here, in this speculative reconstruction of ancestral conditions, that he imagined the essential contours of human attachment had been fashioned: the infant's tendency to seek proximity to a familiar figure, the distress that followed separation, the reassurance that returned when contact was regained.

The ultimate function of attachment, he already believed, was survival: to ensure that the vulnerable human child remained within reach of protection. In this regard, attachment behavior stood alongside the systems governing feeding, mating, and exploration, each an expression of the same underlying imperative to persist.

Yet Bowlby pressed further. In his depiction, humans, more than other creatures, had evolved the capacity to form *internal working models:* complex representations of the environment and the self, constructed from experience and continually revised in response to new information. Borrowing from Craik's earlier speculations, he suggested that the accuracy of these models determined the individual's ability to predict what would come. When models were adequate, they facilitated adaptation, guiding the child toward safety and satisfaction. When they were distorted by inconsistency, neglect, or sudden loss, they could become sources of pathology, entangling the individual in misapprehension and dread.

He saw these internal models as structures that were both social and private. On the one hand, they were influenced by the gestures and utterances of others, like those early exchanges of touch and gaze, later enriched by language. On the other, they furnished the individual with a means of self-regulation, a set of expectations and priorities that oriented behavior even in solitude. Thus, attachment was never merely a reflexive clinging; it was a system of understanding and anticipation, susceptible to reason and imagination, subject to revision but resistant to sudden upheaval.

Having established this theoretical scaffold, Bowlby turned to the specific question of infant-mother attachment. He defined attachment behavior in terms that were almost spare: it was any behavior whose predictable outcome was proximity to a particular figure, and whose evolutionary purpose was protection. This purpose, he insisted, was intrinsic. It could not be explained away as a derivative of feeding or sexual drives; it was a distinct motivational system, organized to preserve the infant's life in the face of danger.

He described how, in the first months, infants directed their signals like crying, smiling, and grasping toward any available caregiver. But over time, these signals became increasingly selective, converging upon those figures who responded consistently, who met the child's needs with sensitivity. This process culminated in the emergence of a secure base: a relationship in which the child felt sufficient safety to explore and sufficient confidence to return when reassurance was needed.

Bowlby drew heavily on Ainsworth's observations to illustrate these dynamics. He quoted her finding that when interactions were smooth, each participant showed pleasure in the other's presence, pleasure that was heightened by expressions of affection. Conversely, in relationships marked by rejection or inconsistency, proximity became a source of anxiety rather than comfort. Children in these relationships did not abandon their bids for connection; instead, their attachment behaviour grew more insistent or more wary, a strategy adapted to an unpredictable world.

And in the final chapters, he discussed how attachment reorganized itself as the child matured. During the preschool years, the infant's simple proximity-seeking gave way to what he called a goal-corrected partnership, a new form of relatedness in which the child began to consider the caregiver's intentions, to negotiate separations and reunions with an emerging sense of perspective. This was not a dissolution of attachment but its *transformation*, a movement toward the understanding that others were separate centers of agency and feeling.

Though the volume was dense with citation of studies by Schaffer and Emerson, Ainsworth's meticulous records of maternal sensitivity, observations of primates and birds, it carried an undercurrent of something more intimate. Beneath the diagrams of plan hierarchies and the schematics of behavioural systems lay Bowlby's conviction that to map the early attachments was to map the secret architecture of human development.

When the first volume of Bowlby's trilogy was published in 1969, after years in the making, it found an atmosphere already dense with the ripening work of others.

Ainsworth's early findings from the Baltimore Study had begun to circulate, drifting across conferences and journals where they provoked conversations, if not outcry. Many who read her papers felt a recoil; they were uneasy with the insistence that avoidant behavior could be understood as defensive rather than independent. They scrutinized the Strange Situation as though it were a stage play rather than a research procedure, failing often to appreciate that each category had been grounded in the slow, exhaustive hours of home observations, when the ordinary business of caregiving unfolded without the artificiality of laboratory walls.

The dissent did not end abruptly; rather, it would taper through the decade. It would take time for a more settled understanding to take shape, but the seeds had been sown.

* * *

The 1970s finally set to rest many of the overdue anxieties of the war years. But a generation that had come of age under Churchill's bullish certainties now found itself in the company of subtler anxieties: economic tremors, emergent social movements, and the uneasy freedoms of modernity.

In psychology, too, the mood had shifted. Where once Freudian doctrine had lain across the field like an iron lattice, dictating the permissible contours of theory, there now rose a hunger for evidence traced in more tangible lines. Bowlby, his spectacles glinting beneath conference lights,

312

appeared both as an heir to old debates and as a herald of unorthodox convictions. The publication of Attachment had unfastened something; his insistence that childhood bonds were not simply fantasies but biological arrangements with measurable consequences had started to colonize the conversations of developmental science.

Yet the dawn of the new decade also brought an undertone of fatigue. The energy that had flared in the 1960s, with its gatherings of researchers and its fluent arguments, began to settle into the slower labor of confirmation and elaboration. Ainsworth, in Baltimore, sifted her data with an almost monastic diligence, while in Minnesota, Alan Sroufe and Everett Waters constructed longitudinal studies that would stretch across years. What had once been a theoretical conjecture now demanded the discipline of replication.

Meanwhile, John Bowlby was working.

As the world beyond his study grew restless with new ideals of freedom and equality, he was not content to rest on his laurels. Having set in motion the dense machinery of Attachment theory, John Bowlby quietly returned to his writing desk and now turned his attention towards a second volume.

Separation.

He approached the topic neither with the fatigue of a man repeating himself nor the haste of one impatient for closure; rather, he seemed drawn forward by the promise that each page would grant fresh purchase on the dark slope of childhood loss. In revisiting Freud's 1926 notion of signal anxiety, he intended to unfasten the neat knots with which psychoanalysis had bound fear to the mere anticipation of danger.

313

His study brimmed with folders lined in pale blue, their corners softened by the handling of years. As daylight slanted across the desk, he studied how the language of instinct and the language of feeling met, sometimes in union, sometimes at blunt angles. Freud had posited that anxiety arose when the ego perceived signals of impending trauma; Bowlby, ever wary of abstractions sealed off from observation, wished to recast this vision in terms of the real and visible. He believed that the child's dread of separation did not flicker in the shadows of the mind alone but erupted in a sequence of cries, withdrawals, and silences that anyone, if they cared to look closely, could chart.

He would draw upon Robertson's patient notations of infants in hospital wards, their faces slack with despair after the first heat of protest subsided. He would lean upon Harlow's experiments, those small tragedies of monkeys clinging to cloth simulacra of mothers. And in the process, he intended to show that separation was not a ghost of anxiety but a force with its own distinct contours.

And so, the year 1973 brought the second volume of Bowlby's trilogy into the world.

In the pages of *Separation*, Bowlby advanced from the descriptive certainties of Attachment to the more intricate terrain of motivation and personality; he undertook the delicate work of unpicking the fibers of fear, yearning, and memory that weave themselves through childhood and, unbidden, persist into maturity. He began with signal anxiety, Freud's term for that anticipatory dread which seizes the child when threatened with loss. Bowlby drew from the old idea but refashioned it until it scarcely resembled its origin. Where Freud had proposed that the child's terror derived from the withdrawal of libidinal satisfaction,

314

Bowlby discerned a subtler pattern. Two distinct currents stirred the mind's alarm: there were the unlearned clues to danger, the flash of a predator's eyes, the boom of thunder, and there was the more devastating absence of the mother or the figure who embodied safety.

These signals did not merge into one shapeless fear. They were governed by separate systems, each ancient and purposeful; he offered, almost as if recalling some precise domestic scene, the example of a ferocious dog interposing itself between mother and child, how the child's frantic impulse to flee tangled with the equally urgent compulsion to scramble into the mother's arms.

This clarity about fear became, in Bowlby's hands, the ground for a broader hypothesis.

He described an organism as situated always within a kind of *dynamic balance*, caught between the homing drift toward safety and the alert movement toward novelty. Attachment and exploration: each had its circuitry, its signals, its deep evolutionary reason. Together, they formed a family of behaviors whose purpose was to maintain a tolerable relation to the environment. Where Freud imagined the mind striving to diminish excitation, Bowlby believed the mind maintained a shifting equilibrium between the familiar and the unknown.

Having revised Freud's model of motivation, Bowlby set about rethinking the inner world itself as an active chamber of representation. Within this private architecture, Bowlby placed what he called the internal working model: the composite record of how the attachment figure had behaved, and of what the self had come to expect. To grow up under the gaze of a parent who both sheltered

315

and respected one's explorations was, he proposed, to assemble a working model of the self as worthy and efficacious. Yet to inhabit the cold or erratic atmosphere of rejection was to fashion a model in which one's needs appeared suspect or doomed to failure. The child, already a small strategist, would use these models to anticipate the caregiver's response, to script their own gestures of plea or retreat. Such models, Bowlby insisted, would endure long past infancy; they became the scaffolding on which the adult personality found its equilibrium or its fracture.

Among the more consequential passages in Separation were those concerned with the transmission of these models across generations. There, Bowlby noted the ways a parent, shaped by their own history of comfort or neglect, communicated their beliefs about worth, reliability, and love. Parents who had learned that attachment could be trusted tended to speak of it plainly; they conveyed to the child that internal models were subject to reflection, to revision, to the clarifying act of shared language. Those raised in more barren or chaotic relational landscapes often lacked this capacity for frankness; they transmitted, without quite intending it, the conviction that connection was perilous or undeserved.

Here, Bowlby made one of his more radical claims: that the inheritance of mental health and ill health was bound to these patterns of expectation, passed along the subtle channels of daily life. Genetic inheritance might possess its own silent power, but the family's microculture shaped the child's interior topography with a comparable force.

In reading these sections, one could sense how Bowlby, so often described as methodical, permitted himself moments of almost literary speculation; he imagined the

316

child's mind as a landscape accumulating the sediments of encounter. Each affectionate touch, each denial or indifference, left its trace. When Bowlby spoke of an internal working model, he was naming a structure both cognitive and emotional, precise yet suffused with the vague atmospheres of remembered experience.

As he neared the end of the manuscript, there arose a tone of provisional summation. He had, in a decade of writing, moved the field away from the Freudian conceptions that once seemed monolithic. Yet he did not pretend the work was complete; he left room for later scholars to test and revise the theory. And in the quiet hours when he drafted the closing chapters, Bowlby remained aware that the patterns of attachment, once disclosed, raised more questions than they resolved.

There was still more work to be done.

Meanwhile, the 70s were seeing attachment theory steadily grow in influence, and not only by John Bowlby's hand. Mary Ainsworth's influence was also slowly making itself known; one student after another carried from her Baltimore rooms the habits of careful observation and the conviction that infancy was saturated with pattern and signal. Her work now began to fan outward in the dissertations and publications of those who had trained beside her, coded with her, and heard her tapes.

Already in 1970, Silvia Bell had probed the liminal space between object permanence and attachment; what did it mean for a child to grasp that something unseen remained existent, and how did that knowledge thread itself into the texture of a relationship? Her findings suggested that memory and expectation, even in their infancy, were already

317

entwined with the emotional scaffolding Bowlby had described. In the same year as the publication of Bowlby's *Separation*, Mary Main stepped forward with her study of toddlers, observing how security, or the absence of it, traced itself into the child's ability to become absorbed in play, to test and reconfigure the world. Mark Cummings turned to the broader implications of caregiving itself; the placement of children in day care was no longer merely a logistical question, but one laden with psychological texture.

There was a turning outward as well. Alicia Lieberman, in 1977, moved into the shared terrain of the preschool world, where peers became mirrors or witnesses to internal working models already forming. Milton Kotelchuck looked to fathers; Robert Marvin to the subtleties of the goal-corrected partnership. Each name carried with it the shape of a new direction, Greenberg's work with deaf children, Waters's steady hand tracking continuity across months that once seemed ungraspable.

Unlike the cult of Freudian ritual, these studies did not cohere into dogma; they offered instead a widening constellation, each body orbiting the twin suns of Attachment Theory and the Strange Situation, while still reaching for other skies.

And slowly, the field was beginning to change.

***

It was now 1980, and a certain expectancy had gathered around the field that, only a generation earlier, remained bound to the vocabulary of drives and defenses.

The ascendance of information processing theories had begun to erode the primacy of the Freudian imagination. Bowlby's work, once regarded as an unsettling departure by traditionalists like those within the Psychoanalytic Society, now stood near the center of a widening conversation about the mechanics of mind. He had been working on the final book of his trilogy off and on for seven years, and in the meantime, concepts of attachment and loss had somehow, seemingly overnight, become part of the psychological lexicon. The intellectual climate had softened, and Mary Ainsworth's Strange Situation had been replicated in diverse settings; longitudinal studies from Minnesota to London had affirmed that early relational experiences could be traced, sometimes with disquieting clarity, across decades.

But for all these contributions, the world in 1980 would be shaken by another great publication by John Bowlby: the third and final volume of his trilogy.

After thorough checking and rechecking, *Loss* appeared in the shelves in that very year. After handling Attachment and Separation, Bowlby turned fully to grief, to the quiet landscapes of mourning, internal rupture, and absence. The book was a widening of the path already trodden; Attachment and Separation had laid the foundation, but Loss moved through the territory with a certain weight of inevitability. It traced the fault lines not only of affect but of cognition; for Bowlby, mourning was not an event, but a process unfolding within systems, among layers of memory, inside the complicated house of the mind.

He turned his attention to internal working models; to the silent architectures of perception and expectation that were, he believed, laid down in the earliest encounters with caregiving. These models, he believed, influenced the

319

patterns of thought and reaction; they guided attention; they rendered some experiences salient and others invisible. And, importantly, once established, they held firm.

Their stability, he observed, came from two forces. First, from the sheer power of *repetition*, interactions that recur often enough become automatic, pulled beneath the level of conscious thought. Second, from the *reciprocity* of relationships, for dyads, once formed, are difficult to unbind. Each party carries an expectation of the other. Mother anticipates the child's cry; the child expects the mother's return. These reciprocal models reinforce each other; they are rehearsed and enacted until they harden.

But time does not stand still.

A world which once suited the model changes; parents die; the secure base vanishes; expectations are confounded. And yet the internal model persists. It filters incoming experience, admits only what is congruent. Information is not received raw; it is processed, transformed, distorted, if necessary, to fit the map already drawn.

Bowlby found support for these mechanisms in the research of others. Dixon and Erdelyi, in their studies of selective attention, had shown that perception was layered, only some of the stimuli reaching the brain would arrive at conscious awareness. He was especially drawn to experiments in dichotic listening, in which participants, presented with two competing auditory streams, would tune out one; and yet, if a personally relevant word appeared in the unattended stream, the listener would jolt, startled. The unattended had been processed after all.

This, Bowlby believed, was the mechanism by which individuals protect themselves from pain. Information, once sensed, is excluded not because it was never perceived, but because it threatens coherence. He called this defensive exclusion.

The individual has heard, has known...yet at some level, *chooses* not to know.

Three circumstances made this form of exclusion more likely in children: when a parent's behavior contradicted their claims; when a parent's actions were too unbearable to integrate; or when the child, out of guilt or shame, suppressed their own feelings or fantasies. In such cases, the result was a division between two sets of internal working models. The model in conscious awareness, often shaped by what the child had been told, painted the parent as benign, perhaps disappointed by the child's inadequacy. The second, excluded from awareness, preserved the raw emotional truth: that the parent had rejected, or frightened, or failed.

Now, the contradiction would be too much.

And so, a rupture followed.

In searching for an explanatory framework, Bowlby turned to Endel Tulving's distinction between semantic and episodic memory. One system stored facts, generalizations, borrowed propositions, what the child had been told. The other held raw, autobiographical events, what had been lived. It was in the contradiction between these systems, Bowlby believed, that psychic conflict took root. When a child's experience of rejection clashed with a caregiver's verbal reassurances, semantic memory might override the episodic; the lived memory is repressed, and semantic knowledge preserved. This dynamic, he thought, played out most sharply in children who had suffered bereavement before the age of three.

But Bowlby also turned to motivation, to the interplay of behavioral systems. Previously, in *Attachment* and *Separation*, he had described these systems as distinct and competitive: attachment versus exploration, comfort versus curiosity. But in *Loss*, he offered a higher-order view. The mind, he now proposed, was not a battlefield of impulses, but a network governed by an executive structure, a controller akin in function to Freud's ego, but rooted in neurobiology rather than metaphor. This structure, embedded in the central nervous system, worked hierarchically, scanning stimuli for relevance; coordinating responses; choosing, sometimes unconsciously, between competing demands.

The brain, in Bowlby's vision, was neither a stage nor a mirror; it was a control center.

The executive system, linked intimately with memory, weighed incoming information against long-term expectations. If relevant, information might rise to the level of conscious scrutiny; if threatening, it might be diverted. But this control structure did not always function smoothly. In some individuals, Bowlby believed the system was fragmented; subsystems failed to communicate; memories could not be retrieved; behavioral patterns failed to activate when needed.

In such cases, what emerged was incoherence. This was nowhere more visible than in disordered mourning. Bowlby saw, in his clinical cases, instances where grief had lost its object; where emotions flickered but their source could not be named. A child, bereaved, might become preoccupied with their own feelings, interpreting sadness as defect, not signal. Or they might redirect care outward, compulsively protecting others; attachment behavior remained, but its direction had shifted.

Such disconnections were the hallmark of pathological mourning, and the consequences were plain. The attachment system, once disrupted and never restored, could spiral into distortions of personality, cognition, and relational life.

And as with his earlier volumes, the impact was both immediate and slow-burning. Loss did not settle debates; it stirred them. But it offered a vocabulary; it clarified a problem that had long been obscured beneath metaphors of detachment and denial. Bowlby had little interest in preserving past schematics for their own sake. He was in it for good faith and good science; he offered falsifiable but rigorous data in the place of platitudes and reliabilities.

And even now, more questions interested him. The scientific spirit within John Bowlby demanded from him even more avenues of inquiry, and he had no trouble answering this call.

Chapter 15.

Darwin

In the coming years, he sat often by the window of his study; the movement of the trees, the shifting translucence of afternoon light on the brick walls across the garden, seemed to mirror the slow unpeeling of memory that he had come to regard as the final, necessary work.

He had spent decades clarifying the ordinary mysteries of infancy, and now he often found himself preoccupied by a few new interests. The first was the extension of his life's work: the question of what became of those earliest models of his theory once the child grew into a reasoning, suffering adult. To this end, a notion settled gradually into his writing: the idea that psychotherapy itself must be understood in attachment terms. The client came bearing not only the burden of conscious narrative but the more tenacious inheritance of early relational patterns; these internal working models, forged out of the parent's acceptance or refusal, the parent's silence or gaze, exerted a persistent, almost mineral pressure on perception. A person with models too brittle to accommodate new experience might bend each relationship to fit the old, injurious shape.

Transference, thus, was not a singular aberration like Freud believed; it was the predictable consequence of attachment systems that had once secured safety but had never been revised.

But increasingly, he was beginning to find that the seeds of his theory were now being spread forth more by others than himself. Now that his days were no longer consumed by his three-volume magnum opus, he had more time: time to be a husband, time to be a father, and time to be a man who could look back at his life and reflect on it. And with the passage of time, he found himself spending his afternoons reading until it was dark, letting the yellow light of his bedside lamp pool over the pages. He went back and read quite a few of the original texts he had failed to quite appreciate when he was a younger man, and one of those texts was by one of the most famous, or infamous, writers in history…

…Charles Darwin.

***

He had always admired Darwin; that strange, solitary figure who stood at the threshold between theology and geology, between the easy certainties of his century and the perplexities of all centuries to follow. His own interest in ethological and evolutionary disciplines meant he was quite familiar already with Darwin, but learning more about the figure fascinated him. So in the evenings, when the tide of correspondence had receded and the house settled into its hush, he would sometimes study the life of that strange man.

In particular, he found himself strangely drawn to the peculiar case of Charles Darwin's illness. It was a fascination that arose from a recognition: the patterns of sickness, recurrence, and hidden dread that he had studied in the minds of children seemed refracted, on a grand historical scale, in the life of this man whose thought had reshaped the comprehension of life itself.

Bowlby now studied Darwin's letters and diaries, examining not only the famous words in which the naturalist described his intellectual revelations but also the passages marked by hesitation, fatigue, and the intimate perplexities of the flesh. As a young man at Edinburgh, Darwin had discovered that his constitution rebelled against the raw realities of surgery; he recoiled from the sound of bone saws and the sweetish tang of blood. This revulsion pressed the youth toward another domain of inquiry: natural history, whose specimens and landscapes did not so directly implicate the senses in suffering. Later, when he was sent to Cambridge to prepare for a life in the clergy, his imagination was already alight with the prospect of a more empirical calling.

It was in December of 1831, as Darwin waited in Plymouth for the Beagle to embark, that the first undeniable symptoms presented themselves. He felt sharp pain in his chest, a disordered drumming of the heart that he could not name without fear it might tether him permanently to England's shores. So he chose secrecy and set sail under the burden of an unspoken frailty. The voyage itself, however, was punctuated by spells of debilitation. The ocean's movement sickened him beyond bearing; the small cabin, always shifting on an uncertain, drunk fulcrum, became a cause for endless bouts of nausea. Yet it was on land, in the midst of discovery, that he found himself most violently undone.

In Argentina, he collapsed with a fever that had already lead to the death of a young shipmate; he lay in the dark hold of a riverboat, listening to his own breath as though it belonged to a stranger. Later, in September 1834, returning from the Andes, he succumbed again, this time in Valparaiso, where a month in bed did little to restore the equilibrium he had once assumed invulnerable. He wrote of the *benchuca*, the black bug whose bite he recorded almost as a curiosity, never suspecting that the parasite it carried might, decades later, provide an explanation for his lifetime of indisposition.

The Beagle returned him to England in 1836, and by then the pattern had been set: a brilliant mind yoked to an unreliable body.

He was scarcely thirty when the palpitations resumed; he was counseled to withdraw to the countryside, to abandon the press of correspondence and lectures. In October 1837, he confessed in his journal that any emotional agitation brought a storm of symptoms: heart racing, a suffocating sense that life was unspooling faster than his capacity to contain it. Even as he pressed forward with his secret speculations on transmutation, ideas that would mature into the theory of evolution, he felt himself eroded by invisible forces.

In the spring of 1838, the toll of overwork became undeniable. He suffered stomach convulsions, headaches so intense that he lay inert for days, incapable of thought or movement. A brief interlude in Scotland seemed to restore

327

him, but the truce was short-lived. Illness returned with an almost ritual regularity. He married Emma Wedgwood in January 1839, and by December, as she advanced toward childbirth, Darwin again descended into exhaustion, his energies so depleted that he could produce scarcely any work.

Bowlby lingered over the accounts of these decades, these forty years in which Darwin was afflicted by a shifting assemblage of symptoms. There were days marked by vertigo, a sensation that the floor had slipped a few degrees beneath his feet; there were nights when muscle spasms twisted his limbs and left him trembling. He recorded fits of vomiting that emptied him of strength; bloating and colics that confined him to bed. There were intervals when vision grew uncertain; black specks danced across the page, and with them came the conviction that reason itself might dissolve.

At times, Darwin described a lassitude so profound that he could not summon the will to lift a pen; in other seasons, he wrote of tremors, headaches, and eczema that crept across his scalp. His letters contained the language of despair, he confessed to crying without cause, to the dread of imminent death, to moments of consciousness dissolving into a blank oblivion. Tachycardia arrived unpredictably, with the force of calamity. At night, he could not sleep. When at last sleep came, it was invaded by tinnitus, a dull roaring that grew into a crescendo of panic.

The pattern, Bowlby thought, was itself a kind of argument: the past leaves an impression upon the nervous system as surely as it marks memory. The interplay of biology and temperament, of infection and constitution, created a narrative no less complex than the emotional biographies he had traced in his own work.

The illness that bothered Darwin, Bowlby decided, had to be psychosomatic.

Around this time, he began writing a book on the matter as well. It was not written with the passionate ardor of his other books, but as something to the side, a project that he could work on without being consumed by. It gave him a kind of pleasure, after all, to write about and study the father of evolutionary science. For one thing, he quite respected the modesty with which Darwin had borne his debility. Despite the daily reckonings with weakness, he had built a theory so elegant that it transformed the scaffolding of science. Yet he could not help but see in these chronic illnesses the deeper theme that preoccupied his own last years: the consequences of fear unspoken, pain unacknowledged. When Darwin hid his palpitations in Plymouth, when he refused to name the full measure of his distress, he had obeyed an instinct that Bowlby knew intimately.

John Bowlby could immediately see that the child who must conceal sorrow to preserve attachment becomes, in adulthood, the scientist who suppresses the knowledge of his own fragility lest it interrupt the work that gives life its coherence. Bowlby believed that such concealment, though necessary at times, exacted a cost, a steady attrition of vitality, a withdrawal from the immediacy of experience.

Bowlby realized quickly that Darwin's adult life had *always* borne the unmistakable mark of a premorbid vulnerability; a delicate responsiveness to stress and the implicit threat of judgment. Even in youth, Darwin's spirit had seemed unusually susceptible to the corrosive power of

329

censure. He recoiled from criticism as though it were a physical injury; the merest suggestion of disapproval could draw from him an acute turmoil of stomach pains, palpitations, and nervous exhaustion. Across the margins of Darwin's letters, Bowlby saw this sensitivity coiled like a hidden wire, waiting to spark.

Even Darwin's episodes of abdominal distress often erupted at the threshold of some public obligation or challenge. Each time he was compelled to defend his views, which by their nature unsettled the prevailing doctrines, his body answered with nausea, vomiting, dizziness. His intestines became a theatre of protest, and his mind succumbed to dread.

Bowlby read of these spells and saw a sad truth: a life nearly torn in two by the unrelenting tension between intellectual daring and emotional fragility. He could not quite tell why, but in some way, he was beginning to see in Charles Darwin a strange sense of kinship.

***

As the 1980s continued to trickle by, John Bowlby continued his quiet, deliberate movement between his Hampstead study and the rooms at Tavistock, the pavements slicked with rain, the air always bearing that peculiar London damp that curled paper and set the joints to aching. Buses went glacially along Euston Road as Thatcher's policies lifted and sank lives by invisible pulleys. The city was new and yet how it had always been; the eternally grey skies blotted out by soot-blunted spires in the process of transitioning into the angular glass of financiers.

Still, the ironwork railings, the small front gardens with their marigolds and their litter, preserved the memory of another age, when John Bowlby and his brother had trudged along on their way to school...

As he walked those paths now, it was as a kindly and venerable older man. Time had aged him into a figure at once visible and oddly peripheral, a man whose work had become an unspoken foundation beneath so much of modern thought about the child and the mother. Young researchers, flush with fresh grants and American journals, nodded politely when they met him in the corridors of the Tavistock but did not quite perceive the originality of what he had pressed into being.

He thought, often, of the course his life had taken; he thought about the European cities he had visited for his WHO report, about the many children he had helped treat, about friends and family he had lost over the years. He thought of people like his friend Durbin, of his old instructors, even of his rivals in the early days of his practice.

Time had the strange habit of making one look back, and he did so often now. He thought of his own upbringing, about his beloved nurse Minnie, about the distant silhouette of his father, and the hour of maternal presence he experienced every day at supper. He thought of the cold walls of the nursery, of distant boarding schools, and of a life spent trying to understand the toll affection of separation had on him and the world at large.

Of course, these musings only increased his connection to Darwin as he continued his book. For John

Bowlby, now felt sure he could trace the beginnings of Darwin's long illness, the loss of his mother.

***

It was 1817, and at eight years old, Charles Darwin had lost his mother.

As far as John Bowlby was concerned, that early bereavement had a determinative gravity. It was no small thing, he believed, to be deprived of a mother's presence at the most impressionable stage of emotional development. The loss, though cushioned by the attentions of older sisters who strove to provide consistency, had left Darwin with a wound that never fully closed. And though his childhood had been described as generally happy, Bowlby knew such summaries concealed the subterranean life of feeling, which persisted long after grief had been officially set aside.

Bowlby had observed in countless patients that the experience of separation, the irremediable fact of an absent figure who once anchored the child's sense of safety, could crystallize in adult life as *panic*. The connection between the two was not merely symbolic; it was functional, encoded in the patterns by which the nervous system learned to anticipate danger. In Darwin's case, Bowlby detected that same associative logic.

It struck Bowlby as especially telling that Darwin's disease displayed a variable intensity of symptoms over decades, along with a chronic, unremitting course. There was no steady deterioration of the organs, no inevitable decline in the tissues themselves. This fact, more than any

332

other, suggested to Bowlby that the illness belonged to the realm of the psychosomatic, where mind and body collude in the production of suffering. Such a conclusion did not diminish Darwin's legitimacy as a patient, nor did it suggest the symptoms were less real. On the contrary, it affirmed that the body can be the most unyielding archive of loss.

Panic disorder, he knew, tended to arise during adolescence or early adulthood, usually in connection with critical life changes. For Darwin, the death of his mother may have set in motion the vulnerability that later flourished into incapacitating dread.

Perhaps the most striking evidence of Darwin's unresolved grief lay in the instances of denial that littered the record. In one letter of condolence, Darwin wrote, seemingly without irony, that he had "never in my life lost one near relation." The sentence glimmered on the page with an uncanny dissonance; it was as if he had excised the fact of his mother's death so thoroughly that it no longer belonged to his autobiographical narrative. In another episode, recorded almost incidentally by a family observer, Darwin participated in a word game resembling Scrabble. Another player added the letter "M" to the word "OTHER," forming the word "MOTHER."

Darwin stared at the arrangement as though it were a cipher he could not interpret. Then, in an agitated voice, he exclaimed:

"There's no such word as M-OTHER!"

Having made this proclamation, he fell silent.

Bowlby read this vignette again and again, each time with the same mixture of fascination and pity. He believed that such denial was not simply an error or an evasion; it was a protective gesture, evolved to spare the mind an encounter with unbearable pain. Yet the protection came at a price. Darwin's body, deprived of any sanctioned means to remember or grieve, became the medium in which sorrow was perpetually enacted. The convulsions, palpitations, and exhaustion were not accidents but expressions, messages sent by a mind unable to acknowledge what it had lost.

As Bowlby inched further into this study, he began to see Darwin's illness further and further in the light of his own theory. As he saw it, the child who endures an early rupture of attachment grows up to confront every fresh challenge with a covert apprehension; the adult life becomes a sequence of efforts to secure reassurance in a world that feels perpetually unstable. When such reassurance fails, or when the prospect of exposure threatens to reveal hidden inadequacies, the body supplies its own pretext for withdrawal. In this light, Darwin's retreats, his spells of invalidism, his withdrawal to Down House, and even his avoidance of controversy could be understood as defensive maneuvers. They were at once genuine necessities and symbolic enactments.

Illness, for instance, allowed him to remain apart, to avoid the overmastering obligations that public life demanded. At the same time, the periodic recoveries permitted him to continue the work that animated his intellect. The cycle of collapse and restoration, like the alternation of attachment and exploration in the child, was the rhythm by which he sustained himself.

It is strange but not difficult to see some parallels between Bowlby and Darwin, and it is not difficult to see why Bowlby was so drawn to the man. After all, both men occupied paradoxical positions in their respective times: insiders who saw too clearly; rebels disguised as gentlemen. Darwin's ideas dismantled the stability of species, of divine intention, of a fixed human order. He did it slowly, almost apologetically, his sentences hedged and folded, but the effect was seismic. Bowlby, in turn, broke ranks with the Freudians, challenged the sentimentalities of mid-century childcare, and insisted that early attachments mattered profoundly, permanently. He, too, published carefully, cited rigorously, and avoided excess. But beneath the surface was the same determination to overturn received wisdom.

Of course, there were differences. Darwin worked in an age of empire and discovery, when nature seemed a wild ledger waiting to be read. In contrast, Bowlby came of age in a time marked by loss and reassembly: the First War, the Second, the long cold afternoons of rationing and recovery. Darwin's Beagle voyage lasted five years; Bowlby's expedition lasted half a century and required only the rare departure from England. After all, his terrain was the human bond, its ruptures and repairs. Yet for both men, science was not a discipline apart from life but rather a way of making sense of the personal. To this end, each observed their subjects with care, avoiding grand pronouncements in favor of patterns. And each, in his way, confronted resistance. Darwin feared the scandal of his conclusions; he delayed publication for years. Bowlby was met with polite rebukes, accusations of oversimplification, charges that he reduced the complexity of the mind to mere maternal fuss.

Solitude marked them both; it was the price of their work, of seeing what others avoided. And yet, neither man had truly worked alone. Darwin had Emma, his cousin and wife, a woman who read proofs and bore children and

335

watched her husband decline. Bowlby had colleagues, analysts, critics; he had the Tavistock and the World Health Organization; he had his own children, his own life, his own losses.

And perhaps this is what drew John Bowlby apart the most from Charles Darwin; a certain ease in his own skin and life, a certain contentment that Darwin, sadly, had not quite been able to muster.

**

Meanwhile, as John Bowlby continued to chronicle the legend of one great man of the sciences, his own legend was slowly entering into the crimson-gold hue of its final sunset.

Outside, London continued to change with that particular brusqueness the city reserves for late decades; the cranes punctuated the skyline, traffic thickened around Russell Square, and the pace of psychiatric research, its journals, its conferences, its alliances with pharmacology, outstripped even the patience of men like Bowlby, who still wrote with pens and held conversation as a form of inquiry. He was a man of his time, though the times seemed to be passing him by; yet, he was at peace with this, too. He had lived a good life by his reckoning, was happy with his children and cared for them deeply, though he was always averse to the word *love*. Too often, that word had masked too many different feelings for him to view it as anything but an ambivalent and roughly arbitrary four-lettered word…yet, perhaps he understood its meaning better than most.

The subject of love, however, did interest him. He had continued to work on projects aside from the Darwin biography, and in 1988, he published *A Secure Base*, a work less revolutionary but no less insightful than its predecessors. It was a work that addressed itself to the rather intimate architecture of home life. He believed that love, in actuality, ought not to be a vague emotion or a hazy parental ideal to be aspired toward in sentiment; it was a pattern of dependable acts, of responsiveness and presence, of consistency that held even during strain. To give a child a *secure base* was to grant them the confidence to explore, the strength to return, and the capacity to mourn.

By 1989, his time was narrowing, though not obviously. His stride still carried purpose, and his sentences retained their rhythm. That year, he composed an epilogue to *Attachment Across the Life Cycle*, a volume shaped by those who had carried his theory forward and outward, into domains he himself had not ventured: neuroscience, policy, developmental psychology in its many branches. The epilogue served as both coda and benediction: not a farewell, but a turning outward, as if to say, *this is yours now*. Bowlby had long understood that ideas, once formed and shared, ceased to belong wholly to their authors; they passed into others, were adapted, contested, evolved. And unlike some giants of the past, John Bowlby was uninterested in the trappings of cult, in the construction of a canonical dogma; he knew that the future was its own master, and that the best he could do was to wish it well.

For this reason, he had also come to expect criticism from both old peers and those representing new waves of thought. This, too, he knew was natural; after all, what was the point of science if not to challenge and succeed?

As his hair thinned to a wispy grey, the arguments of decades past still reached him as steady, familiar tides; they came in the form of journal articles, conference remarks, reviews, and, occasionally, the pointed question from a younger colleague. They were not all hostile; many were justified, even illuminating. Others misread him entirely. He had, over the years, become used to both kinds of critique.

He thought often of Michael Rutter's work, and the way it had prised open one of his central formulations: the maternal-deprivation hypothesis. When Bowlby had written of the damage wrought by early separation, he had not been careless, but neither had he been immune to the narrowing effect of a compelling idea. Michael Rutter, who had been interested in Bowlby's work throughout both the 70s and 80s, had amassed a body of work where he had made the distinction between "privation", ie, never forming an attachment at all, and "deprivation", losing one after it had formed. In retrospect, Bowlby saw the utility of the distinction; the clinical presentations of the two were not identical, the developmental pathways diverged. In his early work, he had indeed spoken of separation and the failure to form attachments as though they belonged to a single continuum. The war years had encouraged that collapse of categories, with children evacuated from their homes, institutionalised in orphanages, or abandoned to relatives.

Rutter's second point cut to the question of causation. To speak of deprivation as a direct cause of later difficulties was to ignore the other privations that often accompanied it: malnutrition, lack of stimulation, inadequate schooling. Rutter called deprivation a "risk

338

factor," not a sentence. John Bowlby could perhaps see the point of this, but perhaps he also felt the language of "risk" could soften the urgency he had sought to convey. In the post-war years, policy-makers had needed to be struck, jolted into seeing the unseen harm. A measured "risk factor" might not have been enough to shift the machinery of child welfare.

The notion of a "critical period" had also been forced to give ground. He had once argued that the earliest years, particularly the first two, were decisive in determining the nature and quality of a child's attachments; that a failure here was, if not irreparable, then permanently scarring. But the Koluchova twins in Czechoslovakia had complicated the picture. Isolated until the age of seven, subjected to cruelty and neglect, they had nonetheless gone on to recover under the care of a devoted foster family. Their progress, social, emotional, and intellectual, had been striking. For critics, the case proved that recovery was possible well beyond the "critical" window he had described.

Bowlby had not been blind to such evidence and its implications. By now, he preferred to speak of a "sensitive period", a span of years in which attachment formed most readily, but after which the task became progressively harder, not impossible. The twins did not, in his mind, erase the value of the idea; they merely showed that the organism, under rare and fortunate circumstances, could still repair itself. The sensitive period was not a locked door, but a narrowing passage.

Then there was the matter of monotropy, the almost-popular belief that he had placed too much emphasis on the mother as the primary figure in a child's life. It was not, he still maintained, an invention of his; it came from observation, both clinical and ethological. Young children tended to orient their need for safety toward one figure above all others, and in mid-century Britain that figure was almost invariably the mother. But in print, the argument too easily hardened into a prescription. He had been reproached, and not without cause, for reinforcing traditional gender roles, for placing an emotional weight on women that men were rarely asked to bear. Feminist critics had been quite vocal on this point: by elevating the mother's role, they believed he had risked rendering fathers, siblings, and extended kin invisible in the child's emotional landscape.

It was true that his language, especially in earlier works, had not been careful enough to make the distinction between biological inevitability and cultural norm. Attachment could form with a father, an aunt, a grandmother, or an older sibling; the principle was one of constancy and responsiveness, not maternal exclusivity. Yet the evidence that one figure generally occupied a primary place remained compelling to him. The charge of "overemphasis" was perhaps partly a misunderstanding and partly the result of his own failure to write with more precision about alternative figures.

And then there were the old classics, criticisms that had stuck around for years now. Chief among them was The Forty-Four Juvenile Thieves study, which had been attacked almost from the moment it appeared. The criticisms had dulled with the years, but they remained constant, especially with regard to the matter of confirmation bias. As far as many of his colleagues were concerned, he had been the architect of both the hypothesis and the study's design; the danger that he would see in the data what he expected to see was real. At the time, of course, he had regarded the work less as a definitive proof than as an opening salvo, a way of bringing to light a set of clinical observations that, to him, had been all but self-evident. It had succeeded in that sense, but the methodological weaknesses were fair game, and he had never pretended otherwise in private.

Looking back, Bowlby saw that the criticisms, those grounded in evidence, at least, had forced him to refine, to clarify, to temper. The misunderstandings had been harder to bear, for they could not always be corrected; a phrase once printed could be quoted without its qualifying paragraphs for decades. Ainsworth had been invaluable in that regard; much of her work in furthering attachment theory had also borne the unenviable task of defending it, developing it, and clearing the air around the presuppositions that so often seemed to come hand in hand with it. For this, among other things, John Bowlby continued to appreciate her work.

The house would often sit quiet as he sat with his thoughts; outside, the trees moved in the wind. He was all too aware of time pressing forward, of the years closing in. Yet the debates of the past did not feel entirely finished; somewhere, in a seminar room or a review article, another generation would take them up again. He imagined them: students and scholars, critics and defenders returning to the same questions, arguing them over and over with the same urgency he had shown in the prime of his years.

And as long as these debates continued, John Bowlby was content with the thought that their ultimate result would be for the best: the betterment of the life of the child, and through that, the betterment of the world itself.

***

341

Slowly, the eighties collapsed into the brave new nineties. The year opened expectantly, as in London, the mornings slipped in quietly over brick and frost. In Germany, they said, something immense had shifted, but here the air simply tasted damp; taxis moved through puddles, even as buses groaned their way along and men in suits hurried past the homeless crouched by Bank station. Cutting-edge computers began to blink from desks in government offices, and at Heathrow, a man looked at the arrivals board and thought how impersonal it had become.

Time was moving forward, and the world had changed; John Bowlby knew by now that he had done all he could for his world, but the currents that had carried the post-war decades now pulled in directions that he could not quite fathom. This, he knew, would be the work and struggle of his successors and colleagues.

Still…one final book remained.

That very year, John Bowlby found himself looking at the finished draft of his comprehensive biography of Charles Darwin. Darwin, long his inspiration, had become first a guiding light, and then a shadow in Bowlby's steps; now, John Bowlby felt he understood the man more intimately than ever before. The book that had emerged from this arduous process went beyond biography, and had become a kind of text on psychological archaeology: almost a study of how loss for one great man had become illness, and how his silence had ossified into somatic pain.

It was only fitting, then, that this psychological reckoning with history was the last he saw to completion. As

342

if, in closing the arc of Darwin's life, he had also gathered together the threads of his own.

**

In that final year of 1990, he travelled to the Isle of Skye, to the house he kept for retreat and rest.

The Isle was a mist-laced and angular thing that rose from the water like a thought half-formed, shaped by wind, worn by time. Its ridges curved with defiance, abrupt and hard as old hands folded over one another. To approach it by sea was to feel a coolness gather on the tongue, the scent of brine and peat, moss layered on stone, and salt meeting earth. Light fell upon it in broken phrases, scattered across lochs and marshes; meanwhile, the Cuillin Hills loomed from the centre, their black rock gleaming when the clouds momentarily parted.

At the edges, the cliffs crumbled down into the Atlantic; sheep wandered over slopes too steep for certainty, their coats snagged with the day's weather. One might walk there for hours and encounter no voice but one's own, or the wind speaking its fractured, fluent tongue through the heather. The houses, when they appeared, were whitewashed, slate-roofed, and crouching to avoid the wind. Here and there, rusted farm gates swung open with no land to guard.

In coming to the Isle of Skye, John Bowlby had come to an ancient plot of land, one that had belonged, historically, to no one and to everyone.

Norse kings had named it; Highland clans had bled for it. The MacLeods and MacDonalds had laid claim to it, and though their ghosts had long since grown quiet, the land still endured, remembering them in the Glen Sligachan, in the sharp drops of Kilt Rock. The weather here, meanwhile, could be moody: sun, mist, or hard rain. In the harsher storms, it would be impossible to say where the sky ended and the sea began; nonetheless, John Bowlby found himself visiting in a reasonably placid period, content to let the island soothe his health. He had long preferred solitude to spectacle; he was not drawn to public honors, though they had come. He had been appointed a CBE; he had lectured internationally; his work had shaped social policy.

Yet it was here that he came for peace.

It is difficult to say exactly why John Bowlby was quite so fond of the family estate at the Isle of Skye, but perhaps his childhood visits to Scotland had something to do with it. After all, the Isle must have stirred in him if not memories then sensations: the hush of moss underfoot, the soft pressure of wool against a child's skin, the smell of heather, almost medicinal in its dryness. Perhaps the sound of the water lapping greedily against the cliffs in an endless rhythm, the light falling at a slant in late afternoon, and the pale grass whipped to one side by the wind reminded him of the winds that used to lift his cap and send it tumbling down a slope in the New Forest or in Ayrshire back in those rare family holidays of his childhood...

It had not been a happy childhood, but to go to Scotland in late summer had been to step into another order of time. Even though it was an indulgence of class, as all such rituals were, for the child John, it had also been a space of release. He remembered New Forest too: the stillness of

344

trees holding their breath, the seemingly endless green. But Scotland was wilder, more serious. Perhaps he remembered how, in Ayrshire, they had gone walking for hours, sometimes in silence, his grandfather striding ahead, the rest catching up in fits and starts. Perhaps he remembered hunting trips, watching the rare smile on his mother's face, or the greedy gulps of air after a long trek.

Now, on Skye, in the last season of his life, he was free once more, far freer than he had ever been as a child. He no longer had to explain himself to anyone. He could rise when he wished, walk when he pleased. He had a lifetime behind him and a legacy that would continue for decades ahead of him. And though no one can know what John Bowlby thought or felt in his last days, it is reasonable to assume that he was a man mostly at peace.

On the 2nd of September, he died after a stroke.

He would be survived by his wife and his children, and remembered the world over. In the coming weeks, colleagues gathered their memories, obituaries were drawn out, tributes were written, and conferences convened. Yet the most lasting recognition for John Bowlby would come from his own words and his own work: a lifetime of effort condensed into theory.

Thus, like the intrepid Darwin that had fascinated him for so long, John Bowlby would leave the world and enter into his own contributions and legacy, carried onwards in every policy and practice that aimed to improve the lot of the child and the development of the human being.

Epilogue

When I began Searching for Bowlby, I imagined myself on an intellectual errand, as if I could walk straight to the shelf where "attachment theory" was filed, open the drawer, and find the answers neatly organized. Instead, what I found was a treasure hunt, lost in a place that was more labyrinth than library. What began as an endeavor of intellectual curiosity soon turned into something far more interesting.

You see, I went looking for a theorist. I found, instead, a man.

In hindsight, I had no idea how prophetic the title of 'Searching for Bowlby' would end up being. The search for Bowlby the Theorist revealed instead a multifaceted and interesting player in history, one with fears, frustrations, and motivations. In looking for an academic, I had discovered a teacher, a student, a son, a brother, a father, a husband, and more. And as I now write these ending words, I can say with confidence that discovering the life and work of John Bowlby has felt like finding something rare and essential.

To my surprise, I have also made quite a few personal discoveries during the course of this book. Perhaps Darwin would approve of the fact that my search revealed itself to be evolutionary in nature; what began as my attempt to understand attachment theory became a reckoning with my own fractured bonds, my own haunting questions. Each turn in his story, each new letter, recollection, or account, was like a key that opened new perspectives into his life and into my own past. His struggles with absence, with silence, with love both withheld and sought, became a kind of cipher I could hold up against my own history.

And so, I end my search with a kind of realization. It occurs to me now that perhaps the act of searching *is* the object of the search; perhaps the point of it all is to turn over stones until the landscape of our own life comes into clearer view.

As for me, I now see life in parentheses. Birth and death are the great enclosing marks, the outer brackets around us all. But within them, smaller parentheses open and close: relationships, mentors, moments that quietly frame the meaning of everything else. For Bowlby, Alford was such a parenthesis, a mentor whose presence shaped his direction, opening a chapter that set him firmly on his path. Later, Mary Ainsworth became another, a closing parenthesis that gave his theories empirical weight and narrative resolution.

And between these parentheses was the fascinating life of a man named John Bowlby: a sentence we are still reading today.

Thank You for Reading

I hope *Searching for Bowlby* has given you something meaningful to reflect on. If the book spoke to you, I would be truly grateful if you could take a moment to leave a **5-star review**.

Your feedback not only means a great deal to me personally, but it also helps this book reach more readers. Reviews play a powerful role in the algorithms that recommend books, ensuring that stories like this one remain visible and discoverable.

By sharing your thoughts, you're helping others find their way to Bowlby's story—and, perhaps, to their own search for connection.

Thank you for supporting this work and for being part of the journey.

Stay Connected

Thank you for reading *Searching for Bowlby*. If you'd like to continue the conversation, receive exclusive updates, behind-the-scenes insights, and early previews of upcoming books, please join my newsletter.

▦ Scan the newsletter QR code below to sign up.

Explore Related Books

History: Unattached

If *Searching for Bowlby* made you curious about how attachment—or the lack of it—shaped lives, you'll enjoy *History: Unattached*. In this witty and revealing collection, C. V. Wooster explores historical figures through the lens of their personal struggles and fractured bonds, offering a fun but poignant look at how relationships (or their failures) changed the course of history.

Mrs. Orcutt's Driveway

Step into the Mojave Desert and discover the unforgettable story of Margaret Orcutt, who waged a one-woman battle against bureaucracy and became an unlikely symbol of resilience. *Mrs. Orcutt's Driveway* is a powerful narrative about human strength and survival against all odds—echoing the same themes of resilience found in Bowlby's own life.

Other Works by C. V. Wooster

The Chinese Room – A philosophical thriller about AI, thought, and impossible choices.

The Clockmaker's Apprentice – A novel about mentorship, legacy, and passing wisdom to the next generation.

The Outsider's Club – A story of belonging, courage, and community for those who have always lived at the margins.

Connect with the Author

Visit cvwooster.com to learn more, explore upcoming projects, and discover companion resources.

Follow on:

Linktr.ee

Twitter/X:
@cvwooster

Facebook:
@cvwooster

Instagram:
@cvwooster

TikTok:
@c.v.wooster

✦ **Thank you for being part of the search. May this book inspire your own journey into connection, resilience, and discovery.**

About the Author

C. V. Wooster is a multiple bestselling and award-winning author, historian, and educator whose work bridges biography, psychology, and cultural history.

He has dedicated his life to teaching and writing in ways that bring forgotten lives and overlooked voices back into the light, restoring them to their rightful place in our collective memory. His books are known for blending intellectual rigor with narrative grace, combining a historian's precision with a storyteller's heart. In *Searching for Bowlby*, Wooster turns to one of psychology's most quietly influential figures. Though John Bowlby's attachment theory has shaped how we understand love, parenting, and human connection, his name remains far less familiar than Freud or Jung. With compassion and depth, Wooster reveals the man behind the theory, tracing both his brilliance and his humanity, and showing how personal wounds gave rise to revolutionary insights.

Wooster's body of work reflects a lifelong commitment to illuminating those who shaped the world yet were never fully recognized. His books explore profound philosophical choices in works like *The Chinese Room*, the resilience of ordinary people in histories such as *Mrs. Orcutt's Driveway*, and the importance of paying it forward to the next generation in novels like *The Clockmaker's Apprentice* and *The Outsider's Club*. Whether writing about forgotten eccentrics, cultural thinkers, or overlooked pioneers, he approaches each subject with the conviction that stories untold are stories unfinished.

353

Today, his books spark dialogue among scholars, general readers, and practitioners alike, shedding light on the quiet revolutions and human struggles that define our world. He writes so that those who were once forgotten might be remembered, and so their stories might illuminate our own.

www.ingramcontent.com/pod-product-compliance
Lightning Source LLC
Chambersburg PA
CBHW031940080426
42735CB00007B/198